Contents

Accounting and Finance for Non-Specialists

PETER ATRILL AND EDDIE MCLANEY

PRENTICE HALL

New York   London   Toronto   Sydney   Tokyo   Singapore

First published 1995 by
Prentice Hall Europe
Campus 400, Maylands Avenue
Hemel Hempstead
Hertfordshire, HP2 7EZ
A division of
Simon & Schuster International Group

Typeset in 9½ on 12 pt Palatino
by MHL Typesetting Ltd

Printed and bound in Great Britain by
T. J. Press (Padstow) Ltd

Library of Congress Cataloguing in Publication Data

Atrill, Peter.
    Accounting and finance for non-specialists / Peter Atrill and
    Eddie McLaney.
        p.   cm.
    Includes index.
    ISBN 0-13-309865-6
    1. Accounting.   2. Financial statements.   I. McLaney, E.J.
    II. Title.
    HF5635.A882   1995
    657–dc20   94-13289
                                                        CIP

British Library Cataloguing in Publication Data

A catalogue record for this book is available from
the British Library

ISBN 0-13-309865-6 (pbk)

3 4 5   99 98 97 96

Accounting and Finance for Non-specialists

Preface

This book has been written for those people who wish to achieve a basic understanding of accounting and finance. Such people may be following a course where such an introduction is required, either at undergraduate or at postgraduate/post-experience levels. Alternatively, readers may be those who wish to acquire an understanding of accounting and finance for its own sake, perhaps to help with managing a business.

A broad range of topics is covered in the book. These topics are included in areas usually known as financial accounting, management accounting, financial management and treasury management.

We have tried to make accounting and finance as accessible as possible. In doing this we have assumed that readers have no prior knowledge of the subject and that they are not familiar with its jargon. An attempt has been made to introduce each topic very carefully and to build gradually. Where technical terms are used, we have endeavoured to give clear explanations of them.

Since many readers will have either no access or very limited access to tutorial help, we have provided a large number of worked examples and tasks in an attempt to aid learning. There are three types of task which readers can attempt. 'Activities' are relatively short questions interspersed throughout the text. These seek to involve readers more actively in their progress through the book. The activities either enable readers to check that they have understood the point made immediately before or encourage the reader to relate the topic to others already covered in earlier chapters. The answers to activities are given immediately following them, as part of the text. There are self-assessment questions which enable readers to test their understanding of a fairly large amount of material, often a whole chapter. The answers to these questions are given at the end of the book. At the end of each chapter there are 'exercises' similar to self-assessment questions, which will give further opportunity for practice. Answers to the first exercise in each chapter are given at the end of the book; the rest are contained in a separate Teacher's Manual.

We hope that readers will find this book readable as well as helpful.

We should like to thank the Chartered Association of Certified Accountants for permission to use questions from the Certified Diploma examinations at various points in the book.

PETER ATRILL

EDDIE McLANEY

February 1994

CHAPTER ONE

Introduction to Accounting

1.1 Introduction

People need economic information to help them to make decisions and judgements about businesses. Whether we are talking about managers within a business making decisions on what is the most appropriate level of production, a bank manager responding to a request from the business for a bank loan, or trade unionists deciding on the level of pay increase to seek for their members, accounting information should help them with their decision. In this chapter we look at accounting as a tool in the decision-making, planning and control process. We shall look in some detail at one of the basic accounting statements — the balance sheet.

1.2 Purpose

When you have completed your study of this chapter you should be able to:

♦ Explain the nature and practice of decision-making, planning and control, and the role of accounting in that context.
♦ Explain why those interested in a business need more than one type of accounting report in order to make judgements about the business.
♦ Prepare and explain a simple balance sheet.
♦ List and explain the accounting conventions on which the balance sheet is based.

1.3 Accounting for Decision-making, Planning and Control

Accounting is concerned with the collection, analysis and communication of economic information. Such information can be used as a tool of decision-making, planning and control. This is to say that accounting information is useful to those who need to make decisions and plans about businesses and for those who need to control these businesses. Although managers working within a particular business will almost certainly be significant users of accounting information, they are by no means the only people who are likely to use such information about that particular business.

[Though the points which will be made in this chapter and throughout this book apply to a great extent to all organizations (e.g. nationalized industries, local authorities, charities, etc.), we are concentrating specifically on private-sector businesses. More specifically we shall focus on limited companies.]

ACTIVITY ───

Apart from its managers, which other groups of people are likely to find accounting information about a business of use and for what purposes?

Other possible user groups and their uses would include the following:

Users	Purpose
Customers	To assess the ability of the business to continue in business and to supply the needs of the customers.
Suppliers of goods and services	To assess the ability of the business to pay for the goods and services supplied. (Most suppliers to other businesses allow a period of credit.)
Government	To assess how much tax the business should pay. (This figure is substantially based on accounting profit.)
Owners	To assess how effectively the managers are running the business and to make judgements about likely levels of risk and return in the future.
Lenders of finance	To assess the ability of the business to meet its obligations to pay interest and to repay the principal in due course.
Employees	To assess the ability of the business to continue to provide employment and to reward employees for their labour.

The 'purposes' shown here are intended only as examples.

We shall return shortly to consider the types of accounting information that are produced by businesses, but before we do that it may be useful to give some consideration to the subjects of decision-making, planning and control.

1.4 Decision-making and Planning

It is vitally important that businesses plan their future. Whatever a business is trying to achieve it is unlikely to be successful unless its managers have clear in their minds what the plans are. Planning is vital for businesses of all sizes, but where a business involves more than one manager it is vital also that the actions of all of the managers are co-ordinated. For example, it is crucial to a manufacturing business that production levels and sales levels are related to one another. It is not feasible for sales and production to go their own separate ways. It is necessary therefore that plans exist which will lead to production and sales levels matching one another. This is not to say that plans once made are incapable of being revised. Unexpected changes in the market or unforeseen production problems may well demand revision of the plans but they require revision of all of the plans which are likely to be affected by the new circumstances.

Closely linked to planning is decision-making. Planning involves making decisions about what course of action is best to plan for.

1.4.1 Steps in the Planning Process

Planning is usually broken down into three stages:

1. Setting the *objectives* or mission of the business, i.e. what the business is basically trying to achieve. These are likely to reflect the attitudes of owners (shareholders) and of the managers. Objectives tend to be framed in broad, generalized, non-numerical terms. Once the objectives have been established they are likely to remain in force for the long term, e.g. ten years. It is probably true to say that, for most private-sector businesses, wealth-generation is likely to be the main financial/economic objective. This broadly means that businesses tend to take actions which will have the effect of increasing the wealth of the business. Increases in wealth may be paid to the government in taxes, paid to the owners, paid to employees, reinvested in the business or deployed in some other way. Businesses will typically have objectives other than the financial ones, e.g. being environmentally friendly. In practice, therefore, any decision is likely to be the result of a compromise between more than one objective.
2. Setting *long-term plans*. These are plans setting out how the business will work towards the achievement of its objectives over a period of, say, five years. They are likely to deal with such matters as:
   ♦ Types of products or services to be offered by the business.
   ♦ Amounts and sources of finance needed to be raised by the business.
   ♦ Capital investments (e.g. in new plant and machinery) needed to be made.
   ♦ Sources of raw materials.
   ♦ Labour requirements.
   In the case of each of these the pursuit of the established objectives of the business over the planning horizon (perhaps five years) will lay the foundation for the plans. Long-term plans are to a great extent likely to be stated in financial terms.
3. Setting detailed short-term plans or *budgets*. Budgets are financial plans for the short-term, typically one year, and are likely to be expressed mainly in financial terms. Their role is to convert the long-term plans into actionable blueprints for the immediate future. Budgets usually define precise targets in areas like:

- ◆ Cash receipts and payments.
- ◆ Sales, broken down into amounts and prices for each of the products or services provided by the business.
- ◆ Detailed stock requirements.
- ◆ Detailed labour requirements.
- ◆ Specific production requirements.

It must be emphasized that planning (and decision-making) is not the role of accountants; it is the role of managers. However, much of the planning will be expressed in financial terms and much of the data for decision-making is of an accounting nature. Therefore accountants, because of their background and their understanding of the accounting system, are very well placed to give technical advice and assistance to managers in this context. It is the department managers who must do the actual planning. Only in respect of the accounting department, of which the most senior accountant will be the manager, should an accountant be taking decisions and making plans.

1.5 Control

However well-planned the activities of the business may be they will come to nothing unless steps are taken to try to achieve them. The process of making planned events occur is known as control. Control can be defined as compelling events to conform to plan. This definition of control is valid in any context. For example, when we talk about controlling a motor car we mean making the car do what we plan that it should do. In the case of a car the plan may only be made split-seconds before the plan is enacted, but if the car is in control it is doing what the driver intended that it should do.

In a business context, accounting is very useful in the control process because it is possible to state both plans and outcomes in accounting terms, thus making comparison between actual and planned outcomes an easy matter. Where actual outcomes are at variance with budgets (plans) this should be highlighted by the accounting information. Managers can then take steps to get the business back on track towards the achievement of the budgets. Figure 1.1 shows the decision-making, planning and control process in diagrammatic form.

In this book we shall look in some detail at the way in which accounting and finance can help managers in the various aspects of decision-making, planning and control. For the remainder of this chapter and in the next one we consider the nature and sources of data for traditional accounting reports — the balance sheet, the profit and loss account and the cash flow statement. Chapters 3 and 4 consider the interpretation of the three traditional statements. Chapter 5 deals with financial planning and looks at the nature of financial decision-making. Chapter 6 considers costs for decision-making, including short-term tactical decisions, and ascertains the cost of the output for the purpose of pricing and other decisions. Chapter 7 deals with decisions involving capital investment in such assets as plant and machinery. Chapter 8

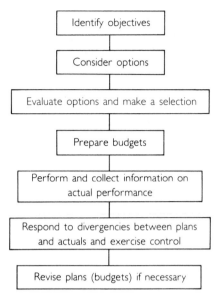

Figure 1.1 The decision-making, planning and control process.

considers how control can be exercised with the help of accounting information. Chapter 9 looks at the control of the short-term assets and liabilities of the business. Chapter 10 is concerned with the sources of finance for private-sector businesses.

1.6 The Traditional Accounting Statements

Perhaps the best way to introduce the accounting statements is to look at an example of a very simple business. From this we shall be able to see the sort of information which the accounting statements can usefully provide.

EXAMPLE

Andy wanted to earn some money in his spare time. Although shops in the area sold posters of pop and film stars, Andy felt that the retail price was unnecessarily high and saw this as a considerable business opportunity. He made some enquiries with a local poster printer who offered to supply a range of posters to Andy on a cash-with-order basis at a price of £1.00 each. Some friends of Andy ran a pub which was very popular with younger people. They agreed with Andy's request that for a trial period he could sell his posters in the pub and that they would not charge him for this facility.

Andy had £40 of spare cash and he decided to use this to buy 40 posters and try his luck at selling them. During his lunch hour on Monday Andy went to the printers and selected a range of posters which he thought would sell. He took over a small corner of one of the bars of his friends' pub and started trading. To his delight all 40 of the posters were sold during the evening.

Andy was keen to keep a record of his trading so when he arrived home on Monday evening he made a brief statement of his achievement, as follows:

Andy's posters — Monday

	£
Cash received from poster sales (40 × £1.50)	60.00
Less: Cash paid for posters (40 × £1.00)	40.00
Increase in cash (profit)	£20.00

The following day Andy went again to the poster printers at lunchtime and used all of his cash to buy 60 more posters. By pub closing time on Tuesday evening Andy found that he had sold 44 of his 60 posters. When he arrived home he again tried to make a statement of his trading. The statement he produced was as follows:

Andy's posters — Tuesday

	£
Cash received from poster sales (44 × £1.50)	66.00
Less: Cash paid for posters (60 × £1.00)	60.00
Increase in cash (profit?)	£6.00

Andy was a bit perplexed by this statement. He knew that he had only £6.00 more than he started the day with, so to that extent the statement seemed logical. What did not seem right to him was that he had sold four more posters than he had done on Monday, yet Monday's profit was £20.00. Andy tried to puzzle it out but it was late by this time so he gave up and went to bed.

When Andy arrived at his day job the next morning he went straight to see the business' accountant to see if any light could be shed on the subject of Tuesday's poster sales. The accountant explained to Andy that the excess of cash receipts over cash payments was not the same as profit. The accountant quickly jotted down the following statements:

Andy's posters — Profit and loss account for Tuesday

	£
Poster sales (44 × £1.50)	66.00
Less: Cost of posters sold (44 × £1.00)	44.00
Profit for the day	£22.00

Andy's posters — Balance sheet as at pub closing time on Tuesday

	£
Cash	66.00
Stock of posters (16 × £1.00)	16.00
Andy's business wealth	£82.00

Andy's posters — Cash flow statement for Tuesday

	£
Cash received from poster sales (44 × £1.50)	66.00
Less: Cash paid for posters (60 × £1.00)	60.00
Increase in cash	£6.00

The accountant explained that one statement did not tell Andy all that he needed to know about Tuesday evening's trading. To get the full picture three statements were necessary.

The first, the profit and loss account (or income statement), showed by how much Andy's wealth had increased on Tuesday evening. Andy had turned stock-in-trade which had cost him £44.00 into cash of £66.00, and made himself £22.00 richer as a result.

The second statement, the balance sheet, showed how the wealth that Andy had invested in the business was currently deployed, i.e. £16.00 in as yet unsold posters and £66.00 in cash. The accountant went on to explain that Andy's business wealth had derived as follows:

	£
Monday's cash investment in the business	40.00
Monday's profit	20.00
Tuesday's profit	22.00
	£82.00

The third statement showed what had happened to cash during Tuesday. The accountant explained that although cash was just another business asset like stock-in-trade, it was such a crucial asset without which no business can function that we tend to pay a lot of attention to its movements, hence the third statement.

The accountant explained that these three statements are those which most businesses are required to prepare and make public at least once a year. She also drew Andy's attention to the fact that the profit and loss account and the cash flow

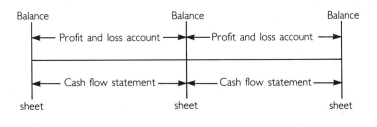

Figure 1.2 **The relationship between the balance sheet, the profit and loss account, and the cash flow statement.**

statement summarize the events of a period (in this case Tuesday evening) whereas the balance sheet showed the position as at a particular point in time, namely the end of Tuesday evening. The accountant drew a simple diagram to help explain this to Andy. This is shown in Figure 1.2.

Andy followed all of the points which the accountant had made, but he could not understand why the statement which Andy himself had prepared on Monday seemed to tell him all he wanted to know.

ACTIVITY ──

Why was Andy's statement for Monday fairly easy to understand whereas the statement produced by Andy on Tuesday seemed to be thoroughly misleading?

The reason that Andy's statement was so easy to follow on Monday was that he had no unsold stock left at the end of the day. As a result his net increase in cash for the day exactly equalled his profit. It also meant that all of Andy's business wealth was tied up in cash. On Tuesday the situation was slightly more complicated by the fact that part of Andy's business wealth was still tied up in stock-in-trade at the end of the evening.

ACTIVITY ──

On Wednesday Andy bought 50 new posters at £1.00 each and took these with his existing stock to the pub. By the end of the evening Andy had sold the remaining stock from Tuesday plus 27 of the new posters, all for £2.00 each.

Prepare the three statements for Wednesday evening's activities.

Andy's posters — *Profit and loss account for Wednesday*

	£
Poster sales (43 × £2.00)	86.00
Less: Cost of posters sold (43 × £1.00)	43.00
Profit for the day	£43.00

Andy's posters — *Balance sheet as at pub closing time on Wednesday*

Assets	£
Cash (£66.00 + 86.00 − 50.00)	102.00
Stock of posters (23 × £1.00)	23.00
	£125.00

Andy's business wealth:	£
Position at Tuesday evening	82.00
Wednesday's profit	43.00
	£125.00

Andy's posters — *Cash flow statement for Wednesday*

	£
Cash received from poster sales (43 × £2.00)	86.00
Less: Cash paid for posters (50 × £1.00)	50.00
Increase in cash	£36.00

1.7 The Balance Sheet

Having considered an overview of the three traditional accounting statements, we now go on in this chapter and the next to look at each of them in a little more detail, starting with the balance sheet.

The balance sheet is essentially two lists. One is of assets and the other one is of claims against those assets. A balance sheet depicts the position at a specified point in time.

Assets are things of value. More formally, for accounting purposes, they can be defined as probable future benefits to the business for which the business controls the right of access which have arisen as a result of some past activity or transaction of the business. Thus, some freehold land owned by the business is an asset because it can either be used in the business to help generate profits or the land could be sold by the business. It will have been acquired as a result of some transaction and the business can deny the right of others to use it. To a business which uses the road network to deliver its product, the existence of the road network is an asset, using the word 'asset' in its non-accounting sense — it is valuable to the business. This would not fall within the definition of an asset for accounting purposes, however.

ACTIVITY ──

Why would the existence of the road network not appear as an asset in the balance sheet of the business referred to above?

───

There are two reasons for this:

1. *The business did not acquire the road network as a result of some past transaction.*
2. *The business cannot restrict the access of others to that road network.*

We consider various examples of assets shortly.

Claims are obligations of the business to provide assets (possibly cash) or services to a person or group of people. To be included on the balance sheet a claim must continue to exist at the date of the balance sheet and be expected to have to be met. Examples of liabilities include an amount owed by a business to a trade creditor as a result of having bought something on credit, and borrowings made by the business from a bank.

Claims fall into two broad classes:

1. Owners (usually referred to as 'capital').
2. Other claimants (usually referred to as 'liabilities').

The balance sheet is really an equation which must always balance. It can be set out as:

Assets = Claims

or expanded to:

Assets = Capital + Liabilities

Probably the best way to approach the balance sheet is through an example.

EXAMPLE ————————————————————————

1. Jack and Jill decide to start a business in the form a company (JJ Limited) and to invest £50,000 each in it by opening a business bank account and each paying into it a cheque drawn on their own personal bank accounts. The balance sheet immediately after this would be:

JJ Limited   Balance Sheet as at . . . .

Assets	£	*Claims*	£
Cash at bank	£100,000	Capital	£100,000

Note the fact that the balance sheet is at a particular point in time which must be specified.

2. The business buys a small shop for £60,000 paying in cash. The balance sheet immediately after this would be:

JJ Limited   Balance Sheet as at . . . .

Assets	£	*Claims*	£
Freehold shop premises	60,000		
Cash at bank (100,000 − 60,000)	40,000	Capital	100,000
	£100,000		£100,000

Note that this transaction does not affect capital. Capital is the investment of the owners in the business, the amount of this is not affected by the business converting part of one asset (cash) into another asset (freehold premises).

3. The business buys some stock-in-trade for £30,000 on credit. The balance sheet immediately after this would be:

JJ Limited   Balance Sheet as at . . . .

Assets	£	Claims	£
Freehold shop premises	60,000	Capital	100,000
Stock-in-trade	30,000	Trade creditor	30,000
Cash at bank	40,000		
	£130,000		£130,000

Trade creditor is the term used for a short-term claimant where the claim has arisen as a result of buying goods and services on credit.

4. The business sells stock which had cost £10,000 for £15,000 on credit. The balance sheet immediately after this would be:

JJ Limited   Balance Sheet as at . . . .

Assets	£	Claims	£
Freehold shop premises	60,000	Capital	
		(100,000 + 15,000 − 10,000)	105,000
Stock-in-trade			
(30,000 − 10,000)	20,000	Trade creditor	30,000
Trade debtor	15,000		
Cash at bank	40,000		
	£135,000		£135,000

Note that capital is affected by this transaction. In fact it is probably better to see this as two transactions. In one of these some wealth of the business passes out of the business into the hands of a customer. This causes a reduction in the wealth of the owners by £10,000. However, this is more than compensated for by wealth flowing into the business in that a customer has contracted to pay the business £15,000 and this has the effect of increasing the investment of the owners by that amount in total. The net effect on the owners is an increase in their wealth by £5,000, i.e. a profit of £5,000.

ACTIVITY ──

The next transaction of JJ Ltd was to sell some stock which had cost £1,000, but which had been damaged, for £800 in cash.

Show the balance sheet immediately following this transaction.

JJ Limited   Balance Sheet as at ....

Assets	£	Claims	£
Freehold shop premises	60,000	Capital	
Stock-in-trade (20,000 − 1,000)	19,000	(105,000 + 800 − 1,000)	104,800
Trade debtor	15,000	Trade creditor	30,000
Cash at bank (40,000 + 800)	40,800		
	£134,800		£134,800

Again capital is affected by this transaction. There is a reduction in the wealth of the owners by £1,000. However, this is partially compensated for by wealth flowing into the business in that a customer has paid the business £800 and this has the effect of increasing the investment of the owners by that amount in total. The net effect on owners is a decrease in their wealth by £200, i.e. a loss of £200.

SELF ASSESSMENT QUESTION

During the following week JJ Ltd did the following:

◆ Borrowed £50,000 from the Commercial Finance Company plc which was paid into the bank.
◆ Bought a delivery van, on credit, for £10,000.
◆ Entered into a contract with KK (Builders) Ltd to carry out some extensive alterations to the shop premises at a total cost of £30,000. The work is not due to start for six weeks and payment will be made in full when the work is complete.
◆ Sold stock, which had cost £11,000, for £15,500 on credit.
◆ Received £13,000 in cash from various trade debtors.
◆ Paid £25,000 in cash to various creditors.
◆ Bought stock-in-trade for cash totalling £10,000 and on credit, totalling £12,500.

Show how these transactions would affect the balance sheet by drawing up the balance sheet of the business as at the end of the week.

There is no need to draw up a series of balance sheets, just one which reflects the accounting transactions for the week.

Solution on p. 249.

1.7.1   Revenues and Expenses

A trading event which gives rise to an increase in capital (the owners' claim) is known as a revenue. Thus the £800 in the last activity and the £15,000 in the previous transaction of JJ Ltd are both examples of revenues. Most businesses use the word 'sales' to refer to their revenues. However, some businesses use other words. For example, insurance broking businesses, whose revenues are commissions earned, would probably call its revenues just that: 'commissions earned'.

A trading event which gives rise to a reduction in capital is known as an expense. Such an event was the £1,000 decrease in stock which occurred as a result of the sale made in the last activity.

Where, in a particular period, the revenues exceed the expenses, a profit is made. A loss is incurred where expenses exceed the revenues.

ACTIVITY —————————————————————————————————

Apart from through incurring an expense, how could the capital of JJ Ltd be reduced?

This can only occur where the owners take out some of the assets (usually cash) of the business. This is, in effect, the opposite of an investment by the owners.

In Chapter 2 we shall look at the laws which restrict withdrawals of the business assets by the owner, where the business trades as a limited company.

ACTIVITY —————————————————————————————————

Jack and Jill, having satisfied themselves that it is perfectly legal to do so, receive a cash divident of £1,000 each from the business.

Show the balance sheet of JJ Ltd immediately following this transaction.

JJ Limited   Balance Sheet as at ....

Assets	£	Claims	£
Freehold shop premises	60,000	Capital (109,300 − 2,000)	107,300
Delivery van	10,000	Commercial Finance	50,000
Stock-in-trade	30,500	Trade creditors	27,500
Trade debtors	17,500		
Cash at bank (68,800 − 2,000)	66,800		
	£184,800		£184,800

1.7.2 The Balance Sheet Equation

The dual aspect convention, of which we have seen numerous examples in recording the transactions of JJ Ltd, means that at all times:

Assets = Capital + Liabilities

This is known as the *balance sheet equation* and the relationship must always hold true. The capital figure at any given moment will be given by:

Capital = Total injections of capital by the owners so far in the life of the business

        + All profits earned by the business so far in the life of the business

        − All losses sustained by the business so far in the life of the business

        − Total withdrawals of capital by the owners so far in the life of the business

ACTIVITY ——————————————————————————————————————

On 1 January the capital of XYZ Ltd was £340,000. During the ensuing year the owners withdrew £15,000 in cash as a dividend, and the expenses of the business totalled £76,000. On 31 December the capital was £364,000.
Deduce the value of the revenues of the business for the year.

- *Capital at 31 December (£364,000) = Capital at 1 January (£340,000) + Capital injections (zero) + Profit for the year − Capital withdrawals for the year (£15,000).*
- *Profit for the year = £364,000 − £340,000 + £15,000 = £39,000.*
- *Profit for the year (£39,000) = Revenues for the year − Expenses for the year (£76,000) Revenues for the year = £39,000 + £76,000 = £115,000.*

1.7.3   The Classification of Assets

Like all accounting statements, the balance sheet is intended to give useful information to those who read it. To this end it is normal for the assets and claims to be classified into their different types and for items in the same class to be shown together in the balance sheet.

Assets are normally divided into two classes: fixed and current assets.

Fixed assets are those that the business acquires with the intention of using them in the business to help to generate revenues. They can be seen as the tools of the business. They are not acquired with the intention of reselling them at a profit, though this may in fact occur. They are typically retained for a relatively long period, though this is not always the case.

ACTIVITY ——————————————————————————————————————

Give some examples of likely fixed assets of a business which publishes newspapers.

Examples might include:

- *Freehold premises.*
- *Printing presses.*
- *Word processors used by staff.*
- *Delivery vans.*

These would, of course, need to fall within the definition of an asset which we have already considered.

Current assets are cash itself and other assets which are expressly intended to turn into cash at some future point, normally a point in the fairly near future. This includes 'circulating' assets, i.e. those which turn over in the normal course of business.

ACTIVITY ───────────────────────────────────

Give some examples of likely current assets of a business which operates in the wholesale trade.

Examples might include:

- *Debtors.*
- *Cash.*
- *Stock-in-trade.*

These would also need to fall within the definition of an asset.

The circulating nature of current assets is depicted in Figure 1.3.

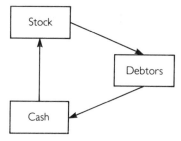

Figure 1.3 The circulating nature of current assets.

ACTIVITY ───────────────────────────────────

Into which category (i.e. fixed or current) would the following assets of a motor car dealer (i.e. retailer) and repair business fall?

Stock of spare parts.
A computer.
A short-term investment.
A desk and chair.
A Ford Escort car.

You should have classified them as follows:

Stock of spare parts	*Current*
A computer	*Fixed*
A short-term investment	*Current*
A desk and chair	*Fixed*
A Ford Escort car	*?*

The car is impossible to classify without some more information. If it was acquired to be resold, i.e. it is an item of stock-in-trade, it is a current asset. It is very common for businesses to supply some staff with a company car. If this car falls into that category then it would be a fixed asset. This provides an example of a situation where a business could own two virtually identical assets, yet one might correctly be classified as a current asset and the other one equally correctly as a fixed asset. It is not the nature of the asset which determines its classification; it is its intended use. This point is particularly important to understand.

1.7.4 The Classification of Claims

As we have already seen, claims are normally classified into *capital* (owners' claim) and *liabilities* (claims of outsiders). Liabilities are further classified into two groups:

1. *Long-term liabilities.* These are amounts which are due for payment in more than twelve months' time.
2. *Current liabilities.* These are due for repayment within twelve months of the balance sheet date.

Unlike assets, intention is not the issue with liabilities. Thus long-term liabilities automatically turn into current liabilities as their time for settlement comes closer.

1.7.5 Balance Sheet Formats

There is an almost infinite number of ways in which the same balance sheet information can be presented. One way follows the style that we adopted with the JJ Ltd examples above, with assets on the left and claims on the right. A more comprehensive example of this style is as follows:

Shockers Car Sales and Repairs Ltd Balance Sheet as at 31 December 19X6

	£000	£000		£000
Fixed assets			*Capital*	207
Freehold premises	200			
Plant and equipment	95			
Motor vehicles	23			
		318	*Long-term liabilities*	
			Loan from bank	150
Current assets			*Current liabilities*	
Stock-in-trade	84		Creditors	67
Debtors	8			
Cash	14			
		106		
		424		424

Note that within each category (fixed assets, current assets, etc.) the items are listed with the least liquid (furthest from cash) first going down to the most liquid last. This is a standard practice which is followed irrespective of the format used.

An obvious alternative to this format is to show claims on the left and assets on the right. Some people prefer that approach because the claims can be seen as the source of finance for the business and the assets are how that finance has been deployed. It could be seen as more logical to show sources first and uses second, though the difference between having assets on the left or on the right is slight.

A more radical departure from this 'horizontal' format is the much more popular 'vertical' or 'narrative' format. With the horizontal format (above) the balance sheet equation is set out as:

Fixed assets + Current assets = Capital + Long-term liabilities + Current liabilities

Using the obvious abbreviations, the vertical format merely rearranges this to:

FA + (CA − CL) − LTL = Capital

Shockers' balance sheet in the vertical format would be:

Shockers Car Sales and Repairs Ltd   Balance Sheet as at 31 December 19X6

	£000	£000	£000
Fixed assets			
Freehold premises			200
Plant and equipment			95
Motor vehicles			23
			318
Current assets			
Stock-in-trade	84		
Debtors	8		
Cash	14	106	
Less: Current liabilities			
Creditors		67	
			39
			357
Less: Long-term liabilities			
Loan from bank			150
			207
Capital			207

This format is probably easier to read than the horizontal format. It usefully highlights the relationship between current assets and current liabilities. We shall consider shortly why this relationship is an important one.

ACTIVITY ──

The following is a list of the assets and claims of Crafty Engineering Ltd at 30 June 19X0:

	£000
Creditors	86
Motor vehicles	38
Loan from Industrial Finance Company	260
Machinery and tools	207
Bank overdraft	116
Stock-in-trade	153
Freehold premises	320
Debtors	185

Prepare the balance sheet of the business as at 30 June 19X0 from the above information using the vertical format.

───

Crafty Engineering Ltd   **Balance Sheet as at 30 June 19X0**

	£000	£000	£000
Fixed assets			
Freehold premises			320
Machinery and tools			207
Motor vehicles			38
			565
Current assets			
Stock-in-trade	153		
Debtors	185		
		338	
Less: Current liabilities			
Creditors	86		
Bank overdraft	116		
		202	
			136
			701
Less: Long-term liabilities			
Loan from Industrial Finance Company			260
			441
Capital			441

1.7.6 Conventions of Accounting

Accounting is based on a number of rules or conventions. Having considered the balance sheet in some detail, it may be useful to look briefly at those conventions which relate particularly to the balance sheet. These are:

- **Money measurement convention.** Accounting only deals with those items which are capable of being expressed in monetary terms, thus potentially useful information which cannot be expressed in monetary terms is omitted.
- **Cost convention.** Assets are shown in accounting statements at a value which is based on cost.
- **Business entity convention.** For accounting purposes the business and its owner(s) are treated as distinct. This is why owners are treated as being claimants against their own business in respect of their investment in the business.
- **Dual aspect convention.** Each transaction has two aspects, both of which must be recorded in the balance sheet.
- **Prudence.** Accountancy tends to err on the side of caution or prudence. When, as is often the case, the outcome of some part-completed transaction is not known with certainty, a cautious view must be taken of the outcome.
- **Objectivity.** As far as possible, accounting statements should be based on objective, verifiable evidence, rather than on matters of opinion, and should be free from bias.

Further conventions are considered in Chapter 2 where we deal with the profit and loss account.

ACTIVITY

Which of the following items of information would you expect to find in a balance sheet?

1. The business owns stock-in-trade which cost it £52,000.
2. A major international competitor has just gone bust which it is confidently expected will have significant beneficial effects on the future sales of the business.
3. One of the business' leading research staff has just resigned, an event which seems likely to have a significant adverse effect on the future prosperity of the business.
4. The owners of the business have just spent £5,000 on a holiday in India.
5. The business owes £4,000 to another business which has supplied it with stock-in-trade on credit.

Only items 1 and 5 would appear on the balance sheet. This is because they fall under the definition of an asset (in the case of item 1) or claim (in the case of item 5) which were given above. None of the other items fall within these definitions, despite the fact that two of them (items 2 and 3) are of possibly great significance to the business.

1.7.7 The Balance Sheet as a Position at a Point in Time

As we have already seen, the balance sheet is a statement of the financial position of the business at a *specified point in time*. This means that each balance sheet must show in its title the precise point in time to which it relates, otherwise it is not likely to be very useful to the reader. Some people make the analogy between a balance sheet and a still photograph, and it is probably a good one. When reading a balance sheet we must be careful to note that the particular point in time to which the balance sheet relates may not be typical. Each UK business is required to prepare a balance sheet as at the close of business on the last day of its accounting year. Businesses in the UK are free to choose their own accounting year. In making their decision on which year-end date to choose, commercial convenience may well be the deciding factor. Thus a business operating in the retail trade may choose to have a year-end date early in the calendar year, e.g. 31 January, because trade tends to be slack during that period and more staff time is available to help with the tasks involved with the preparation of the annual accounting statements. Since trade is slack, it is also a time when the business' holding of stock-in-trade is likely to be untypically low as compared with other times during the year. Thus the balance sheet, though showing a fair view of that which it purports to show, may not show a picture of what is more typically the position of the business over the year.

1.7.8   The Basis of Valuation of Assets in the Balance Sheet

As we have seen, the assets shown in the balance sheet are normally shown at cost. Though this is the general rule, there are three important exceptions to this, these are:

1. Current assets whose market value has fallen below cost will be shown at the market value figure. Here the *prudence* convention takes precedence over the *cost* convention. Thus the balance sheet tends to take a cautious or prudent view of the value of such assets.
2. Some types of fixed assets — typically machinery and vehicles, but some buildings as well — have only a limited useful life. So as to acknowledge that such assets are losing value to the business, part of their cost is treated as an expense in each accounting period. This expense is known as *depreciation*. This is not really a contravention of the cost convention, it is a recognition that part of the asset's value is being lost as a result of wear and tear, etc. We consider the subject of depreciation in Chapter 2.
3. Some fixed assets are revalued upwards in the balance sheet to a value which more closely resembles their market value. It is argued that it can be misleading to show assets at their cost, particularly where prices of goods are increasing with inflation. Wide divergencies between cost and market value are particularly likely to be the case where an asset, like freehold land, is held by the business over a long period. For example, the freehold premises of Crafty Engineering Ltd (in the activity before last) had cost £320,000 when they were acquired. Suppose that they are now estimated to have a market value of £1 million. This would mean that anyone looking at the balance sheet of the business could be misled, if that person were presuming that the balance sheet represents current market values of assets, or at least values not too far removed from current market values.

Accountants would tend to argue that the balance sheet is not intended to represent current values but more to be an historical record of where the funds of the business came from and how they were deployed. Thus when Crafty Engineering Ltd's balance sheet says 'Freehold premises £320,000', this means that this amount of funds were laid out to acquire the premises, not that this is the market value of the asset. Despite this point, many businesses do contravene the *cost* convention and show assets, particularly land and buildings, at a valuation. Not only does this practice contravene the cost convention, it is also at variance with the *objectivity* convention. This is because an opinion of what is the current market value is substituted for a cost figure which is usually a matter of verifiable fact.

We have seen that the figures appearing in the same balance sheet can, in practice, be based on different rules. This can be confusing for the reader of the accounts, though the balance sheet probably remains a fairly useful document for assessing the financial position of the business.

1.7.9 Interpreting the Balance Sheet

Within its limitations the balance sheet can be a useful aid to making judgements about a business. The more important of the judgements which the balance sheet can aid probably fall into three main areas. These are:

1. **Liquidity**. This is the ability of the business to meet its short-term obligations (current liabilities) from its liquid assets. One of the reasons that the 'vertical' or 'narrative' balance sheet layout is preferred by many accounts users is the fact that in this layout the current assets are directly compared with the current liabilities, which highlights the liquidity position of the business. Liquidity is particularly important because business failures occur when the business cannot meet its immediate obligations, whatever the root cause of that inability may be.
2. **Mix of assets**. The relationship between the fixed assets and current assets is also important. Businesses with too much of their funds tied up in fixed assets could be vulnerable to financial failure. This is because fixed assets are typically not easy to turn into cash in order to meet short-term obligations. Converting many types of fixed asset into cash may well lead to substantial losses for the business because such assets are not always worth on the open market what the business paid to acquire the asset or what the asset is worth to the business. For example, a specialized piece of equipment may have little value to any other business, yet it could be worth a great deal to its owner.
3. **Capital gearing**. The relationship between the amount of finance supplied by the owners of the business as compared with that supplied by outside lenders is also important. Borrowings normally involve the business in making regular cash payments for interest and eventually repayment of the loan. These payments are not matters of the discretion of the business, but are legally enforceable obligations. Funds raised from the owners of the business do not impose such obligations.

We shall give further consideration to these matters and to other aspects of inter-pretation of accounts in Chapters 3 and 4.

Summary

In this chapter we have considered the nature of decision-making, planning and control. We have also looked briefly at the role of accounting in aiding implementation of these. We have considered the steps in the planning process. We went on to take an overview of the types of information which are likely to be useful to managers and other users of accounting. We saw that there are three basic statements which are likely to be particularly useful: the balance sheet, the profit and loss account, and the cash flow statement. We then went on to look at the balance sheet in more detail.

EXERCISES ──

1.1 The balance sheet of a business at the start of the week is as follows:

Assets	£	Claims	£
Freehold premises	145,000	Capital	203,000
Furniture and fittings	63,000	Bank overdraft	43,000
Stock-in-trade	28,000	Trade creditors	23,000
Trade debtors	33,000		
	£269,000		£269,000

During the week the following transactions take place:

1. Sold stock for £11,000 cash. This stock had cost £8,000.
2. Sold stock for £23,000 on credit. This stock had cost £17,000.
3. Received cash from trade debtors totalling £18,000.
4. The owners of the business introduced £100,000 of their own money which was placed in the business bank account.
5. The owners brought a motor van, valued at £10,000, into the business.
6. Bought stock-in-trade on credit for £14,000.
7. Paid trade creditors £13,000.

Show the balance sheet after all of these transactions have been reflected.

(Answer on page 260. Answers to exercises 1.2 and 1.3 are given in the Teacher's Manual.)

1.2 The following is a list of assets and claims of a manufacturing business at a particular point in time:

Bank overdraft	22,000
Freehold land and buildings	245,000
Stock of raw materials	18,000
Trade creditors	23,000
Plant and machinery	127,000
Loan from Industrial Finance Corporation	100,000
Stock of finished goods	28,000
Delivery vans	54,000
Trade debtors	34,000

Write out a balance sheet in the standard vertical form incorporating these figures. *Hint*: There is a missing item which needs to be deduced and inserted.

1.3 You have been talking to someone who read the first chapter of an accounting text some years ago. During your conversation the person made the following statements:

(a) The profit and loss account shows how much cash has come into and left the business during the accounting period and the resulting balance at the end of the period.
(b) In order to be included in the balance sheet as an asset an item needs to be worth something in the market, that is all.
(c) The balance sheet equation is:

   Assets + Capital = Liabilities

(d) An expense is an event which reduces capital, so when the owner of the business withdraws some capital, the business has incurred an expense.
(e) Fixed assets are things which cannot be moved.
(f) Current assets are things which stay in the business for less than twelve months.
(g) Working capital is the name given to the sum of the current assets.

Comment critically on each of the above statements, going into as much detail as you can.

Further Reading

Atrill, P., Harvey, D. and McLaney, E., *Accounting for Business*. Butterworth/Heinemann, 1994.
Bull, R., *Accounting in Business*. Butterworth, 1991.
Glautier, M. and Underdown, B., *Accounting Theory and Practice*. Pitman, 1991.

CHAPTER TWO

Measuring Business Performance

2.1 Introduction

In this chapter we continue our consideration of the three major accounting statements which we started in Chapter 1. Firstly we look at the preparation and use of the profit and loss account (income statement). After this we give similar consideration to the cash flow statement. We shall conclude with a brief look at the more important differences between accounting for limited companies and accounting for other types of business.

2.2 Purpose

When you have completed your study of this chapter you should be able to:

◆ Discuss the nature of the profit and loss account.
◆ Explain the conventions which particularly apply to the profit and loss account and discuss problems of profit measurement.
◆ Prepare and interpret a simple cash flow statement.
◆ Discuss the main features of limited company accounting.

2.3 The Nature of the Profit and Loss Account

In Chapter 1 we saw that the capital (owners' claim) of a business can be affected by four different types of transaction. These are:

1. Injections of new capital (i.e. further investment in the business by the owners).
2. Withdrawals of capital by the owners.
3. Revenues (sales).
4. Expenses.

You may recall that revenues and expenses are defined as events which give rise to an increase or a decrease in capital, respectively. For a particular period of time we can say that:

Capital at the beginning of the period

plus

Injections of new capital by the owners

minus

Withdrawals of capital by the owners

plus

The sum of the revenues for the period

minus

The sum of the expenses associated with those revenues

equals

Capital at the end of the period

In the examples and activities which we considered in Chapter 1, injections and withdrawals of capital represented a relatively high proportion of the total transactions. This was not in fact a fair representation of the normal situation in practice. For the typical business, under normal circumstances, 'trading' events, i.e. revenues and expenses, normally occur on a daily basis in vast numbers, whereas injections and withdrawals of capital are relatively rare events.

In practice, the capital figure is not adjusted for each individual revenue or receipt. Normally revenues and expenses of similar types are collected and accumulated. The totals for each of these are periodically compared with one another to deduce the net figure, and the capital figure in the balance sheet is adjusted by this net figure.

There is an important reason why the capital figure is not adjusted for each individual revenue and expense, but these items are first summarized and netted off. By doing so it is possible to see clearly what has occurred in terms of the trading activities of the business over a selected period.

A C T I V I T Y —————————————————————————————————————

What is the usual name for the figure which is deduced from taking the sum of the revenues for a period and deducting the sum of the associated expenses?

The answer is the 'net profit' for the period if total revenues exceed total expenses, or 'net loss' if total expenses exceed total revenues. In some types of business, e.g. professional practices (solicitors, accountants, etc.), the words 'surplus' and 'deficit' are used as alternatives to net profit and net loss, respectively.

If profit (or loss) is the difference between the revenues for a period and the associated expenses, and revenues and expenses are trading events which give rise to a change in owners' capital, then profit (or loss) is the increase (or decrease) in capital caused by trading events. Since the owners' capital represents the owners' investment of their personal wealth in the business, profit represents an increase in their wealth and loss is a reduction in their wealth.

The statement in which the comparison is made between revenues and expenses is normally known either as the 'profit and loss account' or the 'income statement'.

2.4 Recording Expenses and Revenues

As we have just seen, although revenues and expenses strictly represent adjustments to the capital of the business, they are, in the first instance, collected and analyzed separately. To illustrate how this is done we continue our consideration of JJ Limited which was the subject of one of the activities in Chapter 1.

EXAMPLE

When we left JJ Limited in Chapter 1, the balance sheet was as follows:

JJ Limited   Balance Sheet as at ....

Assets	£	Claims	£
Freehold shop premises	60,000	Capital	107,300
Delivery van	10,000	Commercial Finance Co. plc	50,000
Stock-in-trade	30,500	Trade creditors	27,500
Trade debtors	17,500		
Cash at bank	66,800		
	£184,800		£184,800

During the following week the following transactions took place:

- Sold stock which had cost £3,000 for £4,000 on credit.
- Paid wages for the week of £800.
- Bought petrol for the delivery van, for cash, costing £80, all of which was used during the week.
- Sold stock which had cost £500 for £700 for cash.

The following is the balance sheet of the business, after recording these transactions, keeping the revenues and expense items separate from the main balance sheet at present:

JJ Limited   Balance Sheet as at ....

Assets	£	Claims	£
Freehold shop premises	60,000	Capital	107,300
Delivery van	10,000	Commercial Finance	50,000
Stock-in-trade			
(30,500 − 3,000 − 500)	27,000	Trade creditors	27,500
Trade debtors			
(17,500 + 4,000)	21,500		
Cash at bank			
(66,800 − 800 − 80 + 700)	66,620		
	£		£

Revenues and expenses	£
Sales (4,000 + 700)	+4,700
Cost of stock sold	−3,500
(−3,000 − 500)	
Wages	−800
Petrol	−80

It should be clear that the revenues and expenses list simply contains the items which could have been used directly to adjust the capital figure in the balance sheet. The other side of each entry on this list appears in the balance sheet somewhere. For example, the cash spent to pay for the petrol is shown as a reduction in the cash figure in the balance sheet.

At present the two sides of the balance sheet do not agree. If we calculate the net figure for revenues and expenses (i.e. a profit of £320) and add it to the capital figure in the balance sheet it will agree, as follows:

JJ Limited   Balance Sheet as at ....

Assets	£	Claims	£
Freehold shop premises	60,000	Capital (107,300 + 320)	107,620
Delivery van	10,000	Commercial Finance	50,000
Stock-in-trade	27,000	Trade creditors	27,500
Trade debtors	21,500		
Cash at bank	66,620		
	£185,120		£185,120

The statement that summarizes the revenues and expenses is the profit and loss account. This example illustrates the fact that the profit and loss account is simply an appendix to the 'capital' part of the balance sheet.

The profit and loss account would more likely be set out as follows:

Profit and loss account for the week ended ....

	£	
Sales		4,700
Less: Cost of stock sold		3,500
Gross profit		1,200
Less: Wages	800	
Petrol	80	
		880
Net profit for the week		£320

Using a layout something like this can turn the profit and loss account from a list of figures which can be used to find the net profit or loss to a statement which can be used to gain a greater insight to the way in which the profit or loss has arisen. Note particularly that it is normal for businesses that sell goods to deduce the 'gross profit' as a step in deducing the net profit. The gross profit is simply the difference between the price at which the goods sold during the period concerned were sold and how much they cost. The gross profit can be useful in making judgements about the pricing policy of the business.

Note also that the classifications for the revenue and expense items, as with the classification of various assets and claims, is in principle a matter of judgement of those within the business who design the accounting system. In this example there is no reason of principle that the wages and petrol should not have been put under one heading — say general expenses. Such decisions are based entirely on the usefulness, to users of the profit and loss account, of analyzing and classifying revenues and expenses in one way rather than some other way.

Though for businesses which trade as limited companies there are statutory rules which dictate the classification of various items which appear in the accounts, most companies produce accounts for their own management purposes in a form which matches their needs.

ACTIVITY ————————————————————————————————

Look back at the profit and loss account appearing in the last example. From your own background knowledge and from what you know of the business concerned, do you feel that this statement includes all of the expenses which the business will have incurred during the week concerned? Which expenses seem to have been omitted?

The following expenses seem pretty certain to have been incurred, though they have been omitted from the profit and loss account:

◆ *Local authority rates on the freehold premises.*

- *Insurance on the building.*
- *Road fund licence on the van.*
- *Insurance on the van.*
- *Depreciation on the van.*
- *Interest on the loan from the Commercial Finance Co.*

There could also be others.

The reason for their omission is that none of these items has so far given rise to a transaction in the way that the items which we have included did. We return to the way in which such items should be handled after we have established some theoretical underpinning for dealing with such items by considering the accounting conventions which deal with the derivation of the profit figure.

2.5 The Accounting Conventions

You will recall that there are several ground rules on which accounting is based. We met some of these in Chapter 1 in the context of the balance sheet.

ACTIVITY ──

Jot down the conventions that you met in Chapter 1, with a brief outline of each of them.

───

You may have come up with the following:

- Money measurement convention. *Accounting only deals with those items which are capable of being expressed in monetary terms, thus potentially useful information which cannot be expressed in monetary terms is omitted.*
- Cost convention. *Assets are shown in accounting statements at a value which is based on cost.*
- Business entity convention. *For accounting purposes the business and its owner(s) are treated as being distinctly separate. This is why owners are treated as being claimants against their own business in respect of their investment in the business.*
- Dual aspect convention. *Each transaction has two aspects both of which must be recorded in the balance sheet.*
- Prudence. *Accountancy tends to err on the side of caution or prudence. When, as is often the case, the outcome of some part-completed transaction is not known with certainty, a cautious view must be taken of the outcome.*
- Objectivity. *As far as possible, accounting statements should be based on objective, verifiable evidence, rather on matters of opinion and should be free from bias.*

To these we can add some more:
- *Realization*. Revenues (sales) are recognized at the time when the work towards making the sale has been substantially completed, the value of the sale (i.e. how

much the good or service will be sold for) is known and it is confidently expected that the cash will be received from the customer. For most types of business this usually means that we say that a sale has occurred and we take account of it when the goods or service has passed to the customer and the customer has accepted it. In effect this rule establishes in which period's profit and loss account credit is taken for a particular sale. It is important that some such rule exists because otherwise there could be misleading inconsistency as to whether, for example, a credit sale should be included as a revenue for the period in which the sale is made or for the period in which the cash is received.

We have already encountered this rule because, in the example earlier in this chapter, we included a sale on credit for £4,000 as a revenue for the week even though the cash had yet to materialize.

- *Matching.* The expenses associated with a particular revenue must be taken into account in deducing the profit from a particular sale. In other words, in the profit and loss account in which the sale is recognized the associated assets must also be taken into account.

We also saw the effect of this rule in the earlier example, where we accounted for the cost of the goods sold as an expense in the same accounting period as we recognized the sale.

- *Accruals.* This says that the profit (or loss) for a period is the difference between revenues and expenses *not* the difference between cash receipts and payments.
- *Consistency.* Where there is a need to exercise judgement that judgement should be exercised consistently from one accounting period to the next.
- *Materiality.* Where the amounts are trivial, given the size of the other figures involved, it is not necessary slavishly to follow other conventions.
- *Going concern.* Unless it is believed not to be the case, it is assumed that the business will continue in business indefinitely.
- *Stable monetary unit.* This convention asserts that we assume that the value of money is constant. In other words it is assumed that £1 today is worth precisely as much as £1 ten years ago. This is obviously not a justified assumption. It leads to accounting statements which, it is argued, are potentially misleading.

It may not be obvious at the moment as to how some of these conventions are applied. Reference will be made to them in the next few pages and this should make their application clear.

2.6 The Profit and Loss Account — Some Further Issues

We are now going to consider how to deal with the types of expenses which were mentioned in the last activity, namely situations where an expense is incurred, but where the correct amount of the expense will not automatically be taken into account merely by correctly recording the explicit transactions which occur during the accounting period under review. The more important areas where problems occur are given below.

1.   *Where the amount taken into account is less than the full expense for the period because the business has yet to be charged for part of the expense — accrued expenses.*

Say a business has reached the end of its accounting year and it has only been charged for electricity for the first three quarters of the year, simply because the electricity board has yet to send out bills for the quarter which ends on the same date as the business' year-end. If the business takes no action on this, it will mean that the profit and loss account will not reflect the full expense for the year. This will contravene the *matching* convention because not all of the expenses associated with the revenues of the year will have been 'matched' in the same profit and loss account.

Where this problem exists, an estimate is made of the electricity expense outstanding (i.e. the bill for the last three months of the year is estimated). This figure is dealt with as follows:

- Electricity expense in the profit and loss account is increased by the amount of the estimate.
- A new category (accrued expense) is opened on the claims side of the balance sheet and the amount of the estimate entered.

This combination will have the desired effect of increasing the electricity expense to the correct figure for the year in the profit and loss account, presuming that the estimate is reasonably accurate. It will also have the effect of showing that at the end of the accounting year the business owed the amount of the last quarter's electricity bill. It will also have the effect of maintaining the balance sheet equation.

When the electricity bill is eventually paid, it will be dealt with as follows:

- Reduce cash on the balance sheet by the amount of the bill.
- Reduce the amount of accrued expenses in the balance sheet.

If the estimate was accurate then this treatment should precisely cancel the accrued expense item. If there is a slight error it will leave a small amount (either negative or positive depending on the direction of the error) which can be treated as part of the following year's expense. Treating the estimation error in this way is not strictly correct, but the amount is likely to be trivial.

2.   *Where the amount paid during the year is more than the full expense for the period because the business has paid for part of the following year's expense in advance — prepaid expenses.*

Suppose that during an accounting year a business has paid rent for the first two months of the following year, simply because the tenancy agreement is to pay rent annually in advance and the rental year is two months different from the accounting year of the business. If the business takes no action on this, it will mean that the profit and loss account will show more than the full expense for the year. This too will contravene the *matching* convention because more than the expenses associated with the revenues of the year will have been matched in the same profit and loss account.

This problem is overcome by dealing with the rental payment as follows:

- Reduce cash in the balance sheet to reflect the full amount of the rent payment.
- A new category (prepaid expense) is opened on the asset side of the balance sheet and the amount of the prepayment (two months' rent) entered.
- Increase the rent expense item in the profit and loss account by the expense for the year under review (ten months' rent).

This combination will have the desired effect of making the rent payable expense the correct figure for the year in the profit and loss account. It will also have the effect of showing that at the end of the accounting year the business was owed two months' rent, or, at least, the right to occupy the premises for two more months — an asset. This will also have the effect of maintaining the balance sheet equation.

When the two months have elapsed (in the following accounting year), the prepaid expense item in the balance sheet will be dealt with as follows:

- Reduce prepaid expenses on the balance sheet by the amount of the two months' rent (i.e. eliminate the balance unless there are other prepaid expenses).
- Increase the rent payable expense in the new year's profit and loss account by the amount of the two months' rent.

The practical treatment of both accrued expenses and of prepaid expenses provides a good example of how the *materiality* convention is applied. Where the amounts involved are trivial, and particularly where discovering the amount involved is time consuming, the existence of accruals and prepayments is ignored so that expenses fall into the accounting period in which they are paid, rather than being strictly matched to the revenues to which they strictly relate. For example, at the end of an accounting year it is known that there is a bill outstanding for about £5-worth of stationery which was received and used during the year. A business of any size would ignore this when preparing the profit and loss account for the year under review and allow the bill to be treated as an expense of the following year.

3. *Where the business uses particular fixed assets for more than one accounting period.*
   This is fairly straightforward, but does require judgement on behalf of those who are responsible for preparing the profit and loss account. Basically the problem is that some assets (e.g. items of machinery) lose value to the business as a result of factors such as wear and tear and their becoming obsolete. For example, a business pays £50,000 for a machine to be used in manufacturing a product. The management of the business believes that the asset will have a useful working life of five years and is expected to be sold after that time for £5,000. This is to say that it is expected that the expense of owning the asset (over and above the running and maintenance costs) is estimated at £45,000 over the whole five years. Since businesses need to account more frequently than at five year intervals, it is necessary to divide this total expense between the accounting periods concerned. Failure to do this would again contravene the *matching* convention. This is because an expense, the capital cost of owning the machine, would not be matched to the revenues which the machine helped to generate.

The most obvious way of dividing the £45,000 between the five years is simply to give each year an equal share, i.e. £9,000 per year. In fact most businesses use this approach. Some businesses, for various reasons, tend to weight the earlier years of the asset's life with a higher share than the later years. We should be clear, however, that the objective here is simply to apportion part of the estimated expense of owning the asset fairly over the years concerned.

Accounting for purchasing and depreciating fixed assets is quite easy. When the asset is purchased:

♦ Reduce cash in the balance sheet by the full amount paid for the asset.
♦ Increase fixed assets in the balance sheet by the same amount.

At the end of each accounting period in the asset's life:

♦ Reduce the fixed asset in the balance sheet by the annual estimated depreciation expense (£9,000 in the above example).
♦ Show an expense of the same figure in the profit and loss account for the period.

It is important that you are clear that the object of depreciating fixed assets is to match expenses to their associated revenues in the same accounting year. Depreciation is not intended to have the effect of reducing the balance sheet value of assets to their market value. The balance sheet is not meant to be a statement of market values. This is probably a good illustration of the way in which the *going concern* convention is applied. The fact that it is normally assumed that the business will continue trading indefinitely means that there is no need to concern ourselves with the fact that the balance sheet values and the market values of depreciating fixed assets fall out of step with one another. This is because the planned life of individual fixed assets in the business are not expected to be overstatements by virtue of the business ceasing to trade. In other words, the expected life of the asset within the business can actually occur in practice, rather than be thwarted as a result of the business collapsing or closing down for some other reason.

The *consistency* convention is also important in the context of depreciation. As we have seen, the way in which depreciation is calculated is a matter of judgement. The consistency convention simply says that whatever judgement is applied in the first year of the life of a fixed asset should be continually applied throughout the asset's life, unless circumstances alter materially.

4. *Where debtors arising from credit sales cannot be forced to meet their obligations —* bad debts.

Under the *realization* convention, a revenue is taken into account in the profit and loss account during the period when the goods or service passes to the customer, not when payment is received from the customer. Clearly businesses will not sell on credit to those whom the business' management does not expect to pay, but misjudgements inevitably occur from time to time.

While the debt seems likely to be honoured it remains an asset. When it becomes clear that payment will not be forthcoming it ceases to be an asset and becomes an expense. In this eventuality the necessary entries are:

- Reduce trade debtors in the balance sheet by the amount of the debt concerned.
- Show the same amount as an expense (bad debts) in the profit and loss account.

It is important to understand that a debt turning bad does not cancel the original sale. Thus it would be perfectly correct to show a particular sale under revenues and the consequential debt, which has subsequently proved to be bad, as an expense in the same profit and loss account.

Probably the best way to bring the various points together here is through an activity.

ACTIVITY

TT Limited is a new business which started trading on 1 January 19X5. The following is a summary of transactions which occurred during the first year of trading:

1. The owners introduced £50,000 of capital which was paid into a bank account opened in the name of the business.
2. Premises were rented from 1 January 19X5 at an annual rental of £20,000. During the year, rent of £25,000 was paid to the owner of the premises.
3. Rates on the premises were paid during the year as follows:
   For the period 1 January 19X5 to 31 March 19X5   £500
   For the period 1 April 19X5 to 31 March 19X6   £1,200
4. A delivery van was bought on 1 January for £12,000. This is expected to be used in the business for four years and then to be sold for £2,000.
5. Wages totalling £33,500 were paid during the year. At the end of the year the business owed £630 of wages for the last week of the year.
6. Electricity bills for the first three quarters of the year were paid totalling £1,650. After 31 December 19X5, but before the accounts had been finalized for the year, the bill for the last quarter arrived showing a charge of £620.
7. Stock-in-trade totalling £143,000 was bought on credit.
8. Stock-in-trade totalling £12,000 was bought for cash.
9. Sales on credit totalled £152,000 (cost £74,000).
10. Cash sales totalled £35,000 (cost £16,000).
11. Receipts from trade debtors totalled £132,000.
12. Payments to trade creditors totalled £121,000.
13. Van running expenses paid totalled £9,400.

At the end of the year it was clear that a trade debtor who owed £400 would not be able to pay any part of the debt.

Prepare a balance sheet as at 31 December 19X5 and a profit and loss account for the year to that date.

TT Limited   Balance Sheet as at 31 December 19X5

Assets	£	Claims	£
Delivery van	9,500	Capital (50,000 + 26,900)	76,900
(12,000 − 2,500)			
Stock-in-trade (143,000 +			
12,000 − 74,000 − 16,000)	65,000	Trade creditors (143,000	
		− 121,000)	22,000
Trade debtors (152,000			
− 132,000 − 400)	19,600	Accrued expenses (630	
		+ 620)	1,250
Cash at bank (50,000 − 25,000			
− 500 − 900 − 300 − 12,000			
− 33,500 − 1,650 − 12,000			
+ 35,000 − 9,400 + 132,000			
− 121,000)	750		
Prepaid expenses (5,000 + 300)	5,300		
	£100,150		£100,150

Profit and Loss Account for the year ended 31 December 19X5

	£
Sales (152,000 + 35,000)	187,000
Less: Cost of stock sold	
(74,000 + 16,000)	90,000
Gross profit	97,000
Less:	
Rent	20,000
Rates (500 + 900)	1,400
Wages (33,500 + 630)	34,130
Electricity (1,650 + 620)	2,270
Bad debts	400
Van depreciation	2,500
Van expenses	9,400
	70,100
Net profit for the year	£26,900

The balance sheet could now be rewritten in a more stylish form as follows:

TT Limited   Balance Sheet as at 31 December 19X5

	£	£	£
Fixed assets			
Motor van			9,500
Current assets			
Stock-in-trade	65,000		
Trade debtors	19,600		
Prepaid expenses	5,300		
Cash	750		
		90,650	
Less: Current liabilities			
Trade creditors	22,000		
Accrued expenses	1,250		
		23,250	
			67,400
			£76,900
Capital			
Original			50,000
Retained profit			26,900
			£76,900

2.6.1   Deducing the Cost of Stock Sold Figure

In the examples which we have considered so far, when a sale has been made, the cost of the stock sold has been identified simultaneously. This reflects what happens in practice in many cases. For example, the more sophisticated supermarkets tend to have point-of-sale (checkout) devices which record each sale, in the records of the business, and pick up the cost to the business of the items sold at the same time. Businesses which sell a relatively few, high-value, items (e.g. a car retailer) find it easy and convenient to know the cost of each item sold, as it is sold, and to make the necessary transfer from 'stock' to 'cost of stock' sold, on a continual basis.

Some businesses, for example small retail businesses, do not find it practical to match each sale to a particular cost as the accounting period progresses. They find it easier, and just as useful, to deduce the cost of stock sold figure at the end of the accounting period. They do this by knowing the value of the stock at the beginning of the period, by valuing the stock at the end of the period and by knowing the cost of the stock bought during the period.

ACTIVITY ───────────────────────────────────────

Can you set out how we calculate the cost of stock sold when we know the opening and closing stock values and the cost of the stock purchased during the accounting period?

It is as follows:

	Opening stock
Plus:	Purchases
Less:	Closing stock
Equals:	Cost of stock sold

ACTIVITY ───────────────────────────────────────

See if you can do this calculation for TT Limited in the activity before last.

	Opening stock	zero	(new business)
Add:	Purchases (143,000 + 12,000)	155,000	
		155,000	
Less:	Closing stock (from the balance sheet)	65,000	
	Cost of stock sold	90,000	

Note that the cost of stock sold is identical however it is deduced, as should always be the case.

2.6.2 Interpreting the Profit and Loss Account

The profit and loss account is intended to do more than just provide the 'bottom line' figure of profit or loss, important though that figure is. By setting the statement out in a logical way and by analyzing and classifying revenues and expenses likewise, much more can be derived from it.

From the simple example provided by the last activity, it is possible to see how, in total terms, the selling prices compared with the costs of the goods which were sold. It is also possible to see how the net profit related to the sales revenue and how much of the gross profit was eaten away by the overheads (i.e. expenses not directly linked to the sale, e.g. rent). It would be possible to undertake further analysis to see how the various individual overhead expenses related to the total for the overheads. By making comparisons between this year's figures and those of other years or those of other businesses in the same trade, some assessment of TT Limited's effectiveness and efficiency can be made.

Chapters 3 and 4 are particularly concerned with detailed interpretation of the accounting statements, including the profit and loss account.

2.7 The Cash Flow Statement

As we saw in Chapter 1, in the context of Andy's poster sales business, users of accounts find it helpful not only to know what has happened in terms of profit for a period, but also what has happened to the cash of the business.

The cash flow statement is basically as follows:

Sources of cash

less

Uses of cash

equals

Net effect on cash

2.7.1 Sources of Cash

Typically, sources of cash are:

1. **Cash from sales.** If the business sells on credit, the actual cash received from this source during the year will probably not be the same as the sales figure in the profit and loss account.

    It is worth noting that for most UK businesses, of all sizes, cash from sales, net of the expenses which were incurred in order to make those sales, is overwhelmingly the most important source of cash.
2. **Injections of new capital by the owners.** In practice this is not a very important source for most businesses except when they are first starting in business.
3. **Long-term borrowing.** These would include long-term bank loans.
4. **Sales proceeds from any disposals of fixed assets.** This is the cash receivable on the sale of any of the fixed assets of the business at the point where the business disposes of them.

2.7.2 Uses of Cash

The major uses of cash for the typical business are:

1. *Cash to meet trading expenses.* This includes materials, labour and other expenses.
2. *Purchases of new fixed assets.*
3. *Repayments of long-term loans.*
4. *Tax paid.* Businesses are normally responsible for paying tax on their profit, usually due exactly nine months after the end of their accounting year.
5. *Withdrawals of capital by the owners.* These are quite rare events: in many businesses

no more than one or two withdrawals a year. The way in which owners withdraw funds from a business, which trades as a company, is discussed later in this chapter.

Net effect on cash

Any excess of sources over uses or of uses over sources will manifest itself in a net increase or decrease in cash over the year.

EXAMPLE ————————————————————————————————

To illustrate the cash flow statement, we shall pick up the first year of trading of TT Limited, which appeared in the activity on page 35 of this chapter (you should turn back to this activity and the solution). The cash flow statement is simply an analysis of the movements of cash during the year, where the cash arising from each type of transaction is grouped and shown as one figure. The statement should, therefore, explain how the cash balance, which started the year at zero, ended the year at £750 (in funds). The statement is as follows:

TT Limited Cash Flow Statement for the year ended 31 December 19X5

	£	£
Sources of cash (inflows of cash)		
From: Customers for sales (35,000 + 132,000)	167,000	
Owners (capital injections)	50,000	
		217,000
Uses of cash (cash payments)		
To: Suppliers of stock and services		
(25,000 + 500 + 1,200 + 33,500 + 1,650 + 12,000		
+ 121,000 + 9,400)	204,250	
Suppliers of fixed assets	12,000	
		216,250
Net increase in cash during the year		£750

Most large businesses, which trade as limited companies, are required to produce a cash flow statement which must be sent to the owners of the business (shareholders) and made available to any member of the public who wishes to see it. The form of the required statement is not exactly the same as the one given above, but the difference is slight.

Most businesses also produce a projected cash flow statement for future periods as a planning device. We deal with this in some detail in Chapter 5.

SELF ASSESSMENT QUESTION

The following is the balance sheet of TT Limited at the end of its first year of trading (from the last activity).

TT Limited Balance Sheet as at 31 December 19X5

	£	£	£
Fixed assets			
Motor van: Cost			12,000
Depreciation			2,500
			9,500
Current assets			
Stock-in-trade	65,000		
Trade debtors	19,600		
Prepaid expenses	5,300		
Cash	750		
		90,650	
Less: Current liabilities			
Trade creditors	22,000		
Accrued expenses	1,250		
		23,250	
			67,400
			£76,900
Capital			
Original			50,000
Retained profit			26,900
			£76,900

During 19X6, the following transactions took place:

1. The owners withdrew capital in the form of cash of £20,000.
2. Premises continued to be rented at an annual rental of £20,000. During the year, rent of £15,000 was paid to the owner of the premises.
3. Rates on the premises were paid during the year as follows:
   For the period 1 April 19X6 to 31 March 19X7   £1,300
4. A second delivery van was bought on 1 January for £13,000. This is expected to be used in the business for four years and then to be sold for £3,000.
5. Wages totalling £36,700 were paid during the year. At the end of the year the business owed £860 of wages for the last week of the year.

6. Electricity bills for the first three quarters of the year were paid totalling £1,820. After 31 December 19X6, but before the accounts had been finalized for the year, the bill for the last quarter arrived showing a charge of £690.
7. Stock-in-trade totalling £67,000 was bought on credit.
8. Stock-in-trade totalling £8,000 was bought for cash.
9. Sales on credit totalled £179,000 (cost £89,000).
10. Cash sales totalled £54,000 (cost £25,000).
11. Receipts from trade debtors totalled £178,000.
12. Payments to trade creditors totalled £71,000.
13. Van running expenses paid totalled £16,200.

Prepare a balance sheet as at 31 December 19X6, a profit and loss account and a cash flow statement for the year to that date.

Solution on p. 250.

2.8 Accounting for Limited Companies

In the UK most business, except the very smallest, trade in the form of limited companies. A limited company is an artificial legal person. Normally companies are owned by at least two people who are known as members or shareholders. The ownership of a company is normally divided into a number, frequently a large number, of shares of equal size and each shareholder owns one or more shares in the company.

A limited company is legally separate from those who own and manage it. This fact gives rise to the important features of a limited company, and these are discussed below.

Perpetual life

The life of the company is not related to the life of the individuals who own or manage it. When an owner of part of the shares of the company dies, that person's shares pass to the beneficiary under the will. Shares may be sold by an existing shareholder to another person who wishes to become a shareholder.

Limited liability

Since the company is a legal person in its own right it must take responsibility for its own debts and losses. This means that once the shareholders have paid what they have agreed to pay for the shares, their obligation to the company and to the company's creditors is satisfied. Thus shareholders can limit their losses to that which they have paid or agreed to pay for their shares.

Restriction of the right of shareholders to make drawings of capital

Limited companies are required by law to distinguish between that part of their capital (shareholders' claim) which may be withdrawn by the shareholders and that part which may not.

The withdrawable part is that which has arisen from trading profits and from realized profits on the disposal of fixed assets, to the extent that tax payments (on these profits and gains) and previous drawings have not extinguished this part of the capital.

The non-withdrawable part is that which arose from funds injected by shareholders buying shares in the company and that which arose from upward revaluations of company assets which still remain in the company.

That part of the shareholders' fund which is not share capital is known as *reserves*. Thus reserves can either be non-withdrawable (capital reserves) or withdrawable (revenue reserves).

ACTIVITY

Why are limited companies required to distinguish different parts of their capital, whereas sole trading businesses are not?

The reason for this is the limited liability, which company shareholders enjoy, but which owners of unincorporated businesses do not. If a sole trader withdraws all of the owner's claim or even an amount in excess of this, the position of the creditors of the business is not weakened since they can legally enforce their claims against the sole trader as an individual. With a limited company, where the business and the owners are legally separated, such legal right does not exist. However, to protect the company's creditors the law insists that a specific part of the capital of a company cannot legally be withdrawn by the shareholders.

The law does not specify how large the non-withdrawable part of a particular company's capital should be, simply that anyone dealing with the company should be able to tell from looking at the company's balance sheet how large it is. In the light of this, a particular prospective lender, or supplier of goods or services on credit, can make a commercial judgement as to whether to deal with the company or not.

ACTIVITY

Can you think of circumstances in which the non-withdrawable part of the company's capital can legally be reduced?

It can be reduced, but only as a result of the company sustaining trading losses or losses on disposal of fixed assets which exceed the amount of the withdrawable portion of the company's capital.

Drawings may be made by shareholders basically in two ways:

1. Dividends, where all shareholders receive a payment in proportion to the number of the company's shares which are owned.
2. Redemption of share capital, where the company buys the shares from shareholders.

Directors

It is not usually possible for all of the shareholders to be involved in the general management of the company, so they elect directors to act on their behalf. The law imposes on directors the following duties:

1. To maintain appropriate accounting records.
2. To prepare an annual profit and loss account, balance sheet and cash flow statement which shows a 'true and fair' view of events and to make this available to all shareholders and to the public at large.

Company law goes quite a long way in prescribing the form and content of the accounting statements which the directors must publish. A copy of each year's accounts must be made available not only to all of the company's shareholders but also to the general public. This is achieved by the company submitting a copy to the Department of Trade and Industry which allows anyone who wishes to do so to inspect these accounts.

Auditors

Shareholders are required to elect a qualified and independent person or, more usually, a firm to act as auditor. The auditors' main duty is to make a report as to whether in their opinion the statements do what they are supposed to do, namely, show a true and fair view and comply with statutory requirements. In order to make such a statement, the auditors must scrutinize the annual accounting statements prepared by the directors and the evidence upon which they are based. The auditors' opinion must be included with the accounting statements which are sent to the shareholders and to the Department of Trade and Industry.

The relationship between the shareholders, directors and auditors is illustrated in Figure 2.1. The figure shows that the shareholders elect the directors to act on their behalf in the day-to-day running of the company. The directors are required to 'account' annually to the shareholders on the performance, position and cash flows

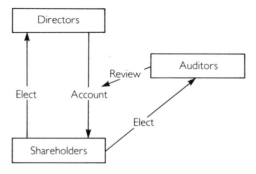

Figure 2.1 The relationships among the shareholders, directors and auditors.

of the company. The shareholders also elect auditors whose role it is to give the shareholders an impression of the extent to which they can regard the accounting statements prepared by the directors as reliable.

Company accounts

The approach and the principles applied to company accounting is more or less identical to that for any other private-sector business. There is one area, though where the accounts of limited companies differ from those of sole trading businesses: this is the appropriation account.

The appropriation account is an appendix to the company's profit and loss account. In the appropriation account, appropriations of the profit for the period are made. These will typically and principally be appropriations to pay the company's corporation tax obligation on its profit for the period and any dividends paid or to be paid from the profit for the period.

EXAMPLE ———

An appropriation account.

Profit and Loss Account for the year ended 31 December 19X5

	£	
Sales		347,000
Less: Cost of stock sold		175,000
Gross profit		172,000
Less:		
Rent	64,000	
Rates	5,000	
Wages	33,000	
Electricity	4,000	
General expenses	13,000	
Depreciation	19,000	
Loan interest	14,000	
Auditors' fee	2,000	
		154,000
Net profit for the year before taxation		18,000
Less: Corporation tax		6,000
Net profit for the year after taxation		12,000
Less: Dividend on ordinary shares		3,000
Unappropriated profit for the year carried forward		£9,000

Summary

In this chapter we began by considering the preparation and nature of the profit and loss account. We then went on to review the conventions of accounting which we have encountered so far. After this we considered the cash flow statement and its preparation. Lastly we took a brief look at accounting for limited companies.

EXERCISES

2.1 You have heard the following statements made. Comment critically on them.

(a) 'If you want to see how the business made its profit you need to look at the balance sheet.'
(b) 'Capital only increases or decreases as a result of the owners putting more cash into the business or taking some out.'
(c) 'The *going concern* convention says that you should always assume that the business will go on indefinitely.'
(d) 'An accrued expense is one that relates to next year.'
(e) 'The auditors of a limited company must make sure that the accounts are correct, that no-one has been "on the fiddle". If the accounts are wrong, the auditor must correct them.'

(Answer on page 261. Answers to exercises 2.2 and 2.3 are given in the Teacher's Manual.)

2.2 The following is the balance sheet of our old friend, TT Limited, as at 31 December 19X6:

TT Limited   Balance Sheet as at 31 December 19X6

	£	£	£
Fixed assets			
Motor van			17,500
Current assets			
Stock-in-trade	26,000		
Trade debtors	20,600		
Prepaid expenses	325		
Cash	49,730		
		96,655	
Less: Current liabilities			
Trade creditors	18,000		
Accrued expenses	1,550		
		19,550	
			77,105
			£94,605

Capital
Original   50,000
Retained profit   44,605
                                                 _____
                                                 £94,605
                                                 ========

During 19X7, the following transactions took place:

1. The owners withdrew capital in the form of cash of £40,000.
2. Premises continued to be rented at an annual rental of £20,000. During the year rent of £25,000 was paid to the owner of the premises.
3. Rates on the premises were paid during the year as follows:

    For the period 1 April 19X7 to 31 March 19X8   £1,400

4. The second delivery van which was bought on 1 January 19X6 for £13,000 has proved to be unsatisfactory. It was part-exchanged for a new van on 1 January 19X7. TT Limited paid cash of £6,000 for the new van. The new van would have cost £15,000 had the business bought it without the trade-in. The new van is expected to be used in the business for four years and then to be sold for £3,000.
5. Wages totalling £36,700 were paid during the year. At the end of the year the business owed £860 of wages for the last week of the year.
6. Electricity bills for the first three quarters of the year were paid totalling £1,820. By the time by which the accounts had to be finalized, the bill for the last quarter had still not arrived.
7. Stock-in-trade totalling £143,000 was bought on credit.
8. Stock-in-trade totalling £12,000 was bought for cash.
9. Sales on credit totalled £211,000 (cost £127,000).
10. Cash sales totalled £42,000 (cost £25,000).
11. Receipts from trade debtors totalled £198,000.
12. Payments to trade creditors totalled £156,000.
13. Van running expenses paid totalled £17,500.

At the end of the year there was a repair bill for repair of the original van amounting to £476, which had not been paid.

Prepare a balance sheet as at 31 December 19X7 and a profit and loss account for the year to that date.

2.3 Prepare a cash flow statement for TT Limited for the year ended 31 December 19X7.

Further Reading

Atrill, P., Harvey, D. and McLaney, E., *Accounting for Business*. Butterworth/Heinemann, 1994.
Bull, R., *Accounting in Business*. Butterworth, 1991.
Glautier, M. and Underdown, B., *Accounting Theory and Practice*. Pitman, 1991.

CHAPTER THREE

The Analysis of Financial Statements — I

3.1 Introduction

In this chapter we consider the analysis, interpretation and evaluation of financial statements. We look especially at how financial ratios can help in developing a financial profile of a business, and the problems which are encountered when applying this technique. This is an important area and we will continue our examination of financial ratios in the following chapter.

3.2 Purpose

When you have completed this chapter you should be able to:

♦ Explain how ratios can be used to evaluate the position and performance of a business.
♦ Calculate important ratios for determining the profitability and efficiency of a business.
♦ Explain the significance of the ratios calculated.
♦ Discuss some of the limitations of financial ratio analysis.

3.3 Financial Ratios

Financial ratios provide a quick and relatively simple means of examining the financial health of a business. A ratio simply expresses one figure appearing in the financial statements in relation to some other figure appearing in the financial statements (e.g. net profit in relation to capital employed) or, perhaps, some resource of the business (e.g. net profit per employee, sales per square metre of counter space, etc.).

By calculating a small number of ratios it is often possible to build up a reasonable picture of the position and performance of a business. Thus, it is not surprising that ratios are widely used by those who have an interest in businesses and business performance. Although ratios are not difficult to calculate, they can be difficult to interpret. For example, a change in the net profit per employee of a business may be due to a number of possible reasons.

ACTIVITY ───

Can you think of five reasons why the net profit per employee ratio may change between one period and another?

You may have thought of the following reasons:

1. Change in the number of employees without a corresponding change in the level of output.
2. Change in the level of output without a corresponding change in the number of employees.
3. Change in the mix of goods and services being offered which, in turn, changes the level of profit.
4. Changes in the level of expenses incurred which, in turn, changes the level of profit.
5. Changes in the quality of employees.

This is not an exhaustive list — you may have thought of other reasons.

It is important to appreciate that ratios are really only the starting point for further analysis. They help to highlight the financial strengths and weaknesses of a business but they cannot, by themselves, explain *why* certain strengths or weaknesses exist or *why* certain changes have occurred. Only a detailed investigation will reveal underlying causes.

Ratios can be calculated in various forms, e.g. as a percentage or as a fraction. The way that a particular ratio is presented will depend on the needs of those who will use the information. Although it is possible to calculate a large number of ratios, only relatively few, based on key relationships, may be required by the user. Many ratios which could be calculated from the financial statements, (e.g. rent payable in relation to taxation) may not be considered because there is no clear or meaningful relationship between the items. We consider here only some of the more important ratios used.

3.3.1 Ratio Classification

Ratios can be grouped according to particular aspects of financial performance or position. The following broad categories provide a useful basis for explaining the nature of the financial ratios to be dealt with:

◆ **Profitability**. Businesses come into being with the primary purpose of creating wealth for the owners. Profitability ratios provide an insight to the degree of success in achieving this purpose. They express the profits made in relation to other key figures in the financial statements or to some business resource.
◆ **Efficiency**. Ratios may be used to measure the efficiency with which certain

resources have been utilized within the business. These ratios are also referred to as *activity* ratios.

♦ **Liquidity**. We have seen in Chapter 2 that it is vital to the survival of a business for there to be sufficient liquid resources available to meet maturing obligations. Certain ratios may be calculated which examine the relationship between liquid resources held and creditors due for payment in the near future.

♦ **Gearing**. Gearing is an important issue which managers must consider when making financial decisions. The relationship between the amount financed by the owners of the business and the amount contributed by outsiders has an important effect on the degree of risk associated with a business.

♦ **Investment**. Certain ratios are concerned with assessing the returns and performance of shares held in a particular business.

3.3.2 The Need for Comparison

Calculating a ratio will not by itself tell you much about the position or performance of a business. For example, if a ratio revealed that the business was generating £100 in sales per square metre of counter space it would not be possible to deduce, from this information alone, whether this level of performance was good, bad or indifferent. It is only when you compare this ratio with some 'benchmark' that the information can be interpreted and evaluated.

ACTIVITY ——

Can you think of any bases which could be used to compare a ratio you have calculated from the financial statements for a particular period?

In answering this activity you may have thought of the following bases:

♦ Past periods. By comparing the ratio you have calculated with the ratio of a previous period it is possible to detect whether there has been an improvement or deterioration in performance. Indeed, it is often useful to track particular ratios over time (say five or ten years) in order to see whether it is possible to detect trends. However, the comparison of ratios from different time periods brings certain problems. In particular, there is always the possibility that trading conditions may have been quite different in the periods being compared. There is the further problem that when comparing the performance of a single business over time, operating inefficiencies may not be clearly exposed. For example, the fact that net profit per employee has risen by 10 per cent over the previous period may at first sight appear to be satisfactory; however, this may not be the case if similar businesses have shown an improvement of 50 per cent for the same period.

♦ Planned performance. Ratios may be compared with the targets that management developed before the start of the period under review. The comparison of planned performance with actual performance may therefore be a useful way of revealing the level of achievement. However, the planned levels of performance must be based on realistic assumptions if they are to be useful for comparison purposes.

◆ Similar businesses. *In a competitive environment a business must consider its performance in relation to that of other businesses operating in the same industry. Survival may depend on the ability to achieve comparable levels of performance. Thus, a useful basis for assessing a particular ratio is the ratio achieved by similar businesses during the same period. This basis is not, however, without its problems. Competitors may have different year-ends and therefore trading conditions may not be identical. They may also have different accounting policies which have a significant effect on reported profits and asset values (e.g. different methods of calculating depreciation, different methods of valuing stock, etc.) Finally, it may be difficult to get hold of the accounts of competitor businesses. Sole proprietorshps and partnerships, for example, are not obliged to publish their financial statements. In the case of limited companies, there is a legal obligation to publish accounts. However, a diversified company may not provide a detailed breakdown of activities sufficient for you to compare with the activity of your particular business.*

There are, however, inter-firm comparison schemes which a business can subscribe to and which provide ratios of similar businesses in the same industry. These ratios have been calculated on financial statements of competitors which have been adjusted to conform to uniform accounting principles. They can therefore provide a useful basis for comparison.

3.4 Ratio Analysis

When employing financial ratios, a sequence of steps is carried out by the analyst. The first step is to undertake an analysis of the ratios. This step involves identifying the key indicators and relationships which require examination and undertaking the necessary calculations. The next step is to interpret the ratios generated. This involves examining the ratios in conjunction with an appropriate basis for comparison and any other information which may be relevant. The significance of the ratios calculated can then be established. The final step is to evaluate the findings. This involves forming a judgement concerning the value of the information uncovered in the analysis and interpretation stages. Whilst calculation is usually straightforward, the interpretation is more difficult and often requires high levels of skill which can only really be acquired through practice. The three steps described are shown in Figure 3.1.

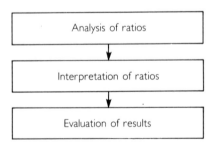

Figure 3.1 **Using financial ratios.**

3.5 The Ratios Examined

Probably the best way to explain financial ratios is to use a set of financial statements, as in the following example, for illustration purposes.

EXAMPLE ───

The following financial statements relate to Alexis plc which owns a small chain of wholesale/retail carpet stores.

Balance Sheets for the year ended 31 March
Fixed assets

	19X2		19X3	
	£000	£000	£000	£000
Freehold land and buildings at cost	451.2		451.2	
Less: Accumulated depreciation	70.0	381.2	75.0	376.2
Fixtures and fittings at cost	129.0		160.4	
Less: Accumulated depreciation	64.4	64.6	97.2	63.2
		445.8		439.4
Current assets				
Stock at cost	300.0		370.8	
Trade debtors	240.8		210.2	
Bank	33.5		41.0	
	574.3		622.0	
Creditors due within one year				
Trade creditors	(221.4)		(228.8)	
Dividends proposed	(40.2)		(60.0)	
Corporation tax due	(60.2)		(76.0)	
	(321.8)	252.5	(364.8)	257.2
		698.3		696.6
Creditors due beyond one year				
12% debentures (secured)		200.0		60.0
		498.3		636.6
Capital and reserves				
£0.50 ordinary shares		300.0		334.1
General reserve		26.5		40.0
Retained profit		171.8		262.5
		498.3		636.6

Profit and Loss Accounts for the year ended 31 March

	19X2		19X3	
	£000	£000	£000	£000
Sales		2,240.8		2,681.2
Less: Cost of sales				
Opening stock	241.0		300.0	
Purchases	1,804.4		2,142.8	
	2,045.4		2,442.8	
Less: Closing stock	300.0	1,745.4	370.8	2,072.0
Gross profit		495.4		609.2
Wages and salaries	137.8		195.0	
Directors' salaries	48.0		80.6	
Rates	12.2		12.4	
Heat and light	8.4		13.6	
Insurance	4.6		7.0	
Interest payable	24.0		6.2	
Postage and telephone	3.4		7.4	
Audit fees	5.6		9.0	
Depreciation:				
Freehold buildings	5.0		5.0	
Fixtures and fittings	27.0	276.0	32.8	369.0
Net profit before tax		219.4		240.2
Less: Corporation tax		60.2		76.0
Net profit after tax		159.2		164.2
Add: Retained profit brought forward		52.8		171.8
		212.0		336.0
Less:				
Transfer to general reserve		—		(13.5)
Dividends proposed		(40.2)		(60.0)
Retained profit carried forward		171.8		262.5

The company employed 14 staff in 19X2 and 18 in 19X3.
All sales and purchases are made on credit.

3.6 Profitability Ratios

The following ratios may be used to evaluate the profitability of the business.

3.6.1 Return on Owners' Equity

This ratio compares the amount of profit for the period available to the owners to the owners' stake in the business. For a limited company the ratio (which is normally expressed as a percentage) is as follows:

Return on owners' equity =

$$\frac{\text{Net profit after taxation and preference dividend (if any)}}{\text{Ordinary share capital + Reserves}} \times 100$$

The net profit after taxation and any preference dividend is used in calculating the ratio as this figure represents the amount of profit available to the owners. In the case of Alexis plc the ratio for the year ended 31 March 19X2 is:

$$\frac{159.2}{498.3} \times 100 = 31.9\%$$

ACTIVITY ——————————————————————

Calculate the return on owners' equity for the company for the year to 31 March 19X3.

The return on owners' equity for the year 19X3 will be:

$$\frac{164.2}{636.6} \times 100 = 25.8\%$$

3.6.2 Return on Capital Employed (ROCE)

ROCE is a fundamental measure of business performance. This ratio expresses the relationship between the net profit generated by the business and the long-term capital invested in the business.

The ratio is expressed as a percentage and is as follows:

$$\text{ROCE} = \frac{\text{Net profit before interest and taxation}}{\text{Share capital + Reserves + Long-term loans}} \times 100$$

Note that, in this case, the profit figure used in the ratio is the net profit *before* interest and taxation. This figure is used because the ratio attempts to measure the returns to suppliers of long-term finance before any deductions for interest payable to lenders or payments of dividends to shareholders are made.

For the year to 31 March 19X2 the ratio is:

$$\frac{243.4}{698.3} \times 100 = 34.9\%$$

Calculate the return on capital employed for the company for the year to 31 March 19X3

For the year ended 31 March 19X3 ROCE is:

$$\frac{246.4}{696.6} \times 100 = 35.4\%$$

ROCE is considered to be a primary measure of profitability. It compares inputs (capital invested) with outputs (profit). This comparison is of vital importance in assessing the effectiveness with which funds have been deployed.

3.6.3 Net Profit Margin

Net profit margin relates the net profit for the period to the sales during that period. The ratio is expressed as follows:

$$\text{Net profit margin} = \frac{\text{Net profit before interest and taxation}}{\text{Sales}} \times 100$$

The net profit before interest and taxation is used in this ratio as it represents the profit from trading operations before any costs of servicing long-term finance are taken into account. This is often regarded as the most appropriate measure of operational performance, for comparison purposes, as differences arising from the way in which a particular business is financed will not influence this measure. However, this is not the only way in which this ratio may be calculated: the net profit after taxation is also used on occasions as the numerator.

For the year ended 31 March 19X2 the net profit margin ratio (based on the net profit before interest and taxation) is:

$$\frac{243.4}{2,240.8} \times 100 = 10.9\%$$

This ratio compares one output of the business (profit) with another output (sales). The ratio can vary considerably between types of business. For example, a supermarket will often operate on low profit margins in order to stimulate sales and thereby increase the total amount of profit generated. A jeweller, on the other hand, may have a high net profit margin but have a much lower sales volume. Factors such as the degree of competition, the type of customer, the economic climate and industry characteristics (such as the level of risk) will influence the net profit margins of a business.

Calculate the net profit margin for the company for the year to 31 March 19X3.

The net profit margin for the year to 31 March 19X3 will be:

$$\frac{246.4}{2,681.2} \times 100 = 9.2\%$$

3.6.4 Gross Profit Margin

The gross profit margin relates the gross profit of the business to the sales generated for the same period. Gross profit represents the difference between sales and the cost of sales. The ratio is therefore a measure of profitability in buying (or producing) and selling goods before any other expenses are taken into account. The ratio is calculated as follows:

$$\text{Gross profit margin} = \frac{\text{Gross profit}}{\text{Sales}} \times 100$$

For the year to 31 March 19X2 the gross profit margin is:

$$\frac{495.4}{2,240.8} \times 100 = 22.1\%$$

ACTIVITY ───────────────────────────────

Calculate the gross profit margin for the company for the year to 31 March 19X3.

The gross profit margin for the year to 31 March 19X3 is:

$$\frac{609.2}{2,681.2} \times 100 = 22.7\%$$

ACTIVITY ───────────────────────────────

Can you think of four reasons why the gross profit margin of a business may increase from one period to another?

You may have thought of the following reasons:

1. An increase in the selling price of goods sold which had not been accompanied by an increase in the cost of goods sold.

2. A decrease in the cost of goods sold through negotiating lower prices with suppliers, finding cheaper sources of supplies, etc. which has not been accompanied by a decrease in the selling price of goods sold.

3. A change in the mix of goods sold so that higher profit margin goods take a greater proportion of total sales.

4. A change in stock valuation method at the year-end which leads to an increase in the closing stock figure (and, therefore, a decrease in the cost of goods sold figure).

Note that an increase in total volume of sales would not lead to a change in the gross profit margin.

The profitability ratios for the company over the two years can be set out as follows:

	19X2	19X3
Return on owners' equity	31.9%	25.8%
ROCE	34.9%	35.4%
Net profit margin	10.9%	9.2%
Gross profit margin	22.1%	22.7%

ACTIVITY ——

What do you deduce from a comparison of the profitability ratios over the two years?

The gross profit margin shows a slight increase in 19X3 over the previous year. This may be due to a number of reasons such as increase in selling prices and a decrease in the cost of sales. However, the net profit margin has shown a slight decline over the period. This means that operating expenses (wages, rates, insurance, etc.) are absorbing a greater proportion of sales income in 19X3 than in the previous year.

The net profit available to equity shareholders has risen only slightly over the period whereas the share capital and reserves of the company have increased considerably (see the financial statements). The effect of this has been to reduce the return to owners equity. The ROCE has improved slightly in 19X3. The slight decrease in long-term capital over the period and increase in net profit before interest and tax has resulted in a better return.

3.7 Efficiency Ratios

Efficiency ratios examine the ways in which various resources of the business are managed. The following ratios consider some of the more important aspects of resource management.

3.7.1 Average Stock Turnover Period

Stocks often represent a significant investment for a business. For some types of business (e.g. manufacturers), stocks may account for a substantial proportion of the total assets held. The average stock turnover period measures the average period for which stocks are being held. The ratio is calculated thus:

$$\text{Stock turnover period} = \frac{\text{Average stock held}}{\text{Cost of sales}} \times 365$$

The average stock for the period can be calculated as a simple average of the opening and closing stock levels for the year. However, in the case of a highly seasonal business, where stock levels may vary considerably over the year, a monthly average may be more appropriate.

In the case of Alexis plc the stock turnover period for the year ended 31 March 19X2 is:

$$\frac{(241 + 300)/2}{1,745.4} \times 365 = 57 \text{ days}$$

This means that, on average, the stock held is being 'turned over' every 57 days. A business will normally prefer a low stock turnover period to a high one as funds tied up in stocks cannot be used for other profitable purposes. In judging the amount of stocks to carry, the business must consider such things as the likely future demand, the possibility of future shortages, the likelihood of future price rises, the amount of storage space available, the perishability of the product, etc.

ACTIVITY ————————————————————————————

Calculate the average stock turnover period for Alexis plc for the year ended 31 March 19X3.

_____

The stock turnover period for the year to 19X3 will be:

$$\frac{(300 + 370.8)/2}{2,072} \times 365 = 59 \text{ days}$$

3.7.2 Average Settlement Period for Debtors

A business will usually be concerned with how long it takes customers to pay the amounts owing. The speed of payment can have a significant effect on the cash flow of the business. The average settlement period calculates how long, on average, credit customers take to pay the amounts which they owe to the business. The ratio is as follows:

$$\text{Average settlement period} = \frac{\text{Trade debtors}}{\text{Credit sales}} \times 365$$

We are told that all sales made by Alexis plc are on credit, and so the average settlement period for debtors for the year ended 31 March 19X2 is:

$$\frac{240.8}{2,240.8} \times 365 = 39 \text{ days}$$

As no figures for opening debtors are available, only the year-end debtors figure is used. This is quite common practice.

ACTIVITY ————————————————————————————

Calculate the average settlement period for debtors for the year ended 31 March 19X3. (For consistency use the year-end debtors figure rather than an average figure.)

_____

The average settlement period for the year to 19X3 is:

$$\frac{210.2}{2,681.2} \times 365 = 29 \text{ days}$$

3.7.3   Average Settlement Period for Creditors

This ratio measures how long, on average, the business takes to pay its trade creditors. The ratio is calculated as follows:

$$\text{Average settlement period} = \frac{\text{Trade creditors}}{\text{Credit purchases}} \times 365$$

For the year ended 31 March 19X2 the average period is:

$$\frac{221.4}{1,804.4} \times 365 = 45 \text{ days}$$

Once again, the year-end figure rather than an average figure for creditors has been employed in the calculations.

ACTIVITY ───────────────────────────────

Calculate the average settlement period for creditors for Alexis plc for the year ended 31 March 19X3. (For consistency, use a year-end figure for creditors.)

The average settlement period is

$$\frac{228.8}{2,142.8} \times 365 = 39 \text{ days}$$

3.7.4   Asset turnover ratio

The asset turnover ratio examines how effective the assets of the business are in generating sales revenue. The ratio is calculated as follows:

$$\text{Asset turnover ratio} = \frac{\text{Sales}}{\text{Total assets employed}}$$

For the year ended 31 March 19X2, this ratio for Alexis plc is:

$$\frac{2,240.8}{445.8 + 574.3} = 2.2 \text{ times}$$

Once again, year-end figures have been employed although an average figure for total assets could also be used if sufficient information were available.

Calculate the asset turnover ratio for Alexis plc for the year ended 31 March 19X3. (For consistency use a year-end figure for total assets.)

The asset turnover ratio for 19X3 will be:

$$\frac{2,681.2}{439.4 + 622.0} = 2.5 \text{ times}$$

Generally speaking, a higher asset turnover ratio is preferred to a lower one. A higher ratio suggests that assets are being used more productively in the generation of revenue. However, a very high ratio may suggest that the business is 'over-trading on its assets', i.e. it has insufficient assets to match the level of sales achieved. When comparing this ratio among businesses, such factors as the age and condition of assets held, the valuation bases for assets and whether assets are rented or purchased outright can complicate interpretation.

A variation of this formula is to use the total assets less current liabilities (which is equivalent to long-term capital employed) in the denominator.

3.7.5 Sales per Employee

This ratio relates sales generated to a particular business resource. It provides a measure of the productivity of the workforce. The ratio is:

$$\text{Sales per employee} = \frac{\text{Sales}}{\text{No. of employees}}$$

For the year ended 31 March 19X2 the ratio is:

$$\frac{£2,240.800}{14} = £160.057$$

It would also be possible to calculate sales per square metre of floor space in order to help assess productivity. This ratio is often used by retail businesses.

Calculate the sales per employee for Alexis plc for the year ended 31 March 19X3.

The ratio for the year ended 31 March 19X3 is:

$$\frac{£2,681.200}{18} = £148.956$$

The activity ratios may be summarized as follows:

	19X2	19X3
Stock turnover period	57 days	59 days
Average settlement period for debtors	39 days	29 days
Average settlement period for creditors	45 days	39 days
Asset turnover	2.2 times	2.5 times
Sales per employee	£160.057	£148.956

ACTIVITY ───

What do you deduce from a comparison of the efficiency ratios over the two years?

A comparison of the efficiency ratios between years provides a mixed picture. The average settlement period for both debtors and creditors has reduced. The reduction may have been the result of deliberate policy decisions, e.g. tighter credit control for debtors, paying creditors promptly in order to maintain goodwill or to take advantage of discounts. However, it must always be remembered that these ratios are average figures and, therefore, may be distorted by a few exceptional amounts owed to or owed by the company.

The stock turnover period has shown a slight decrease over the period but this may not be significant. Overall there has been an increase in the asset turnover ratio which means that the sales have increased by a greater proportion than the assets of the company. Sales per employee, however, have declined and the reasons for this should be investigated.

SELF-ASSESSMENT QUESTION ─────────────────────────────

A plc and B plc operate electrical wholesale stores in the south of England. The accounts of each company for the year ended 30 June 19X4 are as follows:

Balance Sheets for the year ended 30 June

	A plc £000	A plc £000	B plc £000	B plc £000
Fixed assets				
Freehold land and buildings at cost	436.0		615.0	
Less: Accumulated depreciation	76.0	360.0	105.0	510.0
Fixtures and fittings at cost	173.4		194.6	
Less: Accumulated depreciation	86.4	87.0	103.4	91.2
		447.0		601.2
Current assets				
Stock at cost	592.0		403.0	
Debtors	176.4		321.9	
Cash at bank	100.6		109.0	
	869.0		833.9	

	£000	£000	£000	£000
Creditors due within one year				
Trade creditors	(271.4)		(180.7)	
Dividends	(135.0)		(95.0)	
Corporation tax	(32.0)		(34.8)	
	(438.4)	430.6	(310.5)	523.4
		877.6		1,124.6
Creditors due beyond one year				
Debentures		190.0		250.0
		687.6		874.6
Capital and reserves				
£1 ordinary shares		320.0		250.0
General reserves		355.9		289.4
Retained profit		11.7		335.2
		687.6		874.6

Trading and Profit and Loss Accounts for the year ended 30 June 19X4

	A plc		B plc	
	£000	£000	£000	£000
Sales		1,478.1		1,790.4
Less: Cost of sales				
Opening stock	480.8		372.6	
Purchases	1,129.5		1,255.3	
	1,610.3		1,627.9	
Less: Closing stock	592.0	1,018.3	403.0	1,224.9
Gross profit		459.8		565.5
Wages and salaries	150.4		189.2	
Directors salaries	45.4		96.2	
Rates	28.5		15.3	
Heat and light	15.8		17.2	
Insurance	18.5		16.8	
Interest payments	19.4		27.5	
Postage and telephone	12.4		15.9	
Audit fees	11.0		12.3	

Depreciation:				
Freehold buildings	8.8		12.9	
Fixtures and fittings	17.7	327.9	22.8	426.1
Net profit before tax		131.9		139.4
Corporation tax		32.0		34.8
		99.9		104.6
Add: Retained profit brought forward		46.8		325.6
		146.7		430.2
Dividends proposed		135.0		95.0
Retained profit carried forward		11.7		335.2

All purchases and sales are on credit.

Calculate six different ratios which are concerned with profitability and performance. What do you conclude from the ratios that you have calculated?

Solution on p. 252.

Summary

In this chapter we have examined the way in which ratios can be used to assess the profitability and efficiency of a business enterprise. We have seen that ratios are often a useful starting point for a more detailed analysis of a business. Although they can help identify certain strengths and weaknesses concerning financial performance and position they do not identify underlying causes. In Chapter 4 we continue our examination of key financial ratios.

EXERCISES

3.1 C. George (Western) Ltd has recently produced its accounts for the current year. The board of directors met to consider the accounts, at which time concern was expressed that the return on capital employed had decreased from 14 per cent last year to 12 per cent for the current year.

The following reasons were suggested as to why this reduction in ROCE had occurred:

(i) Increase in the gross profit margin.
(ii) Reduction in sales.
(iii) Increase in overhead expenses.
(iv) Increase in amount of stock held.
(v) Repayment of a loan at the year-end.
(vi) Increase in the time taken for debtors to pay.

State, with reasons, which of the above might lead to a reduction in ROCE.

(Answer on page 261. Answers to exercises 3.2 and 3.3 are given in the Teacher's Manual.)

3.2 Extracts from the accounts for the year ended 30 June 19X8 of two companies appear below:

	Dover Printers Ltd	Folkestone Engineers Ltd
	£000	£000
Fixed assets	468	330
Current assets	580	870
	1,048	1,200
Less: Amounts due in under one year:		
Creditors	230	150
Overdraft	160	50
Total assets less current liabilities	658	1,000
Less: Amounts due in over 1 year:		
Loans	460	200
	198	800
Share capital and reserves:		
Ordinary share capital	80	300
Reserves (note 1)	118	500
	198	800
Profit before interest and taxation	95	165
Interest (note 2)	62	45
Profit before taxation	33	120
Taxation	12	42
Profit after taxation	21	78
Less: Ordinary dividends	10	10
Retained	11	68
Note 1: Includes revaluation reserve	—	300
Note 2: Includes overdraft interest	16	15

(a) For each company, calculate the two ratios listed below. You should describe the purpose of each ratio and state to whom they are of most interest. You should include brief notes explaining your calculations.
  (i) Return on capital employed.
  (ii) Return on equity.
(b) Explain the difficulties that may be encountered when attempting to compare the performance of each company on the basis of the ratios above.

3.3 Conday and Co. Ltd has been in operation for three years and produces antique reproduction furniture for the export market. The most recent set of accounts for the company is set out below:

Balance Sheet as at 30 November 19X0

	£000	£000	£000
Fixed assets			
Freehold land and buildings at cost			228
Plant and machinery at cost		942	
Less: Accumulated depreciation		180	762
			990
Current assets			
Stocks		600	
Trade debtors		820	
		1,420	
Less: Creditors: amounts falling due within one year			
Trade creditors	665		
Taxation	95		
Bank overdraft	385	1,145	275
			1,265
Less: Creditors: amounts falling due in more than one year			
12% debentures (note 1)			200
			1,065
Capital and reserves			
Ordinary shares of £1 each			700
Retained profits			365
			1,065

Profit and Loss Account for the year ended 30 November 19X0

	£000	£000
Sales		2,600
Less: Cost of sales		1,620
Gross profit		980
Less: Selling and distribution expenses		
(note 2)	408	
Administration expenses	174	
Finance expenses	78	660

	£000
Net profit before taxation	320
Corporation tax	95
Net profit after taxation	225
Proposed dividend	160
Retained profit for the year	65

Notes:
  1. The debentures are secured on the freehold land and buildings.
  2. Selling and distribution expenses include £170,000 in respect of bad debts.

An investor has been approached by the company to invest £200,000 by purchasing ordinary shares in the company at £6.40 each. The company wishes to use the funds to finance a programme of further expansion.

(a) Analyse the financial position and performance of the company and comment on any features you consider to be significant.
(b) State, with reasons, whether or not the investor should invest in the company on the terms outlined.

Further Reading

Atrill, P., Harvey, D. and McLaney, E., *Accounting for Business* (2nd edn). Butterworth/ Heinemann, 1994.
Bull, R., *Accounting in Business*. Butterworth, 1991.
Glautier, M. and Underdown, B., *Accounting Theory and Practice*. Pitman, 1991.

CHAPTER FOUR

The Analysis of Financial Statements — II

4.1 Introduction

In this chapter we continue our examination of financial ratios. We see how other aspects of financial position and performance can be assessed using appropriate ratios and discuss the limitations of ratio analysis in more detail.

4.2 Purpose

Having completed this chapter you should be able to:

♦ Calculate liquidity, gearing and investment ratios and interpret the results of the ratios you have calculated.
♦ Discuss the importance of gearing to a company and its shareholders.
♦ Discuss the limitations of ratios as a tool of financial analysis.
♦ Explain the impact of inflation on the analysis of financial statements prepared in the conventional manner.

4.3 Alexis plc

In demonstrating how particular ratios are calculated, we continue to use the example of Alexis plc from the previous chapter. For convenience, the example is repeated below (with certain additional information relating to the shares in issue).

EXAMPLE

The following financial statements relate to Alexis plc which owns a small chain of wholesale/retail carpet stores.

Balance Sheets for the year ended 31 March

	19X2		19X3	
Fixed assets	£000	£000	£000	£000
Freehold land and buildings at cost	451.2		451.2	
Less: Accumulated depreciation	70.0	381.2	75.0	376.2
Fixtures and fittings at cost	129.0		160.4	
Less: Accumulated depreciation	64.4	64.6	97.2	63.2
		445.8		439.4
Current assets				
Stock at cost	300.0		370.8	
Trade debtors	240.8		210.2	
Bank	33.5		41.0	
	574.3		622.0	
Creditors due within one year				
Trade creditors	(221.4)		(228.8)	
Dividends proposed	(40.2)		(60.0)	
Corporation tax due	(60.2)		(76.0)	
	(321.8)	252.5	(364.8)	257.2
		698.3		696.6
Creditors due beyond one year				
12% debentures (secured)		200.0		60.0
		498.3		636.6
Capital and reserves				
£0.50 ordinary shares		300.0		334.1
General reserve		26.5		40.0
Retained profit		171.8		262.5
		498.3		636.6

Profit and Loss Accounts for the year ended 31 March

	19X2		19X3	
	£000	£000	£000	£000
Sales		2,240.8		2,681.2
Less: Cost of sales				
Opening stock	241.0		300.0	
Purchases	1,804.4		2,142.8	

	£000	£000	£000	£000
	2,045.4		2,442.8	
Less: Closing stock	300.0	1,745.4	370.8	2,072.0
Gross profit		495.4		609.2
Wages and salaries	137.8		195.0	
Directors' salaries	48.0		80.6	
Rates	12.2		12.4	
Heat and light	8.4		13.6	
Insurance	4.6		7.0	
Interest payable	24.0		6.2	
Postage and telephone	3.4		7.4	
Audit fees	5.6		9.0	
Depreciation:				
Freehold buildings	5.0		5.0	
Fixtures and fittings	27.0	276.0	32.8	369.0
Net profit before tax		219.4		240.2
Less: Corporation tax		60.2		76.0
Net profit after tax		159.2		164.2
Add: Retained profit brought forward		52.8		171.8
		212.0		336.0
Less:				
Transfer to general reserve		—		(13.5)
Dividends proposed		(40.2)		(60.0)
Retained profit carried forward		171.8		262.5

The company employed 14 staff in 19X2 and 18 in 19X3.

All sales and purchases are made on credit.

The market value of the shares of the company at the end of each year was £2.50 and £3.50 respectively. The issue of equity shares during the year ended 31 March 19X3 occurred at the beginning of the year.

4.4 Liquidity Ratios

4.4.1 Current Ratio

The current ratio compares the business' liquid assets (i.e. cash and those assets held which will soon be turned into cash) with its short-term liabilities (creditors due within one year). The ratio is calculated as follows:

$$\text{Current ratio} = \frac{\text{Current assets}}{\text{Current liabilities (i.e. creditors due within one year)}}$$

The current ratio of Alexis plc for the year ended 31 March 19X2 is:

$$\frac{574.3}{321.8} = 1.8 \text{ times (or } 1.8 : 1)$$

The ratio reveals that the current assets cover the current liabilities by 1.8 times. In some texts the notion of an 'ideal' current ratio (usually 2 times, or 2:1) is suggested for businesses. However, this fails to take into account the fact that different types of business require different current ratios. For example, a manufacturing business will often have a relatively high current ratio because it is necessary to hold stocks of finished goods, raw materials and work-in-progress. It will also normally sell goods on credit thereby incurring debtors. A supermarket chain, on the other hand, will have a low ratio as it will hold only stocks of finished goods and will generate mostly cash sales.

The higher the ratio the more liquid the business is considered to be. As liquidity is vital to the survival of a business, a high current ratio is normally preferred to a low one. However, if a business has a very high ratio this may suggest that funds are being tied up in cash or other liquid assets and are not being used as productively as they might otherwise be.

ACTIVITY ───

Calculate the current ratio for Alexis plc for the year ended 31 March 19X3.

───

The current ratio for the year ended 31 March 19X3 is:

$$\frac{622}{364.8} = 1.7 \text{ times (or } 1.7 : 1)$$

4.4.2 Acid Test Ratio

The acid test (or quick) ratio represents a more stringent test of liquidity. It can be argued that, for many businesses, the stock in hand cannot be converted into cash quickly. (Note that, in the case of Alexis plc, the stock turnover period was more than fifty days in both years.) As a result, it may be better to exclude this particular asset from any measure of liquidity. The acid test ratio is based on this idea and is calculated as follows:

$$\text{Acid test ratio} = \frac{\text{Current assets (exc. stock)}}{\text{Current liabilities}}$$

The acid test ratio for Alexis plc for the year ended 31 March 19X2 is:

$$\frac{(574.3 - 300)}{321.8} = 0.9 \text{ times (or } 0.9 : 1)$$

We can see that the 'liquid' current assets do not quite cover the current liabilities and so the business may be experiencing some liquidity problems. In some types of business, however, where cash flows are strong, it is not unusual for the acid test ratio to be below 1.0 without causing liquidity problems.

The current and acid test ratios for 19X2 can be expressed as 1.8:1 and 0.9:1 respectively rather than as a number of times. This form will be found in some texts. The interpretation of the ratios, however, will not be affected by this difference in form.

ACTIVITY ——————————————————————————————————

Calculate the acid test ratio for Alexis plc for the year ended 31 March 19X3.

The acid test ratio for the year ended 31 March 19X3 is:

$$\frac{(622.0 - 370.8)}{364.8} = 0.7 \text{ times (or } 0.7:1)$$

The liquidity ratios for the two-year period may be summarized as follows:

	19X2	19X3
Current ratio	1.8	1.7
Acid test ratio	0.9	0.7

ACTIVITY ——————————————————————————————————

What do you deduce from a comparison of the liquidity ratios over the two years?

The ratios reveal a decrease in both the current ratio and the acid test ratio. These changes suggest a worsening liquidity position for the business. The company must monitor its liquidity carefully and be alert to any further deterioration in these ratios.

4.5 Gearing Ratios

Gearing occurs when a business is financed, at least in part, by contributions from outside parties. The extent to which this happens (i.e. the level of gearing) is often an important factor in assessing risk. Where a business borrows heavily it takes on a commitment to pay interest charges and make capital repayments. This can be a heavy financial burden and can increase the risk of a business becoming insolvent. Nevertheless, it is the case that most businesses are geared to a greater or lesser extent.

Why borrow? A business may borrow for a number of reasons. It may be that the owners have insufficient funds and, therefore, the only way to finance the business adequately is to borrow from others. Another reason is that gearing can be used to increase the returns to owners. This is possible providing the returns generated from borrowed funds exceed the cost of paying interest. An example can be used to illustrate this point.

EXAMPLE ───────────────────────────────────

Two companies X Ltd and Y Ltd commence business with the following long-term capital structures:

	X Ltd	Y Ltd
	£	£
£1 ordinary shares	100,000	200,000
10% loan	200,000	100,000
	300,000	300,000

In the first year of operation they both make a profit before interest and taxation of £50,000. In this case, X Ltd would be considered highly geared as it has a high proportion of borrowed funds in its long-term capital structure. Y Ltd is much lower geared.

The profit available to the shareholders of each company in the first year of operations will be:

	X Ltd	Y Ltd
	£	£
Profit before interest and taxation	50,000	50,000
Interest payable	20,000	10,000
Profit before taxation	30,000	40,000
Taxation (say 25%)	7,500	10,000
Profit available to ordinary shareholders	22,500	30,000

The return on owners' equity for each company will be:

$$\frac{22,500 \times 100}{100,000} \qquad \frac{30,000 \times 100}{200,000}$$

$$\text{i.e. } 22.5\% \qquad\qquad \text{i.e. } 15\%$$

We can see that X Ltd, the more highly geared company, has generated a better return on equity than Y Ltd.

An effect of gearing is that returns to equity become more sensitive to changes in profits. For a highly geared company, a change in profits can lead to a proportionately greater change in the returns to equity.

───

ACTIVITY ───────────────────────────────────

Assume that the profit before interest and tax was 20 per cent higher for each company than stated above. What would be the effect of this on owners' equity?

The revised profit available to the shareholders of each company in the first year of operations will be:

	X Ltd	Y Ltd
	£	£
Profit before interest and taxation	60,000	60,000
Interest payable	20,000	10,000
Profit before taxation	40,000	50,000
Taxation (say 25%)	10,000	12,500
Profit available to ordinary shareholders	30,000	37,500

The return on owners' equity for each company will now be:

$$\frac{30,000 \times 100}{100,000} \qquad \frac{37,500 \times 100}{200,000}$$

$$i.e. \ 30\% \qquad i.e. \ 18.7\%$$

We can see that for X Ltd, the higher geared company, the returns to equity have increased by 33 per cent whereas for the lower geared company the benefits of gearing is less pronounced. The increase in the returns to equity for Y Ltd has only been 25 per cent. The effect of gearing can, of course, work in both directions. Thus, for a high geared company a small decline in profits may bring about a much greater decline in the returns to equity.

ACTIVITY

Assume that the profit before interest and tax was 40 per cent lower for each company than the original £50,000 stated above. What would be the effect of this on owners' equity?

The revised profit available to shareholders will be as follows:

	X Ltd	Y Ltd
	£	£
Profit before interest and taxation	30,000	30,000
Interest payable	20,000	10,000
Profit before taxation	10,000	20,000
Taxation (say 25%)	2,500	5,000
Profit available to ordinary shareholders	7,500	15,000

The return on owners' equity for each company will now be:

$$\frac{7{,}500 \times 100}{100{,}000} \qquad \frac{15{,}000 \times 100}{200{,}000}$$

$$\text{i.e. } 7.5\% \qquad \text{i.e. } 7.5\%$$

We can see that the returns to equity for the higher geared company have fallen by a much greater amount than the returns to equity for the lower geared company. This example illustrates why many equity investors are attracted to high geared companies during periods of economic growth but prefer low geared companies during periods of economic recession.

4.5.1 Gearing Ratio

The following ratio measures the contribution of long-term lenders to the long-term capital structure of a business:

$$\text{Gearing ratio} = \frac{\text{Long-term liabilities (creditors due beyond one year)}}{\text{Share capital} + \text{Reserves} + \text{Long-term liabilities}} \times 100$$

The gearing ratio for Alexis plc for the year ended 31 March 19X2 is:

$$\frac{200}{498.3 + 200} \times 100 = 28.6\%$$

This ratio reveals a gearing ratio which would not normally be considered as high.

The level of gearing adopted by a business will be influenced by various factors including:

- ◆ **The attitude of the owners to risk.** If owners are risk averse, they will prefer less risk to more risk for a particular rate of return. They will only be prepared to take on more risk if there is the opportunity for higher rates of return.
- ◆ **The attitude of management to risk.** Although managers are employed to operate the business on behalf of the owners and should serve the owners' best interests, they may object to high levels of gearing if they feel that this places their job security and remuneration at risk. However, managers may be more prepared to take on greater risk if they feel that there is the opportunity for greater rewards as a result.
- ◆ **The attitude of lenders towards the company.** Lenders will be concerned with the ability of the company to repay the amount borrowed and to pay interest at the due dates. Their attitude towards the company will therefore be influenced by such matters as the profitability of the business, the existing level of borrowing, and security for the loan.
- ◆ **The availability of equity funds.** If the stock market is depressed it may be difficult to raise equity funds and so a company wishing to raise finance may be forced to borrow the amount required.

◆ **The type of industry in which the business operates.** Levels of gearing do vary significantly among industries. Generally speaking, levels of gearing will be higher in industries where profits are stable. Thus, higher levels of gearing are likely to occur in utilities such as electricity, gas and water companies which are less affected by economic recession, changes in consumer tastes, etc. than most businesses.

ACTIVITY

Calculate the gearing ratio of Alexis plc for the year ended 31 March 19X3.

The gearing ratio for the following year will be:

$$\frac{60}{636.6 + 60} \times 100 = 8.6\%$$

4.5.2 Interest Cover Ratio

This ratio measures the amount of profit available to cover interest payable. The ratio may be calculated as follows:

$$\text{Interest cover ratio} = \frac{\text{Profit before interest and taxation}}{\text{Interest payable}}$$

The ratio for Alexis plc for the year ended 31 March 19X2 is:

$$\frac{(219.4 + 24)}{24} = 10.1 \text{ times}$$

This ratio shows that the level of profit is considerably higher than the level of interest payable. Thus, a significant fall in profits could occur before profit levels failed to cover interest payable. The lower the level of profit coverage the greater the risk to lenders that interest payments will not be met.

ACTIVITY

Calculate the interest cover ratio of Alexis plc for the year ended 31 March 19X3.

$$\textit{Interest cover ratio} = \frac{(240.2 + 6.2)}{6.2} = 39.7 \text{ times}$$

ACTIVITY

What do you deduce from a comparison of the gearing ratios over the two years?

The gearing ratios are:

	19X2	19X3
Gearing ratio	28.6%	8.6%
Interest cover ratio	10.1 times	39.7 times

Both the gearing ratio and interest cover ratio have reduced significantly in 19X3. This is due mainly to the fact that a substantial part of the long-term loan was repaid during 19X3. This repayment has had the effect of reducing the relative contribution of long-term lenders to the financing of the company and reducing the amount of interest payable.

The gearing ratio at the end of 19X3 would normally be considered to be very low and may indicate the business has some debt capacity (i.e. it is capable of borrowing more if required). However, the availability of adequate security and profitability must also be taken into account before the debt capacity of a business can be properly established.

4.6 Investment Ratios

There are several ratios available which are designed to help investors assess the returns on their investment.

4.6.1 Dividend per Share

The dividend per share ratio relates the dividends announced during a period to the number of shares in issue during that period. The ratio is calculated as follows:

$$\text{Dividend per share} = \frac{\text{Dividends announced during the period}}{\text{No. of shares in issue}}$$

In essence, the ratio provides an indication of the cash return which an investor receives from holding shares in a company.

Although it is a useful measure, it must be remembered that the dividends received will usually represent only a partial measure of return to investors, dividends being usually only a proportion of the total earnings generated by the company and available to shareholders. A company may decide to plough back some of its earnings into the business in order to achieve future growth. These ploughed-back profits also belong to the shareholders and should, in principle, increase the value of the shares held. When assessing the total returns to investors we must take account of both the cash returns received *plus* any change in the market value of the shares held.

The dividend per share for Alexis plc for the year ended 31 March 19X2 is:

$$\frac{40.2}{600} \text{ (i.e. 300 @ £0.50)} = 6.7\text{p}$$

This ratio can be calculated for each class of share issued by a company. Alexis plc has only ordinary shares in issue and therefore only one dividend per share ratio can be calculated.

ACTIVITY ――――――――――――――――――――――――――――――

Calculate the dividend per share of Alexis plc for the year ended 31 March 19X3.

――

The dividend per share for the year ended 31 March 19X3 is:

$$\frac{60.0}{668.2} = 9.0p$$

Dividends per share can vary considerably among companies. A number of factors influence the amount a company is prepared to issue in the form of dividends to shareholders (e.g. cash availability, future commitments, investor expectations, etc.).

4.6.2 Dividend Payout Ratio

The dividend payout ratio measures the proportion of earnings that a company pays out to shareholders in the form of dividends. The ratio is calculated as follows:

$$\text{Dividend payout ratio} = \frac{\text{Dividends announced for the year}}{\text{Earnings for the year available for dividends}} \times 100$$

In the case of equity shares, the earnings available for dividend will normally be the net profit after taxation and after any preference dividends announced during the period. This ratio is normally expressed as a percentage.

The dividend payout ratio for Alexis plc for the year ended 31 March 19X2 is:

$$\frac{40.2}{159.2} \times 100 = 25.3\%$$

ACTIVITY ――――――――――――――――――――――――――――――

Calculate the dividend payout ratio of Alexis plc for the year ended 31 March 19X3.

――

The dividend payout ratio for the year ended 31 March 19X3 is:

$$\frac{60.0}{164.2} \times 100 = 36.5\%$$

4.6.3 Dividend Yield Ratio

The dividend yield ratio relates the cash return from a share to its current market value. This can help investors assess the cash return on their investment in the company. The ratio (normally expressed as a percentage) is:

$$\text{Dividend yield} = \frac{\text{Dividend per share}/(1-t)}{\text{Market value per share}} \times 100$$

where t is the basic rate of income tax.

The numerator of this ratio requires some explanation. In the UK, investors who receive a dividend from a company also receive a tax credit. This tax credit is equal to the amount of tax that would be payable on the dividends received by a basic rate income tax payer. As this tax credit can be offset against any tax liability arising from the dividends received, this means that the dividends are, in effect, issued net of tax to lower rate income tax payers.

Investors may wish to compare the returns from shares with the returns from other forms of investment. As these other forms of investment are often quoted on a gross (i.e. pre-tax) basis, it is useful to 'gross up' the dividend to facilitate comparison. This can be done by dividing the dividend per share by $1 - t$ where t is the lower rate of income tax.

Assuming a lower rate of income tax of 20 per cent, the dividend yield for Alexis plc for the year ended 31 March 19X2 is:

$$\frac{6.7/(1 - 0.20)}{£2.50} \times 100 = 3.4\%$$

ACTIVITY ——

Calculate the dividend yield for Alexis plc for the year ended 31 March 19X3.

The dividend yield for the year ended 31 March 19X3 is:

$$\frac{9.0/(1 - 0.20)}{£3.50} \times 100 = 3.2\%$$

4.6.4 Earnings per Share

The earnings per share (EPS) of a company relates the earnings generated by the company during a period, and available to shareholders, to the number of shares in issue. For equity shareholders the amount available will be represented by the net profit after tax (less any preference dividend where applicable). The ratio for equity shareholders is calculated as follows:

$$\text{Earnings per share} = \frac{\text{Earnings available to equity shareholders}}{\text{No. of shares in issue}}$$

In the case of Alexis plc, the EPS for the year ended 31 March 19X2 will be:

$$\frac{159.2}{600} = 26.5p$$

This ratio is regarded by many investment analysts as a fundamental measure of share performance. The trend in EPS over time is used to help assess the investment potential of a company's shares.

Although it is possible to make total profits rise through equity shareholders investing more in the company, this will not necessarily mean that the profitability *per share* will rise as a result.

ACTIVITY ───

Calculate the earnings per share of Alexis plc for the year ended 31 March 19X3.

The EPS for the year ended 31 March 19X3 will be:

$$\frac{164.2}{668.2} = 24.6p$$

In this case, the new issue of shares occurred at the beginning of the financial year. Where an issue is made part the way through the year, a weighted average of the shares in issue will be taken based on the date at which the new share issue took place.

It is not usually very helpful to compare the EPS of one company with that of another. Differences in capital structures can render any such comparison meaningless. However, it can be useful to monitor the changes that occur in this ratio for a particular company over time.

4.6.5 Price/Earnings Ratio

The price/earnings (P/E) ratio relates the market value of a share to the earnings per share. This ratio can be calculated as follows:

$$\text{Price earnings ratio} = \frac{\text{Market value per share}}{\text{Earnings per share}}$$

The P/E ratio for Alexis plc for the year ended 31 March 19X2 will be:

$$\frac{£2.50}{26.5p} = 9.4 \text{ times}$$

This ratio reveals that the capital value of the share is 9.4 times higher than its current level of earnings. The ratio is, in essence, a measure of market confidence concerning the future of a company. The higher the P/E ratio the greater the confidence in the future earning power of the company and, consequently, the more investors are prepared to pay in relation to the earnings stream of the company.

P/E ratios provide a useful guide to market confidence concerning the future and therefore can be helpful when comparing different companies. However, differences in accounting conventions between businesses can lead to different profit and EPS figures which can distort comparisons.

ACTIVITY ———————————————————————————

Calculate the P/E ratio of Alexis plc for the year ended 31 March 19X3.

The P/E ratio for the year ended 31 March 19X3 is:

$$\frac{£3.50}{24.6p} = 14.2 \text{ times}$$

The investment ratios for Alexis plc over the two-year period are as follows:

	19X2	19X3
Dividend per share	6.7p	9.0p
Dividend payout ratio	25.3%	36.5%
Dividend yield ratio	3.4%	3.2%
Earnings per share	26.5p	24.6p
P/E ratio	9.4 times	14.2 times

ACTIVITY ———————————————————————————

What do you deduce from the investment ratios set out above?

There has been a significant increase in the dividend per share in 19X3 when compared with the previous year. The dividend payout ratio reveals that this can be attributed in part to an increase in the proportion of earnings distributed to equity shareholders. However, the payout ratio for the year ended 31 March 19X3 is still fairly low. Only about one-third of earnings available for dividend are being distributed. The dividend yield has changed very little over the period and remains fairly low at less than 4.0%.

Earnings per share shows a slight fall in 19X3 when compared with the previous year. However, the price/earnings ratio shows a significant improvement. The market is clearly much more confident about the future prospects of the business at the end of the year to 31 March 19X3.

Investment ratios can vary significantly between companies. However, to give you some indication of average ratios, the following two average investment ratios, derived from listed Stock Exchange companies included in the broadly based Financial Times All Share Index as at 26 June 1993, are provided:

Dividend yield 3.89%
P/E ratio   21.60

SELF-ASSESSMENT QUESTION ——————————————————

A plc and B plc operate electrical wholesale stores in the south of England. The accounts of each company for the year ended 30 June 19X4 are as follows:

Balance Sheets for the year ended 30 June 19X4

	A plc		B plc	
	£000	£000	£000	£000
Fixed assets				
Freehold land and buildings at cost	436.0		615.0	
Less: Accumulated depreciation	76.0	360.0	105.0	510
Fixtures and fittings at cost	173.4		194.6	
Less: Accumulated depreciation	86.4	87.0	103.4	91.2
		447.0		601.2
Current assets				
Stock at cost	592.0		403.0	
Debtors	176.4		321.9	
Cash at Bank	100.6		109.0	
	869.0		833.9	
Creditors due within one year				
Trade creditors	(271.4)		(180.7)	
Dividends	(135.0)		(95.0)	
Corporation tax due	(32.0)		(34.8)	
	(438.4)	430.6	(310.5)	523.4
		877.6		1,124.6
Creditors due beyond one year				
Debentures		190.0		250.0
		687.6		874.6
Capital and reserves				
£1 ordinary shares		320.0		250.0
General reserve		355.9		289.4
Retained profit		11.7		335.2
		687.6		874.6

Trading and Profit and Loss Accounts for the year ended 30 June 19X4

	A plc		B plc	
	£000	£000	£000	£000
Sales		1,478.1		1,790.4
Less: Cost of sales				
Opening stock	480.8		372.6	
Purchases	1,129.5		1,245.3	
	1,610.3		1,617.9	
Less: Closing stock	592.0	1,018.3	403.0	1,214.9
Gross profit		459.8		575.5

Wages and salaries	150.4		189.2	
Directors' salaries	45.4		96.2	
Rates	28.5		15.3	
Heat and light	15.8		17.2	
Insurance	18.5		26.8	
Interest payable	19.4		27.5	
Postage and telephone	12.4		15.9	
Audit fees	11.0		12.3	
Depreciation:				
Freehold buildings	8.8		12.9	
Fixtures and fittings	17.7	327.9	22.8	436.1
Net profit before tax		131.9		139.4
Less: Corporation tax		32.0		34.8
Net profit after tax		99.9		104.6
Add: Retained profit brought forward		46.8		325.6
		146.7		430.2
Dividends proposed		135.0		95.0
Retained profit carried forward		11.7		335.2

All purchases and sales are made on credit.

The market value of the shares in each company at the end of the year were £6.50 and £8.20 respectively.

Calculate six different ratios which are concerned with liquidity, gearing and investment. What can you conclude from the ratios you have calculated?

Solution on p. 253.

4.7 Trend Analysis

It is important to see whether there are trends occurring which can be detected from the use of ratios. Thus, key ratios can be plotted on a graph to provide managers with a simple visual display of changes occurring over time. The trends occurring within the company may be plotted against trends occurring within the industry as a whole for comparison purposes. An example of trend analysis is shown in Figure 4.1.

4.8 Ratios and Prediction Models

Financial ratios, based on current or past performance, are often used to help predict the future. In recent years, a considerable amount of research has been undertaken to test the predictive ability of financial ratios, and in particular, their ability to predict

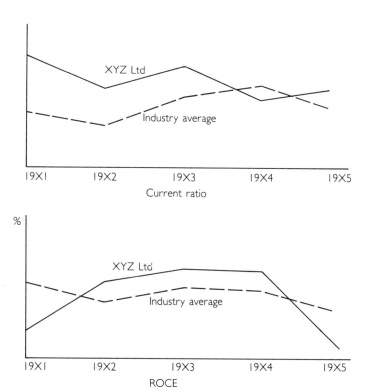

Figure 4.1 **An example of trend analysis.**

financial distress in a business. As a result, a number of models employing ratios have been developed which are claimed to predict financial distress. Researchers have also developed ratio-based models which claim to assess the vulnerability of a company to takeover by another company. These are both areas which are of vital importance to all those connected with the business, and so reliable predictive models can be of great benefit. In the future, it is likely that further ratio-based models will be developed which predict other aspects of future performance.

4.9 Limitations of Ratio Analysis

Although ratios offer a quick and useful method of analysing the position and performance of a business, they are not without their problems and limitations. Some of the more important limitations are considered below.

Quality of financial statements

It must always be remembered that ratios are based on financial statements and the results of ratio analysis are dependent on the quality of these underlying statements.

Ratios will inherit the limitations of the financial statements on which they are based. In the USA there is a saying 'garbage in, garbage out' which, when applied in this context, means that poor quality and unreliable financial statements can only lead to poor quality analysis and interpretation.

In recent years the conventional accounts have been distorted as a result of changing price levels. Traditional accounting assumes, unfortunately, that the monetary unit will remain stable over time even though there have been high levels of inflation during the past few decades. One effect of inflation has been that values for assets held for any length of time may bear little relation to current values. Generally speaking, the value of assets held will be understated in current terms during a period of inflation as they are recorded at their original cost (less any amount written off for depreciation). This means that comparisons, either between businesses or between periods, will be hindered. A difference in, say, an asset turnover ratio may simply be due to the fact that assets in one of the balance sheets being compared were acquired more recently (ignoring the effect of depreciation on asset values).

The value of freehold land in the UK, in particular, increased rapidly during the 1970s and 1980s at least partly as a result of inflation. In order to present a more realistic view of their financial position, some companies began the practice of revaluing their freehold land periodically and showing the revalued amount on the balance sheet. This partial response to inflation, however, can create further problems when comparing ratios. Certain key ratios such as return on capital employed and asset turnover can be greatly changed as a result of changes in the values assigned to freehold land (or indeed other assets).

Another effect of changing prices is to distort the measurement of profit. Sales revenue for a period is often matched against costs from an earlier period. This is because there is often a time lag between acquiring a particular resource and using it in the business. For example, stocks may be acquired in one period and sold in a later period. During a period of inflation this will mean that the costs do not reflect current prices. As a result, costs will be understated in the current profit and loss account and this, in turn, means that profits will be overstated. One effect of this will be to distort the profitability ratios discussed above.

The partial-sightedness of ratios

It is important not to rely on ratios exclusively and thereby lose sight of information contained in the underlying financial statements. Some items reported in these statements can be vital to assessing position and importance. For example, the total sales, capital employed and profit figures may be useful in assessing changes in absolute size which occur over time, or differences in scale between businesses. Ratios do not provide such information. In comparing one figure with another, ratios measure *relative* performance and position and, therefore, provide only part of the picture. Thus, when comparing two businesses, it will often be useful to assess the absolute size of profits as well as the relative profitability of each business. For example, company A may generate £1 million profit and have a ROCE of 15 per cent and company B may generate £100,000 profit and have a ROCE of 20 per cent. Although company B has a higher level of *profitability*, as measured by ROCE, it generates lower total profits.

The basis for comparison

We saw earlier that ratios require a basis for comparison in order to be useful. Moreover, it is important that the analyst compares like with like. When comparing businesses, however, no two are identical, and the greater the differences between the businesses being compared, the greater the limitations of ratio analysis. Furthermore, when comparing businesses, differences in such matters as accounting policies, financing policies and financial year-ends will add to the problems of evaluation.

Balance sheet ratios

Because the balance sheet is only a 'snapshot' of the business at a particular moment in time, any ratios based on balance sheet figures, such as liquidity ratios, may not be representative of the financial position of the business for the year as a whole. For example, it is common for a seasonal business to have a financial year-end which coincides with a low point in business activity. Thus, stocks and debtors may be low at the balance sheet date and the liquidity ratios may also be low as a result. A more representative picture of liquidity can only be gained by taking additional measurements at other points in the year.

Summary

In this chapter we have examined more financial ratios. In particular, we have examined ratios used in the assessment of liquidity, gearing and investment. We have seen that ratios can be used to analyse various aspects of the position and performance of a business. Used properly, they help to provide a thumbnail sketch of a business. However, they require a sound basis for comparison and will only be as useful as the quality of the underlying financial statements permit.

Ratios do not provide the analyst with solutions. Rather they are designed to help in the identification of strengths and weaknesses. Once these have been highlighted further investigation will be required to find out why certain changes or problems have arisen and what the appropriate response should be.

EXERCISES

4.1 The chairman of Diversified Industries plc, a holding company which has interests in engineering, caravan manufacture and a chain of shops selling car accessories, has recently been approached by the managing director of Automobile Care plc, a smaller chain of accessory shops, who wishes to negotiate the merger of his company with Diversified Industries. The following information which has been extracted from Automobile Care's accounts, is available:

	Years ended 31 December		
	19X3	19X4	19X5
	£m	£m	£m
Turnover	18.0	28.0	37.0
Profit before tax	3.2	4.1	7.3
Taxation	1.0	1.7	3.1
Profit after tax	2.2	2.4	4.2
Dividends (net)	0.9	1.1	1.3
Retained	1.3	1.3	2.9
Authorized share capital	6.0	6.0	6.0
Issued share capital			
16 million shares @ 25p	4.0	4.0	4.0
Reserves	8.0	9.1	13.4

The market price per share at the end of December 19X5 was 315p per share.

(a) Calculate the following items for 19X5 and explain the use of each:
  (i) Earnings per share
  (ii) Price/earnings ratio
  (iii) Dividend yield (assume a 20% basic rate)
  (iv) Dividend payout
  (v) Net assets per share
(b) Write some short notes on the factors the chairman of Diversified Industries should take into account when considering the bid. You should use the profit and loss details given in the question together with the figures you calculated in your answer to part (a).

(Answer on page 262. Answers to exercises 4.2 to 4.6 are given in the Teacher's Manual.)

4.2 Threads Limited manufactures nuts and bolts which are sold to industrial users. The abbreviated accounts for 19X8 and 19X7 are given below.

Profit and Loss Account for the years ended 30 June

	19X8 £000	19X8 £000	19X7 £000	19X7 £000
Sales		1,200		1,180
Cost of sales		(750)		(680)
Gross profit		450		500
Operating expenses	(208)		(200)	
Depreciation	(75)		(66)	
Interest	(8)		(—)	
		(291)		(266)
Profit before tax		159		234
Tax		(48)		(80)
Profit after tax		111		154
Dividend — proposed		(72)		(70)
Retained profit for year		39		84

Balance Sheets as at 30 June

	19X8 £000	19X8 £000	19X7 £000	19X7 £000
Fixed assets (note 1)		687		702
Current assets:				
Stocks	236		148	
Debtors	156		102	
Cash	4		32	
	396		282	
Creditors (amounts due within one year):				
Trade creditors	(76)		(60)	
Other creditors and accruals	(16)		(18)	
Dividend	(72)		(70)	
Tax	(48)		(80)	
Bank overdraft	(26)		(—)	
	(238)		(228)	
Net current assets		158		54
Creditors (amounts due after more than one year):				
Bank loan (note 2)		(50)		—
		795		756
Ordinary share capital of £1 (fully paid)		500		500
Retained profits		295		256
		795		756

Note 1: Fixed assets

	Buildings £000	Fixtures and fittings £000	Vehicles £000	Total £000
Cost 1.7.X7	900	100	80	1,080
Purchases	—	40	20	60
Cost 30.6.X8	900	140	100	1,140
Depreciation 1.7.X7	288	50	40	378
Charge for year	36	14	25	75
Depreciation 30.6.X8	324	64	65	453
Net book value 30.6.X8	576	76	35	687

Note 2
The bank loan was taken up on 1 July 19X7 and is repayable on 1 January 19X3. It carries a fixed rate of interest of 12% per annum and is secured by a fixed and floating charge on the assets of the company.

(a) Calculate the following financial statistics for *both* 19X8 and 19X7, using end of year figures where appropriate.
   (i) Return on capital employed
   (ii) Net profit margin
   (iii) Gross profit margin
   (iv) Current ratio
   (v) Liquid ratio (acid-test ratio)
   (vi) Day's debtors
   (vii) Day's creditors
   (viii) Stock turnover ratio
(b) Comment on the performance of Threads Limited from the viewpoint of a company considering supplying a substantial amount of goods to Threads Limited on usual credit terms.
(c) What action could a supplier take to lessen the risk of not being paid should Threads Limited be in financial difficulty?

4.3 Bradbury Ltd is a family-owned clothes manufacturer based in the south west of England. For a number of years the chairman and managing director of the company was David Bradbury. During his period of office the company's sales turnover had grown steadily at a rate of 2–3 per cent each year. David Bradbury retired on 30 November 19X8 and was succeeded by his son Simon. Soon after taking office Simon decided to expand the business. Within weeks he had successfully negotiated a five-year contract with a large clothers retailer to make a range of sports and leisurewear items. The contract will result in an additional £2 million sales during each year of the contract. In order to fulfil the contract new equipment and premises were acquired by Bradbury Ltd.

Financial information concerning the company is given below.

Profit and Loss Account for the year ended 30 November

	19X8	19X9
	£000	£000
Turnover	9,482	11,365
Profit before interest and tax	914	1,042
Interest charges	22	81
Profit before tax	892	961
Taxation	358	385
Profit after tax	534	576
Dividend	120	120
Retained profit	414	456

Balance Sheet as at 30 November

	19X8		19X9	
	£000	£000	£000	£000
Fixed assets				
Freehold premises at cost		5,240		7,360
Plant and equipment (net)		2,375		4,057
		7,615		11,417
Current assets				
Stock	2,386		3,420	
Trade debtors	2,540		4,280	
Cash	127		—	
	5,053		7,700	
Creditors: Amounts falling due within one year				
Trade creditors	1,157		2,245	
Taxation	358		385	
Dividends payable	120		120	
Bank overdraft	—		2,424	
	1,635		5,174	
Net current assets		3,418		2,526
		11,033		13,943
Creditors: Amounts falling due in more than one year				
Loans		1,220		3,674
Total net assets		9,813		10,269

Capital and reserves		
Share capital	2,000	2,000
Reserves	7,813	8,269
Net worth	9,813	10,269

(a) Calculate for each year the following ratios:
    (i) Net profit margin.
    (ii) Return on capital employed.
    (iii) Current ratio.
    (iv) Gearing ratio.
    (v) Day's debtors (collection period).
    (vi) Net asset turnover.
(b) Using the above ratios, and any other ratios or information you consider relevant, comment on the results of the expansion programme.

4.4 Aspley Engineers plc, a medium-sized listed company, is considering two schemes to finance its next expansion. The first is to raise £80 million by means of a term loan from its bankers. Interest would be charged at 2 per cent above base rate which you should assume currently stands at 10 per cent. The loan would be repayable in equal annual instalments over 5 years starting on 1 January 19X0 and finishing on 1 January 19X4. The bank requires a floating charge on the company's assets and an agreement to the following covenants. Firstly, an interest cover of at least 2 times must be maintained and secondly the ratio of debt (i.e. long-term loans) to equity is not to exceed 1 to 1.

The other scheme is to raise £80 million by issuing 20 million ordinary shares at 400p.

The following extracts have been taken from the company's records

Years ended 30 June	19X8	19X7	19X6
No. of £1 ordinary shares (millions)	100	100	100
	£ millions		
Share capital and reserves	360	340	320
Loans	260	200	180
	620	540	500
Profit before interest and tax	93	52	80
Interest payable	30	28	24
Company share price — pence	480	281	546

Currently the chairman of the company and close family members own 42 per cent of its shares. Use a corporate tax rate of 35 per cent in your calculations.

Profit before interest and tax for 19X9 is expected to be £100 million and the net dividend 20p per share. The amount of interest on existing loans is likely to remain unchanged.

(a) Calculate the following ratios for 19X9 for each of the debt and the equity alternatives:
  (i) Interest cover.
  (ii) Earnings per share.
  (iii) Gearing ratio.
(b) Using the information above, state with reasons which scheme you would recommend.

4.5 One of your main suppliers of raw materials is a family-owned company. It is the only available supplier and your company purchases 60 per cent of its output from it. Recently it has run into a severe cash shortage and it requires extra finance to re-equip its factory with modern machinery which is expected to cost £8 million. The machinery's life is expected to be 10 years and savings, before depreciation, arising from its installation, will be £3 million per annum. It has approached you to see if you are able to help and has mentioned that if it can acquire the new equipment your company will be able to share in the benefits through reduced prices for its purchases. An extract of some recent accounts of the company appear below.

Profit and Loss Data
Years ended

	31.12.X7	31.12.X6	31.12.X5
	£ million	£ million	£ million
Sales	9.5	8.0	11.5
Profit before interest and tax	1.9	(2.0)	(0.2)
Interest	1.5	2.4	1.2
Profit before tax	0.4	(4.4)	(1.4)

There was no charge for tax or dividends in these years.

Balance Sheets for the year ended 31 March

	19X7	19X6	19X5
	£million	£million	£million
Fixed assets	24.0	23.9	22.1
Less: Depreciation	14.0	12.0	10.2
	10.0	11.9	11.9
Current assets			
Stock	3.8	3.5	4.3
Debtors	4.1	2.6	2.8
Cash	0.0	0.0	0.0
	7.9	6.1	7.1

	£million	£million	£million
Less: Creditors			
(amounts due in under one year):			
Trade creditors	1.9	1.7	1.4
Overdrafts	4.2	4.1	2.7
	6.1	5.8	4.1
Net current assets	1.8	0.3	3.0
Total assets less current liabilities	11.8	12.2	14.9
Less: Loans	7.4	8.2	6.5
Net assets	4.4	4.0	8.4
Capital and reserves			
Capital	1.0	1.0	1.0
Reserves	3.4	3.0	7.4
	4.4	4.0	8.4

(a) Calculate for each year and comment upon each of the following ratios for the supplier.
  (i) Return on capital employed.
  (ii) Acid test ratio.
  (iii) Stock turnover.
  (iv) Interest cover.
  (v) Gearing ratio.
(b) Prepare a short report stating the financial assistance, if any, your company would be prepared to provide to the supplier. Your recommendations should also state the form that the assistance should take, its amount, and what terms and conditions you would seek to impose.

4.6 The financial statements for Harridges Limited are given below for the two years ended 30 June 19X7 and 19X6. Harridges Limited operates a department store in the centre of a small town.

Harridges Limited
Profit and Loss Account for the years ended 30 June

	19X7		19X6	
	£000	£000	£000	£000
Sales		3,500		2,600
Cost of sales		2,350		1,560
Gross profit		1,150		1,040
Expenses: Wages and salaries	350		320	
Overheads	200		260	
Depreciation	250		150	

	£000	£000
	800	730
Operating profit	350	310
Interest payable	50	50
Profit before taxation	300	260
Taxation	125	105
Profit after taxation	175	155
Dividend proposed	75	65
Profit retained for the year	100	90

Balance Sheet as at 30 June

	19X7		19X6	
	£000	£000	£000	£000
Fixed assets (note 1)		1,525		1,265
Current assets				
Stocks	400		250	
Debtors	145		105	
Cash at bank	115		380	
	660		735	
Creditors: amounts falling due within 1 year				
Trade creditors	(300)		(235)	
Dividend	(75)		(65)	
Other	(110)		(100)	
	(485)		(400)	
Net current assets		175		335
Total assets less current liabilities		1,700		1,600
Creditors: amounts falling due after more than 1 year				
10% loan stock (19X8)		(500)		(500)
		1,200		1,100
Capital and reserves				
Share capital: £1 shares fully paid		490		490
Share premium		260		260
Profit and loss account		450		350
		1,200		1,100

Note 1
Fixed assets schedule

	Freehold* property £000	Fixtures and fittings £000	Motor vehicles £000	Total £000
Cost or valuation				
At 1.7.X6	905	620	80	1,605
Additions	—	480	30	510
Disposals	—	—	(20)	(20)
At 30.6.X7	905	1,100	90	2,095
Depreciation				
At 1.7.X6	—	300	40	340
Disposals	—	—	(20)	(20)
Charge for year	—	220	30	250
At 30.6.X7	—	520	50	570
Net book value	905	580	40	1,525

* The freehold property is the department store operated by Harridges Limited which was valued at £905,000 in June 19X2. The directors consider the property to be worth at least this amount at June 19X7.

(a) Choose and calculate eight ratios which would be helpful in assessing the performance of Harridges Limited. Use end of year values and calculate for 19X6 and 19X7.

(b) Using the ratios calculated in (a) and any others you consider helpful, comment on the performance of Harridges Limited from the viewpoint of a prospective purchaser of a majority of the shares of Harridges.

Further Reading

Atrill, P., Harvey, D. and McLaney, E. *Accounting for Business* (2nd edn). Butterworth/ Heinemann, 1994.
Bull, R., *Accounting in Business*. Butterworth, 1991.
Glautier, M. and Underdown, B. *Accounting Theory and Practice*. Pitman, 1991.

CHAPTER FIVE

Projected Financial Statements

5.1 Introduction

In this chapter we consider the preparation and usefulness of projected (pro forma) financial statements. We see that projected financial statements can be useful for both internal planning purposes and for providing information to prospective investors or lenders.

5.2 Purpose

Having completed this chapter you should be able to:

♦ Prepare a simple projected cash flow statement, profit and loss account and balance sheet for a business.
♦ Explain the usefulness of each of the above statements for planning and decision-making purposes.
♦ Explain the way in which sensitivity analysis can help in evaluating projected information.
♦ Discuss the role of spreadsheets in the preparation of projected financial statements.

5.3 The Role of Projected Financial Statements

Projected financial statements can be valuable when developing long-term strategic plans. When making such plans, it is important for managers to consider the financial consequences to the business as a whole of pursuing a particular course of action. Often, managers will be confronted with a number of possible options. Where these are mutually exclusive, it will be necessary to decide which gives the best return in relation to the risks involved. Projected financial statements can be prepared for each option and can be used to assess the likely future returns. On the basis of these statements, an informed decision can then be made.

You will recall from Chapter 1 (Figure 1.1) that the first three steps in the decision-making, planning and control process were:

1. Identify objectives.
2. Consider objectives.
3. Evaluate options and make a selection.

It is this third step where projected financial statements have a valuable role.

Where managers are considering only one course of action, projected financial statements can still be extremely useful. The preparation of projected statements will provide a useful insight to the effect on future financial performance and position for the business as a whole. They can identify future financing needs and can help assess whether the expected outcomes from the particular course of action are acceptable. Plans may have to be modified to take account of the likely financial outcomes which are revealed.

Where there is considerable uncertainty about the future, managers may wish to examine more than one set of financial statements for a particular course of action. For example, managers may wish to examine projected financial statements prepared according to different possible states of the world. Thus, projected statements may be prepared on the basis of:

- An optimistic view of likely future events.
- A pessimistic view of likely future events.
- A 'most likely' view of future events.

This type of scenario analysis, as it is sometimes called, can help in assessing the level of risk involved. The degree of probability associated with each state of the world would also require careful assessment.

Projected financial statements are usually prepared for internal purposes only. Managers are usually reluctant to share this information with those outside the business, feeling that its publication could damage the competitive position of the business. They may also feel that those outside the business might not fully understand the nature of projected statements and may not, therefore, appreciate that the projections may prove to be inaccurate. There may be a significant difference between projected and actual financial outcomes, particularly where the business operates in a turbulent environment. Nevertheless, there are certain occasions when managers are prepared to release projected information to those outside the business.

ACTIVITY ——

Can you think of any circumstances under which managers might be prepared to provide projected financial information to those outside the business?

——

Managers will often be prepared to provide projected financial statements when trying to raise finance for the business. Prospective lenders may require projected financial statements before considering a loan application. When making an offer of new shares to the public, projected statements are published by the company in order to attract investor interest. Projected statements may also be published if the managers feel the business is under threat. For example, a company which is the subject of a takeover bid to which the managers are opposed may publish projected financial statements in order to give its shareholders confidence in the future of the company as a separate entity and to encourage them to retain their shares in the company.

5.4 Preparing Projected Financial Statements

For most businesses, the most important item in the preparation of projected statements is the projections of sales. The expected level of sales for a period will be influenced by a number of factors including the degree of competition, the planned expenditure on advertising, the quality of the product, changes in consumer tastes and the general state of the economy. Only some of these factors will be under the control of the business. A reliable sales projection is essential as many other items including certain expenses, stock levels, fixed asset and financing requirements will be determined partially or completely by the level of sales for the period. Other expenses, however, may be unaffected by the level of sale for a period.

ACTIVITY ——

Can you name two expenses which are likely to vary directly with the level of sales and two expenses which are likely to stay constant irrespective of the level of sales?

_____

You may have identified cost of sales, materials consumed, and salesforce commission as examples of expenses which vary directly with sales output. Other expenses such as depreciation, rent, rates, insurance and salaries may stay constant during a period irrespective of the level of sales generated. Some expenses have both a variable and a fixed element, and so may vary partially with sales output. Heat and light may be an example of such an expense. A certain amount of heating and lighting costs will be incurred irrespective of the level of sales. However, if overtime is being worked due to heavy demand, this expense will increase. The behaviour of different types of expenses to changes in the level of output is an important issue and we return to this in Chapter 6.

The sales projection of a business may be developed in a number of ways. It may be done by simply aggregating the projections made by the salesforce. These projections may rely heavily on subjective judgement and will usually attempt to take account of various aspects of the market and likely changes in market conditions. However, sales projections may also be based on certain statistical techniques or (in the case of large businesses) economic models. There are no hard-and-fast rules concerning the most appropriate method of projecting into the future for a business. Each business must assess the available methods, in terms of reliability and accuracy for their particular situation, and associated costs. The particular techniques of projecting into the future are not the subject of this chapter. Rather we are concerned with the preparation of projected financial statements and their subsequent evaluation.

Projected financial statements are prepared using the same methods and principles as we have discussed in relation to historic financial statements. The only real difference lies in the fact that the statements are prepared using *projected* rather than *actual* information. This means that projected statements are less reliable and rely more on the use of judgement.

In order to illustrate the preparation of financial statements let us consider the following example.

EXAMPLE

Designer Dresses Limited is a small company to be formed by James and William Clark to sell an exclusive range of dresses from a boutique in a fashionable suburb of London. On 1 January 19X9 they plan to invest £50,000 cash to purchase 25,000 £1 shares each in the company. Of this, £30,000 is to be invested in new fittings in January. These fittings are to be depreciated over three years on the straight line basis (their scrap value is assumed to be zero at the end of their lives). A half year's depreciation is to be charged in the first six months. The sales and purchases projection for the company are as follows:

	Jan.	Feb.	Mar.	Apr.	May	June	Total
£000							
Sales	10.2	30.6	30.6	40.8	40.8	51.0	204.0
Purchases	20.0	30.0	25.0	25.0	30.0	30.0	160.0
Other costs*	9.0	9.0	9.0	9.0	9.0	9.0	54.0

* These include wages but exclude depreciation.

The sales will all be made by credit card. The credit card company will take one month to pay and will deduct its fee of 2 per cent of gross sales before paying amounts due to Designer Dresses. One month's credit is allowed by suppliers. Other costs shown above do not include rent and rates of £10,000 per quarter, payable on 1 January and 1 April. All other costs will be paid in cash. Closing stock at the end of June is expected to be £58,000.

Ignoring taxation, and working to the nearest £000, we now use these figures to prepare the following:

(a) A cash projection for the six months to 30 June 19X9.
(b) A projected profit and loss account for the same period.
(c) A projected balance sheet at 30 June 19X9.

(a) Projected cash flow statement

We have seen in an earlier chapter that the cash flow statement is fairly straightforward to prepare. This statement simply records the cash inflows and outflows of the business. When preparing this statement for management purposes, the cash flow statement is usually broken down into monthly periods. This helps managers to monitor closely changes in the cash position of the business.

There is no set format for the cash flow statement. Managers are free to decide on the form of presentation which best suits their needs. Below is an outline cash flow statement for Designer Dresses for the six months to 30 June 19X9. This format is widely used and we recommend that you use it when preparing this type of statement.

Projected Cash Flow Statement for the six months to 30 June 19X9

	Jan. £000	Feb. £000	Mar. £000	Apr. £000	May £000	June £000
Cash inflows						
Issue of shares						
Credit sales	___	___	___	___	___	___
	___	___	___	___	___	___
Cash outflows						
Credit purchases						
Other costs						
Rent and rates						
Fittings	___	___	___	___	___	___
	___	___	___	___	___	___
Net cash flow						
Opening balance	___	___	___	___	___	___
Closing balance	___	___	___	___	___	___

In this outline each column represents a monthly period. At the top of each column the cash inflows are set out. Below these cash inflows the cash outflows are set out. The difference between the cash inflows and outflows is the net cash flow for the period. If we add this net cash flow to the opening cash balance brought forward from the previous month we derive the cash balance at the end of the month.

When preparing a cash flow statement there are two questions you must ask when considering each item of information presented to you. The first question is:

♦ *Does the item of information concern a cash transaction (i.e. does it involve cash inflows or outflows)?*

If the answer to this question is 'no' then the information should be ignored for the purposes of preparing this statement. You will find that there are various items of information relating to a particular period, such as the depreciation charge, which do not involve cash movements.

If the answer is 'yes' then a second question must be asked:

◆ *When did the cash transaction take place?*

It is important to identify the particular month in which the cash movement takes place. Often the cash movement will occur after the period in which a particular transaction has been agreed: for example, where sales and purchases are made on credit.

Problems in preparing cash flow statements usually arise because the two questions above have not been properly addressed.

ACTIVITY ───

Fill in the outline cash flow statement for Designer Dresses Ltd for the six months to 30 June 19X9 using the information contained in the example.

──

Your answer to the above activity should be as follows:

Projected Cash Flow Statement for the six months to 30 June 19X9

	Jan. £000	Feb. £000	Mar. £000	Apr. £000	May £000	June £000
Cash inflows						
Issue of shares	50					
Credit sales	—	10	30	30	40	40
	50	10	30	30	40	40
Cash outflows						
Credit purchases		20	30	25	25	30
Other costs	9	9	9	9	9	9
Rent and rates	10			10		
Fittings	30					
	49	29	39	44	34	39
Net cash flow	1	(19)	(9)	(14)	6	1
Opening balance	—	1	(18)	(27)	(41)	(35)
Closing balance	1	(18)	(27)	(41)	(35)	(34)

Notes

1. The receipts from credit sales will arise one month after the sale has taken place. Hence, January's sales will be received in February, etc. Similarly, trade credits are paid one month after the goods have been purchased.

2. The closing cash balance for each month is deduced by adding to (or subtracting from) the opening balance the cash flow for the month

(b) Projected profit and loss account

When preparing the projected profit and loss account it is important to include all revenues which are realized in the period (whether or not the cash has been received) and all expenses (including non-cash items) which relate to those revenues. Remember that the purpose of this statement is to show the wealth generated during the period and this may bear little relation to the cash generated.

The format for the projected profit and loss account will be as follows:

Projected Profit and Loss Account for the six months to 30 June 19X9

	£000	£000
Credit sales		
Less: Cost of sales		
Purchases		
Less: Closing stock	——	——
Gross profit		
Credit card discounts		
Rent and rates		
Other costs		
Depreciation of fittings	——	——
Net profit		══

ACTIVITY ──────────────────────────────

Fill in the outline profit and loss account for Designer Dresses Ltd for the six months to 30 June 19X9 using the information contained in the example.

Your answer to this activity should be as follows:

Projected Profit and Loss Account for the six months to 30 June 19X9

	£000	£000
Credit sales		204
Less: Cost of sales		
Purchases	160	
Less: Closing stock	58	102
Gross profit		102
Credit card discounts	4	
Rent and rates	20	
Other costs	54	
Depreciation of fittings	5	83
Net profit		19

Note: The credit card discount is shown as a separate expense and not deducted from the sales figure. This approach is more informative than simply netting off the amount of the discount against sales.

(c) Projected balance sheet

The projected balance sheet reveals the end-of-period balances and should normally be the last of the three statements to be prepared since the earlier ones provide information to be used when preparing the projected balance sheet: the projected cash flow statement reveals the end-of-period cash balance and the projected profit and loss account reveals the projected retained profit for the period for inclusion in the share capital and reserves section of the balance sheet. The depreciation charge for the period, which appears in the projected profit and loss account, must also be taken into account when preparing the projected balance sheet.

The format for the projected balance sheet will be as follows:

Projected Balance Sheet as at 30 June 19X9

	£000	£000	£000
Fixed assets			
Fittings at cost			
Less: Accumulated depreciation			———
Current assets			
Stock			
Debtors		———	
Less: Creditors due within one year			
Trade creditors			
Bank overdraft	———	———	———
Net assets			═══
Share capital and reserves			
Share capital			
Retained profit			———
			═══

ACTIVITY

Fill in the outline balance sheet for Designer Dresses Ltd as at 30 June 19X9 using the information contained in the example.

Your answer to this activity should be as follows:

Projected Balance Sheet as at 30 June 19X9

	£000	£000	£000
Fixed assets			
Fittings at cost			30
Less: Accumulated depreciation			5
			25
Current assets			
Stock		58	
Debtors (£51,000 less 2%)		50	
		108	
Less: Creditors due within one year			
Trade creditors	30		
Bank overdraft	34	64	44
Net assets			69
Share capital and reserves			
Share capital			50
Retained profit			19
			69

Note: *The debtors figure represents June credit sales (less the credit card discount). Similarly, the creditors represents June purchases.*

5.5 Evaluation of Projected Statements

Projected financial statements must be evaluated in order to ensure that sensible financial decisions are made. When evaluating such statements you must ask yourself a number of key questions. These include the following:

♦ How reliable are the projections which have been made?
♦ What underlying assumptions have been made and are they valid?
♦ Are the cash flows satisfactory? Can they be improved by changing policies or plans, e.g. delaying capital expenditure decisions, requiring debtors to pay more quickly, etc.?
♦ Is there a need for additional financing? Is it feasible to obtain the amount required?
♦ Can any surplus funds be profitably reinvested?
♦ Is the level of projected profit satisfactory in relation to the risks involved? If not, what could be done to improve matters?
♦ Are the levels of sales and individual expense items satisfactory?
♦ Have all relevant expenses been included?

◆ Is the financial position at the end of the period acceptable?
◆ Is the level of gearing acceptable? Is the company too highly geared?

ACTIVITY ——

Evaluate the projected financial statements of Designer Dresses Ltd. Pay particular attention to the projected profitability and liquidity of the business.

The projected cash flow statement reveals that the company will have a bank overdraft throughout most of the period under review. The maximum overdraft requirement will be £41,000 in April 19X9. Although the company will be heavily dependent on bank finance in the early months, this situation should not last for too long providing the company achieves and then maintains the level of projected profit.

The company is expected to achieve a net profit margin of 9.3 per cent and a return on owners' equity (using end-of-period figures) of 27.5 per cent. This level of return for a new business may be considered acceptable. The return on equity, in particular, seems to be high. However, the business is of a high-risk nature and therefore the owners will be looking to make high returns. As this is a new company involved in a high-risk business it may be very difficult to project into the future with any real accuracy. Thus, the basis on which the projections have been made require careful investigation.

Some further points regarding profitability can be made. It is not clear from the question whether the wages included in the profit and loss account include any remuneration for James and William Clark. If no remuneration for their efforts has been included, the level of profit shown may be overstated. It may not be possible to extrapolate the projected revenues and expenses for the six-month period in order to obtain a projected profit for the year. It is likely that the business is seasonal in nature, and therefore the following six month period may be quite different.

ACTIVITY ——

Dalgleish Ltd is a wholesaler supplier of stationery. In recent months the company has experienced liquidity problems. The company has an overdraft at the end of November 19X1 and the bank has been pressing for a reduction in this overdraft over the next six months. The company is owned by the Dalgleish family who are unwilling to raise finance through long-term borrowing.

The balance sheet of the business as at 30 November 19X1 is as follows:

Balance Sheet as at 30 November 19X1

	£000	£000	£000
Fixed assets			
Freehold land and premises at cost		250	
Less: Accumulated depreciation		24	226
Fixtures and fittings at cost		174	
Less: Accumulated depreciation		38	136
			362

	£000	£000	£000
Current assets			
Stock at cost		142	
Debtors		120	
		262	
Creditors: amounts falling due within one year			
Trade creditors	145		
Bank overdraft	126		
Corporation tax	24		
Dividends	20	315	(53)
			309
Capital and reserves			
£1 ordinary shares			200
Profit and loss account			109
			309

The following projections for the six months ended 31 May 19X2 are available concerning the business:

1. Sales and purchases for the six months ended 31 May 19X2 will be as follows:

	Sales £000	Purchases £000
December	160	150
January	220	140
February	240	170
March	150	110
April	160	120
May	200	160

2. Seventy per cent of sales are on credit and 30 per cent are cash sales. Credit sales are received in the following month. All purchases are on one month's credit.
3. Wages are £40,000 for each of the first three months. However, this will increase by 10 per cent as from March 19X2. All wages are paid in the month they are incurred.
4. The gross profit percentage on goods sold is 30 per cent.
5. Administration expenses are expected to be £12,000 in each of the first four months and £14,000 in subsequent months. These figures include a monthly charge of £4,000 in respect of depreciation of fixed assets. Administration expenses are paid in the month they are incurred.
6. Selling expenses are expected to be £8,000 per month except for May 19X2 when an advertising campaign costing £12,000 will also be paid for. The advertising campaign will commence at the beginning of June 19X2. Selling expenses are paid for in the month they are incurred.
7. The dividend outstanding will be paid in December 19X1.
8. The company intends to purchase, and pay for, new fixtures and fittings at the end of April 19X2 for £28,000. These will be delivered in June 19X2.

You are required to:

(a) Prepare a cash flow projection for Dalgleish Ltd for each of the six months to 31 May 19X2.
(b) Prepare a projected profit and loss account for the six months to 31 May 19X2.
(c) Briefly discuss ways in which the company might reduce the bank overdraft as required by the bank.

Your answer to this activity should be along the following lines:

Cash Flow Projection for the six months to 31 May 19X2

	Dec. £000	Jan. £000	Feb. £000	Mar. £000	Apr. £000	May £000
Cash inflows						
Credit sales	120	112	154	168	105	112
Cash sales	48	66	72	45	48	60
	168	178	226	213	153	172
Cash outflows						
Purchases	145	150	140	170	110	120
Administration expenses	8	8	8	8	10	10
Wages	40	40	40	44	44	44
Selling expenses	8	8	8	8	8	20
Fixtures					28	
Dividend	20					
	221	206	196	230	200	194
Cash flow	(53)	(28)	30	(17)	(47)	(22)
Opening balance	(126)	(179)	(207)	(177)	(194)	(241)
Closing balance	(179)	(207)	(177)	(194)	(241)	(263)

Projected Profit and Loss Account for the six months to 31 May 19X2

	£000	£000
Sales		1,130
Less: Cost of sales (balancing figure)		791
Gross profit (30% of sales)		339
Wages	252	
Selling expenses (exc. advertising campaign)	48	
Admin. expenses (inc. depreciation)	76	376
Net loss		(37)

Note: The advertising campaign relates to the next financial period and will therefore be charged to the profit and loss account of that period.

In answering part (c) you may have thought of a number of possible options. The following (or perhaps, some combination of these) might be feasible:

- *New equity finance injected by the Dalgleish family or others.*
- *Reduce stock levels.*
- *Delay purchase/payment of fixtures.*
- *Sell fixed assets.*
- *Increase proportion of cash sales.*
- *Delay payment of trade creditors.*

Note: The Dalgleish family have ruled out the possibility of raising a loan.
   Each of the above options has advantages and disadvantages and these must be carefully assessed before a final decision is made.

5.6 Sensitivity Analysis

Sensitivity analysis is useful when evaluating projected financial statements. The technique involves taking a single variable (e.g. volume of sales) and examining the effect of changes in the chosen variable on the likely performance and position of the business. An assessment can then be made of the sensitivity of performance and position to changes in that variable. Although only one variable is examined at a time, a number of variables, considered to be important to the performance of a business, may be examined consecutively.

In essence, a series of 'what if' questions is posed. In relation to sales, for example, the following questions might be asked:

- What if sales volume is 5 per cent higher than expected?
- What if sales volume is 10 per cent lower than expected?
- What if sales price is reduced by 4 per cent?
- What if sales price could be increased by 6 per cent?

In answering these questions it is possible to develop a better 'feel' for the effect of projection inaccuracies on the final outcomes. However, this technique does not assign probabilities to each possible change nor does it consider the effect of more than one variable on projected outcomes at a time.

5.7 Projections Using Spreadsheets

Preparing projected financial statements is facilitated by the use of spreadsheet packages. In essence, a spreadsheet package is simply a matrix of rows and columns which can be loaded into a computer and viewed on the computer screen. The intersection of a row and a column is referred to as a cell into each of which it is possible to insert numbers, equations or descriptions. A simple model can be built using this matrix. For example, the projected cash flow statement for Dalgleish Ltd, dealt with earlier, may be prepared using the rows and columns of a spreadsheet package as follows:

A	B	C	D	E	F	G
1	Dec.	Jan.	Feb.	Mar.	Apr.	May
2	£000	£000	£000	£000	£000	£000
3 *Cash inflows*						
4 Credit sales	120	112	154	168	105	112
5 Cash sales	48	66	72	45	48	60
6	168	178	226	213	153	172
7						
8 *Cash outflows*						
9 Purchases	145	150	140	170	110	120
10 Admin. expenses	8	8	8	8	10	10
11 Wages	40	40	40	44	44	44
12 Selling expenses	8	8	8	8	8	20
13 Fixtures					28	
14 Dividend	20					
15	221	206	196	230	200	194
16						
17 Cash flow	(53)	(28)	30	(17)	(47)	(22)
18 Opening balance	(126)	(179)	(207)	(177)	(194)	(241)
19 Closing balance	(179)	(207)	(177)	(194)	(241)	(263)

Cell B6 can be made equal to the sum of cells B4 and B5, cell C6 can be made equal to the sum of C4 and C5, etc. so that all calculations are carried out by the package. The spreadsheet package is useful if managers wish to carry out sensitivity analysis on the projected statements. One variable may be altered and the spreadsheet will quickly recalculate the totals to show the effect of the change.

SELF-ASSESSMENT QUESTION ————————————————————

Quardis is an importer of high-quality laser printers which can be used with a range of microcomputers. The balance sheet of Quardis Ltd as at 31 May 19X0 is as follows:

	£000	£000	£000
Fixed assets			
Freehold premises at cost		460	
Less: Accumulated depreciation		30	430
Fixtures and fittings at cost		35	
Less: Accumulated depreciation		10	25
			455

	£000	£000	£000
Current assets			
Stock		24	
Debtors		34	
Cash at bank		2	
		60	
Creditors: amounts falling due within one year			
Trade creditors	22		
Taxation	14		
Dividends	10	46	14
			469
Creditors: amount falling due within one year			
Loan — Highland Bank			125
			344
Capital and reserves			
£1 ordinary shares			200
Retained profit			144
			344

The following information is available for the year ended 31 May 19X1:

1. Sales are expected to be £280,000 for the year. Sixty per cent of sales are on credit and it is expected that, at the year-end, three months' credit sales will be outstanding. Sales revenues accrue evenly over the year.
2. Purchases of stock during the year will be £186,000 and will accrue evenly over the year. All purchases are on credit and at the year-end it is expected that two months' purchases will remain unpaid.
3. Fixtures and fittings costing £25,000 will be purchased and paid for during the year. Depreciation is charged at 10 per cent on the cost of fixtures and fittings held at the year end.
4. Depreciation is charged on freehold premises at 2 per cent on cost.
5. On 1 June 19X0 £30,000 of the loan from the Highland Bank is to be repaid. Interest is at the rate of 13% per annum and all interest accrued to 31 May 19X1 will be paid on that day.
6. Stock-in-trade at the year end is expected to be 25 per cent higher than at the beginning of the year.
7. Wages for the year will be £34,000. At the year-end it is estimated that £4,000 of this total will remain unpaid.
8. Other overhead expenses for the year (excluding those mentioned above) are expected to be £21,000. At the year-end it is expected that £3,000 of this total will still be unpaid.

9. A dividend of 5p per share is expected to be announced at the year-end. The dividend outstanding at the beginning of the year will be paid during the year.
10. Corporation tax is payable at the rate of 35 per cent. Corporation tax outstanding at the beginning of the year will be paid during the year.

You are required to:

(a) Prepare a projected profit and loss account for the year ended 31 May 19X1.
(b) Prepare a projected balance sheet as at 31 May 19X1.
(c) Comment on the significant features revealed by these statements.

All workings should be shown to the nearest £000.
Note: A cash flow statement is not required. The cash figure in the balance sheet will be a balancing figure.

Solution on p. 254.

Summary

In this chapter we have examined the preparation of projected financial statements. We have seen that such statements are used mostly for internal planning purposes. The preparation of projected statements is based on the same principles as those underlying the preparation of historic statements, the only difference being that we employ projected rather than actual data. Projected statements are only useful if the projections made are reliable, hence the starting point in any evaluation of projected statements is to examine the way in which the projected data were developed and any assumptions made. The use of scenario analysis and sensitivity analysis can be helpful in developing a 'feel' for likely future outcomes.

EXERCISES ───

5.1   Prolog Ltd is a small wholesaler of microcomputers. It has in recent months been selling 50 machines a month at a price of £2,000 each. These machines cost £1,600 each. A new model has just been launched and this is expected to offer greatly enhanced performance. Its selling price and cost will be the same as for the old model. From the beginning of January, sales are expected to increase at a rate of 20 machines each month until the end of June when sales will amount to 170 units per month. They are expected to continue at that level thereafter. Operating costs including depreciation of £2,000 per month, are forecast as follows:

	Jan.	Feb.	Mar.	Apr.	May	June
			£000			
Operating costs	6	8	10	12	12	12

Prolog expects to receive no credit for operating costs. Additional shelving for storage will be bought, installed and paid for in April costing £12,000. Corporation tax of £25,000 is due at the end of March. Prolog anticipates that debtors will amount to two months' sales. To give their customers a good level of service Prolog plans to hold enough stock at the end of each period to fulfil anticipated demand from customers in the following month. The computer manufacturer, however, grants one month's credit to Prolog. Prolog Ltd's balance sheet appears below.

Balance Sheet at 31 December 19X4

	£000	£000
Fixed assets		80
Current assets		
Stock	112	
Debtors	200	
Cash	—	
	312	
Creditors: amounts falling due within one year		
Trade creditors	112	
Taxation	25	
Overdraft	68	
	205	
Net current assets		107
Total assets less current liabilities		187
Capital and reserves		
Share capital — 25p ordinary shares		10
Profit and loss account		177
		187

(a) Prepare a cash forecast for Prolog Ltd showing the cash balance or required overdraft for the six months ending 30 June 19X5.
(b) Compute at 30 June 19X5 Prolog's:
  (i) Current ratio.
  (ii) Acid test ratio.
  You should ignore any possible tax liability or proposed dividend.
(c) State briefly what further information a banker would require from Prolog before granting additional overdraft facilities for the anticipated expansion of sales.

(Answer on page 263. Answers to exercises 5.2 and 5.3 are given in the Teacher's Manual.)

5.2 Davis Travel Limited specializes in the provision of winter sports holidays but it also organizes outdoor activity holidays in the summer. You are given the following information:

Abbreviated Balance Sheet as at 30 September 19X7

	£000
Fixed assets	560
Current assets	
Cash	30
	590
Total assets	
Creditors: due in under one year	
Trade creditors	180
Total assets less current liabilities	410
Creditors: due in more than one year	
Loans	110
	300
Share capital	100
Reserves	200
	300

Its sales estimates for the next six months are:

	Numbers of bookings received	Numbers of holidays taken	Promotion expenditure £000
October	1,000		100
November	3,000		150
December	3,000	1,000	150
January	3,000	4,000	50
February		3,000	
March		2,000	
Total	10,000	10,000	450

1. Holidays sell for £300 each. Ten per cent is payable when the holiday is booked and the remainder after two months.
2. Travel agents are paid a commission of 10 per cent of the price of the holiday one month after the booking is made.

3. The cost of a flight is £50 per holiday and a hotel £100 per holiday. Flights and hotels must be paid for in the month when the holidays are taken.
4. Other variable costs are £20 per holiday and are paid in the month of the holiday.
5. Administration costs, including depreciation of fixed assets of £42,000, amount to £402,000 for the six months. Administration costs can be spread evenly over the period.
6. Loan interest of £10,000 is payable on 31 March 19X8 and a loan repayment of £20,000 is due on that date. For your calculations you should ignore any interest on the overdraft.
7. The creditors of £180,000 at 30 September are to be paid in October.
8. A payment of £50,000 for fixed assets is to be made in March 19X8.
9. The airline and the hotel chain base their charges on Davis Travel's forecast requirements and hold capacity to meet those requirements. If Davis is unable to fill this reserved capacity a charge of 50 per cent of those published above is made.

(a) Prepare:
    (i) A cash forecast for the six months to 31 March 19X8.
    (ii) A profit and loss account for the six months ended on that date.
    (iii) A balance sheet at 31 March 19X8.
(b) Discuss the main financial problems confronting Davis Travel.

Ignore taxation in your calculations.

5.3 Changes Limited owns a chain of eight shops selling fashion goods. In the past the company maintained a healthy cash balance. However, this has fallen in recent months and at the end of September 19X6 it had an overdraft of £70,000. In view of this, its managing director has asked you to prepare a cash forecast for the next six months. You have collected the following data:

	Oct. £000	Nov. £000	Dec. £000	Jan. £000	Feb. £000	Mar. £000
Sales forecast	140	180	260	60	100	120
Purchases	160	180	140	50	50	50
Wages and salaries	30	30	40	30	30	32
Rent			60			
Rates						40
Other expenses	20	20	20	20	20	20
Refurbishing shops				80		

Stock at 1 October amounted to £170,000 and creditors were £70,000. The purchases in October, November and December are contractually committed and those in January, February and March, the minimum necessary to restock with spring fashions. Cost of sales is 50 per cent of sales and suppliers allow one month's credit on purchases. Taxation of £90,000 is due on 1 January. The rates payment is a charge for a whole year and other expenses include depreciation of £10,000 per month.

(a) Compute the cash balance at the end of each month, for the six months to 31 March 19X7.
(b) Compute the stock levels at the end of each month for the six months to 31 March 19X7.
(c) Prepare a profit and loss account for the six months ended 31 March 19X7.
(d) What problems might Changes Limited face in the next six months and how would you attempt to overcome them?

Further Reading

Atrill, P., McLaney, E. and Harvey, D. *Accounting for Business*. Butterworth/Heinemann, 1994.

Samuels, J., Wilkes, F. and Brayshaw, E. *Management of Company Finance* (5th edn). Chapman and Hall, 1990.

CHAPTER SIX

Costs for Decision-making

◆

6.1 Introduction

This chapter is concerned with the identification of costs which managers can use to help them to make decisions.

6.2 Purpose

On completion of this chapter you should be able to:

♦ Define and distinguish between relevant costs, outlay costs and opportunity costs and use them to make decisions.
♦ Distinguish between fixed costs and variable costs and use them to deduce the break-even point for some activity.
♦ Make decisions on the use of spare capacity and on the most effective use of scarce resources.
♦ Define the full cost of some activity and distinguish between direct and indirect costs to deduce a job cost.

6.3 What Is Meant by Cost?

The answer to this question is, at first sight, obvious. Most people would say that it is how much was paid for the item or service which is under discussion.

ACTIVITY ───

You own a motor car which cost you £5,000 when you bought it, much below list price, at a recent car auction. You have just been offered £6,000 for this car.

What is the cost to you of keeping the car for your own use (ignore running costs, etc., just consider the 'capital' cost of the car)?

───

The real economic cost of retaining the car is £6,000 since this is what you are being deprived of to retain the car. Any decision which you make with respect to the car's future should logically take account of this figure. This cost is known as the 'opportunity cost' since it is the value of the opportunity forgone in order to pursue the other course of action, which in this case is to retain the car.

In one sense the cost is £5,000 because that is how much you paid for the car. However, this cost, which is known as the 'historic cost', is only of academic interest, as it cannot logically be used to make a decision on the car's future. If you disagree with this point, ask yourself how you would assess another offer for the car of £5,500. Obviously you would compare the offer price of £5,500 with the opportunity cost of £6,000. You would not accept the £5,500 on the basis that it was bigger than £5,000, but would reject it on the basis that it was less than £6,000. The only other figure which should concern you is the value to you, in terms of pleasure, usefulness, etc., which retaining the car would give you. If you valued this more highly than the £6,000 opportunity cost, you would reject both offers.

It may occur to you that the £5,000 is relevant here because if you sold the car either you would make a profit of £500 (i.e. £5,500 − 5,000) or £1,000 (i.e. £6,000 − 5,000). Since you would choose to make the higher profit you would sell the car for £6,000 and make the right decision as a result. Now ask yourself what decision you would make if the car cost you £4,000 to buy. Clearly you would still sell the car for £6,000 rather than for £5,500. What is more, you would reach the same conclusion whatever the historic cost was, thus the historic cost cannot ever be relevant to a future decision.

You should note particularly that even if the car cost, say £10,000, the historic cost would still be irrelevant. If you had just bought a car for £10,000 and find that shortly after it is only worth £6,000, you may well be spitting blood with anger at your mistake, but this does not make the £10,000 a relevant cost. The only relevant costs in a decision on whether or not to sell the car are the £6,000 and the value of the benefits of keeping it.

As we saw in Chapters 1 and 2, the historic cost is normally used in accounting statements like the balance sheet and the profit and loss account. This is logical, however, since these statements are intended to be accounts of what has actually happened after the event. In the context of decision-making, which is always related to the future, historic cost is always irrelevant.

To say that historic cost is irrelevant is not to say that the effects of having incurred that cost are always irrelevant. The fact that you own the car and you are thus in a position to exercise choice as to how you use it is not irrelevant.

It might be useful to formalize what we have discussed so far.

6.4 A Definition of Cost

Cost may be defined as the amount of resources, usually measured in monetary terms, sacrificed to achieve a particular objective. The objective might be to retain the car, to buy a particular house, to make a particular product or to render a particular service. If we are talking about a past cost we are talking about historic costs. If we are considering the future we are interested in *opportunity costs* and *outlay costs*.

An opportunity cost can be defined as the value in montary terms of being deprived of the next best option in order to pursue the particular objective. An outlay cost is an amount of money that will have to be spent in order to achieve that objective. We presently meet plenty of examples of both types of future cost.

6.5 Relevant Costs for Decision-making

In order to be relevant to a particular decision a cost must satisfy both of the following criteria:

1. The cost must relate to the objectives of the business. Most businesses have some wealth/financial enhancement objective. For these businesses, costs which are relevant for other reasons (below) will be relevant to the objectives because costs affect wealth.
2. The cost must differ from one possible decision outcome to the next. Only items which are different between outcomes can be used to distinguish between them. Thus the reason that the historic cost of the car, which we discussed earlier, is irrelevant is that it is the same whichever decision is taken about the future of the car. This means that all past costs are irrelevant because what has happened in the past must be the same for all possible future outcomes; the car had the same historic cost irrespective of what you now decide to do with it.

   It is not only past costs which are the same from one decision outcome to the next. For example, a road haulage business has decided that it will buy a new lorry and the decision lies between two different models. The purchase price, load capacity, fuel and maintenance costs are different from one lorry to the other, so the potential costs and revenues associated with these are relevant items. The lorry will require a driver so the business will need to employ one, but a qualified driver could drive either lorry equally well and for the same wage. The cost of employing the driver is thus irrelevant to the decision as to which lorry to buy. This is despite the fact that this cost is a future one.

   If the decision were whether to operate an additional lorry or not, the cost of employing the driver would be relevant because here it would be a cost which would vary with the outcome.

ACTIVITY

A garage has an old car lying around which it bought several months ago for £3,000. The car needs a replacement engine. It is possible to buy a reconditioned engine for £300. This would take seven hours to fit by a mechanic who is paid £4 an hour. At present the garage is short of work, but the owners are reluctant to lay-off any mechanics or even to cut down their basic working week because skilled labour is difficult to find and an upturn in repair work is expected soon. Without the engine the car could be sold for an estimated £3,500.

What is the *minimum* price for which the garage would have to sell the car, with a reconditioned engine fitted, to justify doing the work?

The minimum price is:

	£
Opportunity cost of the car	3,500
Cost of the reconditioned engine	300
Total	£3,800

The original cost of the car is irrelevant. It is the opportunity cost which concerns us.

The cost of the new engine is relevant because if the work is done then the garage will have to pay out the £300; if the job is not done nothing will have to be paid. This is known as an 'outlay cost'.

The labour cost is irrelevant because the same cost will be incurred whether the mechanic undertakes the work or not. This is because the mechanic is being paid to do nothing if the job is not undertaken, thus the additional cost arising from this job is zero.

It should be emphasized that the garage will not seek to sell the car with its reconditioned engine for £3,800; it will seek to charge as much as possible. On the other hand, any price above the £3,800 will make the garage better off financially than not undertaking the job.

ACTIVITY ───

Assume exactly the same circumstances as in the last activity except that the garage is quite busy at the moment. If a mechanic is to be put on the engine replacement job it will mean that other work which the mechanic could have done during the seven hours, all of which could be charged to a customer, will not be undertaken. The garage's 'labour' charge is £12 an hour.

What is the minimum price for which the garage would have to sell the car, with a reconditioned engine fitted, to justify doing the work under these altered circumstances?

The minimum price is:

	£
Opportunity cost of the car	3,500
Cost of the reconditioned engine	300
Labour cost (7 × £12)	84
Total	£3,884

The relevant labour cost here is that which the garage will have to sacrifice in order to undertake the engine replacement. While the mechanic is working on this job, the garage is losing the opportunity to do work for which a customer would pay £84. Note that the £4 an hour mechanic's wage is still not relevant. This is because the mechanic will be paid the £4 irrespective of whether it is the engine replacement work or some other job which is undertaken.

ACTIVITY ───

Can you think of any other factors which should be taken into account relating to this job?

We can think of two points:

1. *Turning away another job in order to do the engine replacement may lead to customer dissatisfaction. On the other hand, having the car available for sale may be useful commercially for the garage, beyond the profit which can be earned from that particular car sale.*
2. *It has been assumed that the only labour opportunity cost is the charge-out rate for the seven hours concerned. In practice, most car repairs involve the use of some materials, spare parts, etc. These are usually charged to customers at a profit to the garage. Any such profit from a job turned away would be lost to the garage and this lost profit would be an opportunity cost of the engine replacement and should, therefore be included in the calculation of the minimum price to be charged for the sale of the car.*

ACTIVITY ───

A business is considering offering a tender to undertake a contract. Fulfilment of the contract will require the use of two types of raw material, a quantity of both of which is held in stock by the business. All of the stock of these two stock items will need to be used on the contract. Information on the stock is as follows:

Stock item	Quantity (units)	Historic cost (£)	Sales value (£)	Replacement cost (£)
A1	500	5	3	6
B2	800	7	8	10

Stock item A1 is in frequent use in the business on a variety of work. The stock of stock item B2 was bought a year ago for a contract which was abandoned. It has recently become obvious that there seems to be no likelihood of ever using this stock if the contract currently being considered does not proceed.

Management wishes to deduce the minimum price at which it could undertake the contract without reducing its wealth as a result, which can be used as the baseline in deducing the tender price.

How much should be included in the minimum price in respect of the two stock items detailed above?

Stock item   A1: £6 × 500 = £3,000
               B2: £8 × 800 = £6,400

Since A1 is frequently used, if the stock is used on the contract it will need to be replaced. Sooner or later if this stock is used on the contract the business will have to buy 500 units of it additional to that which would have been required had the contract not been undertaken.

Under the circumstances, the only reasonable behaviour of the business, if the contract is not undertaken, is to sell the stock of B2. Thus using this stock has an opportunity cost equal to the potential proceeds from disposal.

6.6   The Behaviour of Costs

It is an observable fact that for many commercial/business activities, costs may be broadly described as:

- ◆ Those which remain the same when changes occur to the volume of activity; and
- ◆ Those which vary according to the level of activity.

These are known as *fixed costs* and *variable costs* respectively.

We shall see later in this chapter that knowledge of how much of each type of cost is involved with some particular activity can be of great value to the decision-maker.

6.6.1   Fixed Costs

The way in which fixed costs behave can be depicted as in Figure 6.1. $0F$ is the amount of fixed costs and this stays the same irrespective of the level of activity.

ACTIVITY ──

A business operates a small chain of hairdressing salons. Can you give some examples of costs which are likely to be fixed for this business?

──

We came up with the following:

Rent
Insurance
Cleaning costs
Staff salaries

Staff salaries and wages are sometimes discussed in books as being variable costs. In fact, they tend to be fixed. People are generally not paid according to the level of output and it is not normal to sack staff when there is a short-term downturn in activity. If there is a long-term downturn in activity, or at least it looks that way to management, redundancies may occur, with fixed cost savings. This, however,

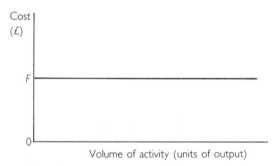

Figure 6.1   Graph of fixed cost against level of activity.

is true of all costs. If there is seen to be a likely reduction in demand the business may decide to close some branches and make rent cost savings. Thus fixed does not mean set in stone for all time, it usually means fixed over the short to medium term.

1. Are fixed costs affected by inflation?
2. Are fixed costs the same amount, whether the time period is one month or one year?

1. *Fixed in this context means that the cost is not altered by changes in the level of activity. If rent (a typical fixed cost) goes up due, say, to inflation a fixed cost will have increased, but not due to a change in the level of activity.*
2. *Fixed costs are almost always 'time-based', i.e. they vary with the length of time concerned. The rent charge for two months is normally twice that for one month. Thus fixed costs normally vary with time, but (of course) not with the level of output.*

Note that when we talk of fixed costs being, say £1,000, we must add the period concerned, say £1,000 per month.

Do fixed costs stay the same irrespective of the level of output, even where there is a massive rise in the level of output? Think in terms of the rent cost for the hairdressing business.

In fact the rent is only fixed over a particular range (known as the 'relevant' range). If the number of people wanting to have their hair cut by the business increased, the business would have to expand its physical size eventually. This might be by opening additional branches, or perhaps by moving existing branches to larger premises. It may be possible to cope with relatively minor increases in activity by using existing space more efficiently, or having longer opening hours. If activity continued to expand, increased rent charges would seem inevitable.

In practice, then, the situation regarding rent cost would look something like Figure 6.2. At lower levels of activity the rent cost would be 0R. As the level of activity expands, the accommodation becomes inadequate and further expansion requires an increase in premises and therefore cost. This higher level of accommodation provision will enable further expansion to take place. Eventually, further costs will need to be incurred if further expansion is to occur.

6.6.2 Variable Costs

Variable costs vary with the level of activity. In a manufacturing business, for example, this would include raw materials used.

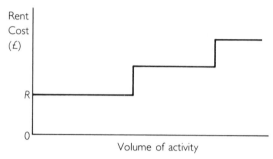

Figure 6.2   **Graph of rent cost against level of activity.**

ACTIVITY ————————————————————————————————————

Can you think of some examples of variable costs in the hairdressing business?

We can think of a couple:

◆ *Lotions and other materials used.*
◆ *Laundry costs to wash towels used to dry the hair of customers.*

Variable costs can be represented graphically as in Figure 6.3. At zero level of activity the cost is zero. This increases in a straight line as activity increases.

ACTIVITY ————————————————————————————————————

The straight line for variable cost in Figure 6.3 implies that the cost of materials will always be the same per unit of activity irrespective of the level of activity concerned. Is this likely in practice to be true of the materials used by hairdressers?

In some cases this is not true because at high levels of output the quantities bought will enable the business to benefit from bulk discounts and general power in the market-place, i.e. economies of scale.

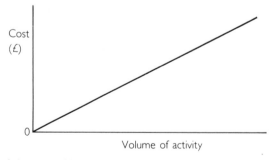

Figure 6.3   **Graph of the cost of lotions and other materials against the level of activity.**

On the other hand, there are circumstances where a high level of demand may cause a shortage of the commodity, thus pushing prices up at the higher end of activity. In the context of materials used by hairdressers, the former seems more likely than the latter.

6.6.3 Semi-fixed and Semi-variable Costs

In some cases costs have an element of both fixed and variable cost. An example might be the electricity cost for the hairdressing business. Some of this will be for heating and lighting and this part is probably fixed, at least until the volume of activity expands to a point where longer opening hours or larger premises are necessary. The other part of the cost will vary with the level of activity. Here we are talking about such things as power for hairdryers, etc.

Usually it is not very obvious how much of each element a particular cost contains, and one must look to past experience. If we have data on what the electricity cost has been for various levels of activity, say the relevant data over several three-month billing periods, we can estimate the fixed and variable portions. This is often done graphically, as shown in Figure 6.4. Each one of the crosses in the graph is a reading of the electricity charge for a particular level of activity (probably measured in terms of sales revenue). The line drawn through them is an estimate of 'the line of best fit', i.e. the line which seemed best to represent the data. A better estimate can usually be made using a statistical technique, which does not involve drawing graphs and making estimates. In practice, it probably does not make too much difference which approach is taken.

From the graph we can say that the fixed element of the electricity cost is the amount represented by the vertical distance from the zero point (bottom left-hand corner) to the point where the line crosses the vertical axis. The variable cost per unit is the amount that the graph rises for each increase in the volume of activity.

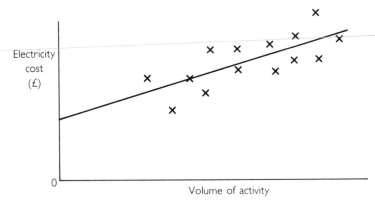

Figure 6.4   Graph of electricity cost against level of activity.

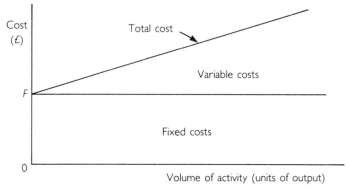

Figure 6.5 **Graph of total cost against level of activity.**

6.7 **Break-even Analysis**

Now that we have considered the nature of fixed and variable costs we can go on to do something useful with that knowledge.

If, in respect of a particular activity, we know the total fixed costs for a period and the total variable cost per unit, we can produce a graph like Figure 6.5.

Figure 6.5 shows the fixed cost area. Added to this is the variable cost — the wedge shaped portion at the top of the graph. The uppermost line is the total cost at any particular level of activity. This total is the vertical distance between the horizontal axis and the uppermost line for the particular level of activity concerned. Logically enough, the total cost at zero activity is the amount of the fixed costs. This increases by the amount of the relevant variable costs as the volume of activity increases.

If we superimpose on this total cost graph a line representing total revenue for each level of activity we obtain the graph shown in Figure 6.6.

Note that at zero level of activity (zero sales) there is zero sales revenue. The profit or loss (total sales revenue less total cost) at various levels of activity is the vertical distance between the total sales line and the total cost line, at that particular level of activity. At break-even point there is no vertical distance between these two lines and thus there is no profit, i.e. the activity breaks even. Below break-even point a loss will be incurred, above break-even point there will be a profit. The further below break-even point, the greater the loss; the further above, the greater the profit.

The usefulness of being able to deduce break-even point in this way is to compare the planned level of activity with the break-even point and so make a judgement concerning the riskiness of the activity. Operating only just above the level of activity necessary in order to break-even may indicate that it is a risky venture, since only a small fall from the planned level of activity could lead to a loss.

Deducing break-even points by graphical means is a laborious business. Fortunately, since the relationships in the graph are all straight line ones, it is easy to calculate the break-even point. We know that at break-even point (but not at any other point):

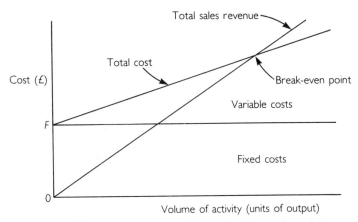

Figure 6.6 A break-even chart.

Total revenues = Total costs

i.e.

Total revenues = Fixed costs + Total variable costs

If we call the number of units of output at break-even point b, then:

b × Sales revenue per unit = Fixed costs + (b × Variable costs per unit)

thus:

(b × Sales revenue per unit) − (b × Variable costs per unit) = Fixed costs

and

b × (Sales revenue per unit − Variable costs per unit) = Fixed costs

giving

b = Fixed costs/(Sales revenue per unit − Variable costs per unit)

If you look back at the break-even chart this looks logical. The variable cost line starts off with an advantage over the sales revenue line equal to the amount of the fixed costs. Because the sales revenue per unit is greater than the variable cost per unit, the sales revenue line will gradually catch up with the variable cost line. The rate at which it will catch it up is dependent on the relative gradients of the two lines, and the amount which it has to catch up (the amount of the fixed costs). Bearing in mind that the slopes of the two lines are the variable cost per unit and the selling price per unit, the above equation for calculating b looks perfectly logical.

ACTIVITY

Cottage Industries Ltd makes baskets. The fixed costs of operating the workshop for a month total £500. Each basket requires materials which cost £2. Each basket takes two hours to make and the business pays the basketmakers £3 an hour. The basketmakers are all on contracts such that if they do not work for any reason, they are not paid. The baskets are sold to a wholesaler for £10 each.

What is the break-even point for basketmaking for the business?

Break-even point (in number of baskets) = Fixed costs/(Sales revenue per unit
$$− \text{ Variable costs per unit}) = £500/[£10$$
$$− (2 + 6)] = 250 \text{ baskets per month}$$

Note that the break-even point must be expressed with respect to a period of time.

6.8 Contribution and Marginal Analysis

The denominator of the break-even formula (i.e. sales revenue per unit minus variable costs per unit) is known as the *contribution* per unit. Thus for the basketmaking activity the contribution per unit is £2. This can be quite a useful figure to know in a decision-making context. It is known as contribution because it contributes to covering the fixed costs and, if there is any excess, it also contributes to profit.

The variable cost per unit is known as the *marginal cost*, i.e. the additional cost of making one more basket.

If you cast your mind back to the start of this chapter when we were discussing relevant costs for decision-making, we concluded that only costs which vary with the decision should be included in the decision analysis. For many decisions which involve relatively small variations from existing practice and/or are for relatively limited periods of time, fixed costs are not relevant to the decision. This is because fixed costs tend to be such that:

♦ They are impossible to alter in the short term, or
♦ Managers are reluctant to alter them in the short term.

Suppose that a business occupies premises which it owns in order to carry out its activities. There is a downturn in demand for the service which the business provides and it would be possible to carry on the business from smaller, cheaper premises. Does this mean that the business will sell its old premises and move to new ones overnight? Clearly it cannot mean this. This is partly because it is not usually possible to find a buyer for premises at very short notice and it may be difficult to move premises quickly where there is, say, delicate equipment to be moved. Apart from external constraints on the speed of the move, management may feel that the downturn may not be permanent and would thus be reluctant to take such a dramatic step as to deny itself the opportunity to benefit from a possible revival of trade.

The business' premises may provide an example of an area of one of the more inflexible types of cost, but most fixed costs tend to be broadly similar in nature.

6.8.1   Accepting or Rejecting Special Contracts

ACTIVITY

Cottage Industries Ltd (in the last activity) has spare capacity in that it has spare basket-makers, etc. An overseas retail chain has offered the business an order for 300 baskets at a price of £9 each. Without considering any wider issues, should the business accept the order?

Since the fixed costs will be incurred in any case, they are not relevant to this decision. All we need to do is to see whether the price offered will yield a contribution. If it will, then the business will be better off by accepting the contract than by refusing it. We know that the variable costs per basket total £8, thus each basket will yield a contribution of £1 (i.e. £9 − £8); £300 in all. Whatever else may be happening to the business, it will be £300 better off by taking this contract than by refusing it.

ACTIVITY

What other factors do you think the management of Cottage Industries Ltd should take account of before reaching a final decision?

We think that they should consider the following:

♦ *The possibility that spare capacity will be 'sold off' cheaply when there is another potential customer who will offer a higher price, but by which time the capacity is fully committed. It is a matter of commercial judgement as to how likely this will be.*
♦ *The problem that selling the same product, but at different prices, could lead to a loss of customer goodwill. The fact that the two prices will be to customers in different countries may be sufficient to overcome this potential problem.*
♦ *If the business is going to suffer continually from being unable to sell its full production potential at the 'regular' price, it might be better, in the long run, to reduce capacity and make fixed cost savings. Using the spare capacity to produce marginal benefits may lead to the business failing to address this issue.*
♦ *On a more positive note, the business may see this as a way of breaking into the overseas market. This is something that might be impossible to achieve if the business charges its regular price.*

6.9   The Most Efficient Use of Scarce Resources

We tend to think in terms of the size of the market being the brake on output. That is to say that the ability of a business to sell is likely to limit production, rather than the ability to produce limiting sales. Limited production might stem from a shortage of any factor of production — labour, raw materials or production capacity.

The most profitable combination of products will occur where the contribution per unit of the scarce factor is maximized.

EXAMPLE ——

A business makes three different products the details of which are as follows:

Product (code name)	AX107	AX109	AX220
Selling price per unit	£50	£40	£65
Variable cost per unit	25	20	35
Contribution per unit	£25	£20	£30
Labour time per unit	5 hours	3 hours	6 hours

Within reason, the market will take as many units of each product as can be produced, but production is limited by the availability of labour, all of which needs to be skilled. Fixed costs are not affected by the choice of product because all three products use the same production facilities.

The most profitable product is AX109 because it generates a contribution of £6.67 (i.e. £20/3) per hour. The other two only generate £5.00 each per hour (£25/5 and £30/6).

——

ACTIVITY ——

A business makes three different products the details of which are as follows:

Product (code name)	B14	B17	B22
Selling price per unit	£25	£20	£23
Variable cost per unit	10	8	12
Weekly demand (units)	25	20	30
Machine time per unit	4 hours	3 hours	4 hours

Fixed costs are not affected by the choice of product because all three products use the same machine. Machine time is limited to 148 hours a week.

Which combination of products should be manufactured if the business is to produce the highest profit?

——

Product	B14	B17	B22
Selling price per unit	£25	£20	£23
Variable cost per unit	10	8	12
Contribution per unit	£15	£12	£11
Machine time per unit	4 hours	3 hours	4 hours
Contribution per machine hour	£3.75	£4.00	2.75
Order of priority	2nd	1st	3rd

Therefore the business should produce:

20 units of product B17 using	60 hours
22 units of product B14 using	88
	148

This leaves unsatisfied the market demand for a further 3 units of product B14 and 30 units of product B22.

ACTIVITY ────────────────────────────────────

What steps could be contemplated which could lead to a higher level of contribution for the business in the last activity?

The possibilities for improving matters which occurred to us are as follows:

◆ *Contemplate obtaining additional machine time. This could mean obtaining a new machine, subcontracting the machining to another business or, perhaps, squeezing a few more hours per week out of the business' own machine. Perhaps a combination of two or more of these is a possibility.*
◆ *Redesign the products in a way that requires less time per unit on the machine.*
◆ *Increase the price per unit of the three products. This may well have the effect of dampening demand, but the existing demand cannot be met at present and it may be more profitable in the long run to make a greater contribution on each unit sold than to take one of the other courses of action to overcome the problem.*

6.10 Full Costing

We are now going to look at another approach to deducing costs which is widely used in practice. After looking at how it is done we consider the usefulness of it for management purposes.

With full costing we are not concerned with opportunity costs or variable costs, but with all costs involved with achieving some objective. The logic of full costing is that all the costs of running a particular facility, say a factory, are part of the cost of the output of that factory. For example, the rent may be a cost which will not alter merely because we make one more unit of production, but if the factory was not rented there would be nowhere for production to take place so rent is an important element of the cost of each unit of output.

The simplest case for which to deduce the full cost per unit is where the business has only one output, either product or service. Here it is simply a question of adding up all the costs of production incurred in the period — materials, labour, rent, fuel, power, etc. — and dividing this total by the number of units of output for the period.

There can be minor problems deciding exactly how much cost was incurred and precisely how many units of output there were.

More of a problem is where the units of output are not identical. In these circumstances we normally separate costs into two categories, these are:

- **Direct costs**. These are costs which can be identified with specific cost units. That is to say, the effect of the cost can be measured in respect of each unit of output. The normal examples of these are direct materials and direct labour.
- **Indirect costs** (or **overheads**). These are all other production costs.

ACTIVITY ───

Into which category would each of the following fall in respect of a restaurant business, where the objective is to deduce the full cost of each meal?

- The cleaner's salary.
- The cost of heating the restaurant.
- Food.
- A waiter's salary.
- Depreciation of the furniture.

Only the food and the waiter's salary are direct costs. This is because it is possible to measure how much food cost has gone into a particular meal and it is possible to measure how much time a waiter spent serving a particular meal. All of the other costs are general costs of running the restaurant, and as such must form part of the full cost of the meal, but they cannot be directly measured in respect of each meal served.

If the indirect costs of any activity must form part of the cost of each unit of output, yet, by definition, they cannot be directly related individual cost units, a major question is, how are they to be apportioned to individual cost units?

It is reasonable to view the overheads as rendering a service to the cost units. A manufactured product can be seen as being rendered a service by the factory in which the product is made. In this sense it is reasonable to charge each cost unit with a share of the costs of running the factory — rent, lighting, heating, cleaning, building maintenance, etc. It seems reasonable to relate the charge for the 'use' of the factory to the level of service which the product received from the factory.

ACTIVITY ───

Do you have any suggestions as to how the cost of running the factory, which in total is a cost of all production, might be apportioned among individual products which are not similar in size and complexity of manufacture?

One possibility is sharing this overhead cost equally between each cost unit produced in the period. Most of us would not propose this method unless the cost units were close to being identical.

If we are not to propose equal shares, we must identify something observable and measurable about the cost units which we feel provides a reasonable basis for distinguishing between one cost unit and the next in this context.

Direct labour hours is usually the basis which is most popular in practice. Though it must be stressed that this is not the correct way and it certainly is not the only way, we could for example use relative size of products as measured by weight or by relative material cost.

ACTIVITY ———

Johnson Ltd has overheads of £10,000 each month. Each month 2,500 direct labour hours are worked and charged to units of output (the business' products). A particular job undertaken by the business used direct materials costing £46. Direct labour worked on the job was 15 hours and the wage rate is £5 an hour. Overheads are charged to jobs on a direct labour hour basis. What is the full cost of the job?

Firstly let us establish the 'overhead recovery rate', i.e. the rate at which jobs will be charged with overheads. This is £4 (i.e. £10,000/2,500) per direct labour hour. Thus the full cost of the job is:

	£
Direct materials	46
Direct labour (15 × £5)	75
	121
Overheads (15 × £4)	60
	£181

Note that if all of the jobs which are undertaken during the month are apportioned with overheads in a similar manner, all £10,000 of overheads will be charged to the jobs among them. Jobs requiring much direct labour will be apportioned much of the overheads and those with little direct labour will have only a small amount of overheads.

ACTIVITY ———

Can you think of reasons why direct labour hours are regarded as the most logical basis for sharing overheads between cost units?

The reasons which occurred to us are:

♦ *Large jobs should logically attract large amounts of overheads because they are likely to have been rendered more 'service' by the overheads than small ones. The length of time that they are worked on by direct labour may be seen as a rough and ready way of measuring relative size, though other means of doing this may be found, e.g. relative physical size.*

♦ *Most overheads are related to time. Rent, heating, lighting, fixed asset depreciation, supervisors' and managers' salaries and loan interest, which are all typical overheads, are all more or less time-based. That is to say that the overhead cost for one week tends to be about half of that for a similar two-week period. Thus a basis of apportioning overheads which takes account of the length of time that the units of output benefited from the 'service' rendered by the overheads seems logical.*

◆ *Direct labour hours are capable of being measured in respect of each job. They will normally be measured to deduce the direct labour element of cost in any case. Thus a direct labour hour basis of dealing with overheads is practical to apply in the real world.*

It cannot be emphasized enough that there is no correct way to apportion overheads to jobs. Overheads (indirect costs) by definition do not naturally relate to individual jobs. If we wish to take account of the fact that overheads nevertheless are part of the cost of all jobs, we must find some acceptable way of including a share of the total overheads in each job. If a particular means of doing this is accepted by those who are affected by the full cost deduced as a result then the method is as good as any other method. In practice the method which gains the most acceptability is the direct labour hour method.

6.10.1 Uses of Full Cost Information

Why do we need to deduce full cost information? There are probably two reasons:

1. For pricing purposes. In some industries and circumstances, full costs are used as the basis of pricing. Here the full cost is deduced and a percentage is added for profit. This is known as 'cost-plus' pricing. Garages probably provide an example of this.

   In many circumstances suppliers are not in a position to deduce prices on a cost-plus basis, however. Where there is a competitive market, a supplier will probably need to accept the price which the market offers, i.e. most suppliers are 'price-takers' not 'price-makers'.

2. For income measurement purposes. As we saw in Chapters 2 and 3, it is necessary to match (following the matching convention of accounting) expenses with the revenues realized (recognized) in the same accounting period. Where manufactured stock is made or partially made in one period but sold in the next, or where a service is partially rendered in one accounting period but the revenue is realized in the next, the full cost (including an appropriate share of overheads) must be carried from one accounting period to the next. Unless we are able to identify the full cost of work done in one period, which is the subject of a sale in the next, the profit figures of the period concerned will become meaningless.

SELF-ASSESSMENT QUESTION ──────────────────────────────────

Andrews and Co. Ltd has been invited to tender for a contract to produce 10,000 metres of a cable in which the business specializes. The estimating department of the business has produced the following information relating to the contract:

Materials: The cable will require a steel core which the business buys in. The steel core is to be coated with a special plastic, also bought-in, using a special process. Plastic for the covering will be required at the rate of 0.10 kg per metre of completed cable.

Direct labour: Skilled   10 minutes per metre
                 Unskilled   5 minutes per metre

The business already has sufficient stock of each of the materials required to complete the contract. Information on the cost of stock is as follows:

	Steel core	Plastic
	£ per metre	£ per kg
Historic cost	1.50	0.60
Current buying in cost	2.10	0.70
Scrap value	1.40	0.10

The steel core is in constant use by the business for a variety of work which it regularly undertakes. The plastic is a surplus from a previous contract where a mistake was made and an excess quantity ordered. If the current contract does not go ahead this plastic will be scrapped.

Unskilled labour, which is paid at the rate of £3.50 an hour, will need to be taken on specifically to undertake the contract. The business is fairly quiet at the moment which means that a pool of skilled labour exists which will still be employed at full pay of £4.50 an hour to do nothing if the contract does not proceed. The pool of skilled labour is sufficient to satisfy the skilled labour requirement of the contract.

The business charges jobs with overheads on a direct labour hour basis. The production overheads of the entire business for the month in which the contract will be undertaken are estimated at £50,000. The estimated total direct labour hours which will be worked are 12,500. The business tends not to alter the established overhead recovery rate to reflect increases or reductions to estimated total hours arising from new contracts. The total overhead cost is not expected to increase as a result of undertaking the contract.

The business normally adds 12.5 per cent profit loading to the job cost to arrive at a first estimate of the tender price.

You are required to cost this job on a traditional job costing basis *and* to indicate the minimum price at which the contract could be undertaken such that the business would be neither better nor worse off as a result of doing it.

Solution on p. 255.

Summary

In this chapter we have seen that cost can have several meanings. Relevant costs are those which relate to the objectives of the decision-making business and which will vary with the decision. Relevant costs include not only outlay costs, but opportunity costs as well.

We saw that for short-run decisions, all fixed costs (i.e. costs which do not vary with the level of activity) can be assumed to be irrelevant and all variable costs can be assumed to be relevant. This enables us to undertake break-even analysis, i.e. deducing the break-even point for some activity. It also enables us to make decisions on the use of spare capacity and on the most efficient use of scarce resources.

Lastly we say that many businesses deduce a full cost for their units of output. This is derived from the direct costs of the activity plus a share of the overheads of the entire business.

EXERCISES

6.1 The management of your company is concerned at its inability to obtain enough fully trained labour to enable it to meet its present budget projection.

Product:	Alpha £	Beta £	Gamma £	Total £
Direct costs:				
Materials	6,000	4,000	5,000	15,000
Labour	9,000	6,000	12,000	27,000
Expenses	3,000	2,000	2,000	7,000
Allocated fixed costs	13,000	8,000	12,000	33,000
Total cost	31,000	20,000	31,000	82,000
Profit	8,000	9,000	2,000	19,000
Sales	£39,000	£29,000	£33,000	£101,000

The amount of labour that is likely to be available amounts to £20,000. You have been asked to prepare a statement ensuring that at least 50 per cent of the budget sales are achieved for each product and the balance of labour used to produce the greatest profit.

(a) Prepare a statement showing the greatest profit available from the limited amount of skilled labour available, within the constraint stated.
(b) Provide an explanation of the method you have used.
(c) Provide an indication of any other factors that need to be considered.

(Answer on page 264. Answers to exercises 6.2 and 6.3 are given in the Teacher's Manual.)

6.2 The local authority of a small town maintains a theatre and arts centre for the use of a local repertory company, other visiting groups and exhibitions. Management decisions are taken by a committee that meets regularly to review the accounts and plan the use of the facilities.

The theatre employs a full-time staff and a number of artistes at costs of £4,800 and £17,600 per month respectively. They mount a new production every month for 20 performances. Other monthly expenditure of the theatre is as follows:

	£
Costumes	2,800
Scenery	1,650
Heat and light	5,150
Apportionment of administration	
costs of local authority	8,000
Casual staff	1,760
Refreshments	1,180

On average the theatre is half full for the performances of the repertory company. The capacity and seat prices in the theatre are:

200 seats at £6 each
500 seats at £4 each
300 seats at £3 each

In addition the theatre sells refreshments during the performances for £3,880 per month, programme sales cover their costs but advertising in the programme generates £3,360.

The management committee has been approached by a popular touring group to take over the theatre for one month (25 performances). The group is prepared to pay half of its ticket income for the booking. It expects to fill the theatre for 10 nights and achieve two-thirds full on the remaining 15 nights. The prices charged are 50p less than those normally applied in the theatre.

The local authority will pay for heat and light costs and will still honour the contracts of all artistes and pay full-time employees who will sell refreshments and programmes, etc. The committee does not expect any change in the level of refreshments or programme sales if they agree to this booking.

Note: The committee includes allocated costs when making profit calculations. It assumes occupancy applies equally across all seat prices.

(a) On financial grounds should the management committee agree to the approach from the touring group? Support your answer with appropriate workings.
(b) Assume the group will fill the theatre for 10 nights as predicted. What occupancy is required for the remaining 15 nights for the committee to:
  (i) break even for the month?
  (ii) be financially indifferent to the booking?
(c) What other factors may have a bearing on the decision by the committee?

6.3 Lombard Ltd has been offered a contract for which there is available production capacity. The contract is for 20,000 items, manufactured by an intricate assembly operation, to be produced and delivered in the next financial year at a price of £80 each.
The specification is as follows:

Assembly labour   4 hours
Component X   4 units
Component Y   3 units

There would also be the need to hire equipment which would increase next year's fixed overheads by £200,000.

The assembly is a highly skilled operation and the workforce is currently under-utilized. It is company policy to retain this workforce on full pay in anticipation of high demand, in a few years time, for a new product currently being developed. In the meantime all non-productive time (about 150,000 hours per annum) is charged to fixed production overhead at the current rate of pay of £5 per hour.

Component X is used in a number of other subassemblies produced by the company. It is readily available. A small stock is held and replenished regularly. Component Y was a special purchase in anticipation of an order which did not materialize. It is, therefore, surplus to requirements and the 100,000 units which are in stock may have to be sold at a loss. An estimate of alternative values for components X and Y provided by the material planning department are:

	X	Y
	£ per unit	£ per unit
Book value	4	10
Replacement cost	5	11
Net realizable value	3	8

Overhead costs are applied on a labour hour basis. Variable overhead is £2 per hour worked. Provisionally, fixed overheads, before the contract was envisaged, were budgeted next year at £3,560,000 for productive direct labour hours of 1,040,000. There is sufficient time available to revise the budgeted overhead rate.

(a) Analyse the information in order to advise Lombard Ltd on the desirability of the contract and briefly explain your reasoning.
(b) The company employs a system of absorption costing, using actual direct costs and a predetermined overhead rate, when it reports on the results of individual contracts. Show how the contract would be reported in such a system and comment on its usefulness.

Further Reading

Arnold, J. and Hope, A., *Accounting for Management Decisions* (2nd edn). Prentice Hall, 1990.
Glautier, M. and Underdown, B., *Accounting Theory and Practice*. Pitman, 1991.
Pizzey, A., *Cost and Management Accounting* (3rd edn). Paul Chapman Publishing, 1989.

CHAPTER SEVEN

Capital Investment Decisions

7.1 Introduction

In this chapter we look at how businesses make decisions about investment in new plant, machinery, buildings and similar long-term assets. The general decision-making principles being considered can equally well be applied to investments in the shares of companies, irrespective of whether the investment is being considered by a business or by a private individual, or of any other financial investment.

7.2 Purpose

When you have completed your study of this chapter you should be able to:

♦ Explain the nature and importance of investment decision-making.
♦ Identify the four main investment appraisal methods used in practice.
♦ Use each method to reach a decision on an example of an investment opportunity.
♦ Discuss the attributes and defects of each of the methods.

7.3 The Nature of Investment Decisions

The essential feature of investment decisions, irrespective of who is to make the decision, is a time factor. Investment involves making an outlay of something of economic value, usually cash, at one point in time which is expected to yield economic benefits to the investor at some other point in time. Typically, the outlay precedes the benefits. Also the outlay is typically one large amount and the benefits arrive in a stream over a fairly protracted period.

Investment decisions tend to be of crucial importance to the investor because:

♦ Large amounts of resources are often involved. Many investments made by a business involve outlaying a significant proportion of its total resources. If mistakes are made with the decision, the effects on the business could be significant, if not catastrophic.

♦ It is often difficult and/or expensive to 'bail-out' of an investment once it has been undertaken. It is often the case that investments made by a business are specific to its needs. For example, a manufacturing business may have a factory built which has been designed to accommodate the flow of production of that business. This may render the factory of rather small secondhand value to another potential user with different needs. If the business found, after having made the investment, that the product which is being produced in the factory is not selling as well as was planned, the only possible course of action might be to close down production and sell the factory. This would probably mean that much less could be recouped from the investment in the factory than it had originally cost, particularly if the costs of design are included (as logically they should be) as part of the cost.

ACTIVITY

When businesses are making decisions involving capital investments, what should the decision seek to achieve?

The answer must be that any decision must be made in the context of the objectives of the business concerned. For a private-sector business, this is likely to include increasing the wealth of the business through long-term profitability.

7.4 The Methods Used in Practice

Research shows that there are basically four approaches used in practice by businesses in the UK and elsewhere to appraise investment opportunities. It is possible to find businesses which use variants of these four methods. It is also possible to find businesses, particularly smaller ones, which do not use any formal appraisal method, but rely more on 'gut-feeling'. Most businesses, however, seem to use one or more of the four methods which we now review.

To help us to consider each of the four approaches it might be useful to consider how each of them would cope with the particular investment opportunity set out in the example below.

EXAMPLE

Billingsgate Battery Company has carried out some research which shows that it could manufacture and sell a product which the business has recently developed. The production would require investment in a machine which would cost £100,000, payable immediately. Production and sales would take place throughout the next five years, at the end of which time it is estimated that the machine could be sold for £20,000.

Production and sales of the product would be expected to occur as follows:

	Number of units
Next year	5,000
Second year	10,000
Third year	15,000
Fourth year	15,000
Fifth year	5,000

It is estimated that the new product can be sold for £12 a unit and that the relevant material and labour costs will total £8 a unit.

To simplify matters, we assume that the cash from sales and for the costs of production are paid and received, respectively, at the end of each year. (This is clearly unlikely to be so in real life: money will have to be paid to employees on a weekly or monthly basis, and customers will pay within a month or two of buying the product. Nevertheless, it is probably not a serious distortion; indeed, it is a simplifying assumption which is often made in real life and it will make things more straightforward for us now. You should be clear, however, that there is nothing about any of the four approaches which *demands* that this assumption be made.)

Bearing in mind that each product sold will give rise to a net cash inflow of £4 (i.e. £12 − 8), the cash flows (receipts and payments) over the life of the production will be as follows:

		£000
Immediately	Cost of machine	(100)
1 year's time	Net profit before depreciation (£4 × 5,000)	20
2 years' time	Net profit before depreciation (£4 × 10,000)	40
3 years' time	Net profit before depreciation (£4 × 15,000)	60
4 years' time	Net profit before depreciation (£4 × 15,000)	60
5 years' time	Net profit before depreciation (£4 × 5,000)	20
5 years' time	Disposal proceeds from the machine	20

Note that, broadly speaking, the net profit before deducting depreciation equals the net amount of cash flowing into the business.

7.4.1 Accounting Rate of Return (ARR)

The ARR method takes the average accounting profit which the investment will generate and expresses it as a percentage of the average investment in the project as measured in accounting terms. Thus:

$$ARR = \frac{\text{Average annual profit}}{\text{Average investment to earn that profit}} \times 100\%$$

The average profit before depreciation over the five years is:

$$\frac{20,000 + 40,000 + 60,000 + 60,000 + 20,000}{5} = £40,000 \tag{1}$$

Assuming 'straight line' depreciation (i.e. equal annual amounts), the annual depreciation charge will be:

$$\frac{100,000 - 20,000}{5} = £16,000 \tag{2}$$

Thus the average annual profit is equation (1) minus equation (2), i.e.:

$$40,000 - 16,000 = £24,000 \tag{3}$$

The machine will appear in the balance sheet as follows:

£000
At end of year 1 84 (i.e. 100 − 16)
             2 68 (i.e. 84 − 16)
             3 52 (i.e. 68 − 16)
             4 36 (i.e. 52 − 16)
             5 20 (i.e. 36 − 16)

The average investment (at balance sheet values) will be:

$$\frac{84,000 + 68,000 + 52,000 + 36,000 + 20,000}{5} = £52,000 \tag{4}$$

Thus the ARR of the investment is [equation (3)/equation (4)] × 100%, i.e.:

$$\frac{£24,000}{£52,000} \times 100\% = 46\%$$

ACTIVITY

Chaotic Industries is considering an investment in a fleet of ten delivery vans to take its products to customers. The vans will cost £15,000 each to buy, payable immediately. The annual running costs are expected to total £20,000 for each van (including the driver's salary). The vans are expected to operate successfully for six years at the end of which period they will all have to be scrapped with disposal proceeds expected to be about £3,000 per van. At present the business uses a commercial carrier for all of its deliveries. It is expected that this carrier will charge a total of £230,000 each year for the next five years to undertake the deliveries.

What is the ARR of buying the vans?

Note that cost savings are as relevant a benefit from an investment as are actual net cash inflows.

The vans will save the business £30,000 a year [(i.e. 230,000 − (20,000 × 10)], before depreciation, in total. Thus the inflows and outflows will be:

		£000
Immediately	*Cost of vans*	*(150)*
1 year's time	*Net saving before depreciation*	*30*
2 years' time	*Net saving before depreciation*	*30*
3 years' time	*Net saving before depreciation*	*30*
4 years' time	*Net saving before depreciation*	*30*
5 years' time	*Net saving before depreciation*	*30*
6 years' time	*Net saving before depreciation*	*30*
6 years' time	*Disposal proceeds from the vans*	*30*

The total annual depreciation expense (assuming a 'straight-line' approach) will be £20,000 [i.e. 150,000 — 30,000)/6]. Thus the average annual saving, after depreciation, is £10,000 (i.e. 30,000 — 20,000). The vans will appear in the balance sheet as follows:

	£000	
At the end of year 1	*130*	*(i.e. 150 — 20)*
2	*110*	*(i.e. 130 — 20)*
3	*90*	
4	*70*	
5	*50*	
6	*30*	

The average investment (at balance sheet values) will be £80,000 [i.e. (130,000 + 110,000 + 90,000 + 70,000 + 50,000 + 30,000)/6]. Thus the ARR of the investment is 12.5% [i.e. (10/80) × 100%).

In principle, the ARR of a project should be the return on capital employed (ROCE) figure. You will probably recall from Chapter 3 that ROCE is a popular means of assessing the performance of a business *after* the period has passed. By the same logic, ARR can be argued to be a useful means of assessing an investment opportunity *before* it takes place. In theory, if all investments made by Chaotic Industries (in the last activity) actually proved to have an ARR of 12.5 per cent, then the ROCE for that business should be 12.5 per cent. Since private-sector businesses are seeking, probably among other things, to increase the wealth of their owners, ARR seems to be a sound method of appraising investment opportunities. Profit can be seen as a net increase in wealth over a period, and relating profit to the size of investment made to achieve it seems logical.

A user of ARR would require that any investment undertaken by the business was able to achieve a minimum ARR. Perhaps the minimum would be the rate which previous investments had achieved (as measured by ROCE). Perhaps it would be the industry average ROCE.

Where there are competing projects which both seem capable of exceeding the minimum rate, the one with the higher ARR would normally be selected.

ARR suffers from a major defect as a means of assessing investment opportunities. Can you reason out what this is? Take a look back at the Billingsgate Battery example (above).

Hint: The defect is not concerned with the ability of the decision-maker to forecast future events, though this too can be a problem.

The problem with ARR is that is almost completely ignores the time factor. In the Billingsgate Battery example, exactly the same ARR would have been computed under any of the following three scenarios:

		Original	Option 1	Option 2
		£000	£000	£000
Immediately	Cost of machine	(100)	(100)	(100)
1 year's time	Net profit before dep'n	20	10	160
2 years' time	Net profit before dep'n	40	10	10
3 years' time	Net profit before dep'n	60	10	10
4 years' time	Net profit before dep'n	60	10	10
5 years' time	Net profit before dep'n	20	160	10
5 years' time	Disposal proceeds	20	20	20

Since the same total profit over the five years arises in all three cases, the average net profit after depreciation must be the same in each case. In turn, this means that each case will give rise to the same ARR of 46 per cent.

Given a financial objective of increasing the wealth of the business, any rational decision-maker faced with these three scenarios as a choice among three separate investments would strongly favour option 2. This is because most of the benefits from the investment come in within 12 months of spending the £100,000 to establish the project. The original scenario would rank second and option 1 would come a poor third. Any appraisal technique which is not capable of distinguishing between these three situations is seriously flawed.

Clearly, the use of ARR can easily lead to poor decisions being made. Later in this chapter we look in more detail at why timing is so important.

7.4.2 Payback Period (PP)

The payback period method seems to go some way to overcoming the timing problem of ARR, at least at first glance. It might be useful to consider PP in the context of the Billingsgate Battery example. You will recall that the project's costs and benefits can be summarized as:

		£000
Immediately	Cost of machine	(100)
1 year's time	Net profit before dep'n	20
2 years' time	Net profit before dep'n	40
3 years' time	Net profit before dep'n	60
4 years' time	Net profit before dep'n	60
5 years' time	Net profit before dep'n	20
5 years' time	Disposal proceeds	20

Note that all of these figures are amounts of cash to be paid or received. The payback period is the length of time it takes for the initial investment to be repaid out of the net cash inflows from the project. In this case it will be three years before the £100,000 outlay is covered by the inflows.

A decision-maker using PP would need to have a maximum payback period in mind. For example, if Billingsgate Battery had a minimum payback period of three years it would accept the project, but it would not go ahead if its minimum payback period were two years. Similarly, a business which used PP to make investment decisions would select the project with the shorter payback if there were competing projects.

ACTIVITY ————————————————————————————

What is the payback period of the Chaotic Industries project from the activity before last?

The inflows and outflows are expected to be:

		£000
Immediately	*Cost of vans*	*(150)*
1 year's time	*Net saving before depreciation*	*30*
2 years' time	*Net saving before depreciation*	*30*
3 years' time	*Net saving before depreciation*	*30*
4 years' time	*Net saving before depreciation*	*30*
5 years' time	*Net saving before depreciation*	*30*
6 years' time	*Net saving before depreciation*	*30*
6 years' time	*Disposal proceeds from the vans*	*30*

The payback period here is five years, i.e. it is not until the end of the fifth year that the vans will pay for themselves out of the savings which they are expected to generate.

The logic of using PP is that projects which can recoup their cost quickly are economically more attractive than those with longer payback periods. PP is probably an improvement on ARR in respect of the timing of the cash flows. PP is not, however, the whole answer to the problem.

ACTIVITY ──

In what respect, in your opinion, is PP not the whole answer as a means of assessing investment opportunities? Again take a look back at the Billingsgate Battery example (above).

Hint: Again the defect is not concerned with the ability of the decision-maker to forecast future events. This is a problem, but it is a problem whatever approach we take.

───

Consider the Billingsgate Battery example. Exactly the same payback period would have been computed under any of the following three scenarios:

		Original	Option 1	Option 2
		£000	£000	£000
Immediately	Cost of machine	(100)	(100)	(100)
1 year's time	Net profit before dep'n	20	0	80
2 years' time	Net profit before dep'n	40	0	10
3 years' time	Net profit before dep'n	60	100	10
4 years' time	Net profit before dep'n	60	0	200
5 years' time	Net profit before dep'n	20	0	500
5 years' time	Disposal proceeds	20	0	20

Any rational decision-maker would prefer option 2 to either of the other two scenarios, yet PP sees them as being the same, i.e. a three-year payback period. The method cannot distinguish between the original which pays back some of the outlay before year 3 and option 1 which is obviously less favourable because it is not until year 3 that anything comes in. Option 2 is by far the best bet because the cash flows come in earlier and they are greater in total, yet PP would not identify it as the best.

Within the payback period, PP ignores the timing of the cash flows. Beyond the payback period, the method totally ignores the size and the timing of the cash flows.

It seems that PP has the advantage of taking some note of the timing of the costs and benefits from the project, but it suffers the disadvantage of ignoring a great deal of other information. ARR ignores timing to a great extent, but it does take account of all of the benefits and costs.

What we really need to help us to make sensible decisions is a method of appraisal which takes account of all of the costs and benefits of each investment opportunity, but which also makes a logical allowance for the timing of those costs and benefits.

7.4.3   Net Present Value (NPV)

Consider the Billingsgate Battery example, which can be summarized as follows:

		£000
Immediately	Cost of machine	(100)
1 year's time	Net profit before dep'n	20
2 years' time	Net profit before dep'n	40
3 years' time	Net profit before dep'n	60
4 years' time	Net profit before dep'n	60
5 years' time	Net profit before dep'n	20
5 years' time	Disposal proceeds	20

Given that the principal financial objective of the business is probably to increase wealth, it would be easy to assess this investment if all of the cash flows were to occur now (i.e. all at the same time). All that we should need to do would be to add up the benefits (total £220,000) and compare the total with the cost (£100,000). This would lead us to the conclusion that the project should go ahead because the business would be better off by £120,000. Of course, it is not as easy as this because time is involved. The cash outflow (payment) will, if the project is undertaken, occur immediately. The inflows (receipts) will arise at a range of later times.

The time factor arises because normal people do not see paying out £100 now in order to receive £100 in a year's time as being equivalent in value. If you were to be offered £100 in 12 months' time, provided that you paid £100 to that person now, you would not be prepared to do so, unless you wished to do that person a favour.

ACTIVITY ───────────────────────────────────

Why would you see £100 to be received in a year's time as unequal in value to £100 to be paid immediately? (We believe that there are basically three reasons.)

Our three reasons are:

1. Interest lost.
2. Risk.
3. Effects of inflation.

We now take a closer look at these three factors in turn.

Interest lost

If you were able to be deprived of the use of your money for a year, you could equally well be deprived of its use by placing it on deposit in a bank or building society. In this case, at the end of the year you could have your money back and have interest as well. Thus unless the opportunity to invest will offer similar returns you will be incurring an *opportunity cost*. An opportunity cost occurs where one course of action, e.g. making an investment in a computer, deprives you of the opportunity to derive some benefit from an alternative action, e.g. putting the money in the bank.

From this we can see that any investment opportunity must, if it is to make you more wealthy, do better than the returns which are available from the next best opportunity. Thus, if Billingsgate Battery Company sees putting the money in the bank on deposit as the alternative to investment in the machine, the return from investing in the machine must be better than that from investing in the bank.

Risk

Buying a machine, to manufacture a product to be sold in the market, on the strength of various estimates made in advance of buying the machine, is risky.

ACTIVITY ──

Can you suggest some areas where things could go other than according to plan?

──

We came up with the following:

- *The machine might not work as well as expected; it might break down. leading to loss of production and to loss of sales.*
- *Sales of the product may not be as buoyant as expected.*
- *Labour costs may prove to be higher than was expected.*
- *The sale proceeds of the machine could prove to be less than was estimated.*

It is important to remember that the decision whether or not to invest in the machine must be taken *before* any of these things are known. It is only after the machine has been purchased that we realize that the level of sales, which had been estimated before the event, are not going to be achieved. It is not possible to wait until we know for certain whether the market will behave as we expected before we buy the machine. We can study reports and analyses of the market. We can commission sophisticated market surveys and these may give us more confidence in the likely outcome. We can advertise strongly and try to expand sales. Ultimately, however, we have to jump into the dark and accept the risk.

Normally, people expect to receive greater returns where they perceive risk to be a factor. Examples of this in real life are not difficult to find. One such example is the fact that a bank will tend to charge a higher rate of interest to a borrower whom the bank perceives to be more risky, than to one who can offer good security for the loan and can point to a regular source of income.

Going back to Billingsgate Battery Company's investment opportunity, it is not logical to say that we would advise making the investment where the returns from it are only as high as those from investing in a bank deposit. Clearly we would want returns above the level of bank deposit interest rates because the logical equivalent investment opportunity to investing in the machine is not putting the money on deposit: it is making an alternative investment which seems to have a risk similar to that of the investment in the machine.

In practice, we tend to expect a higher rate of return from investment projects where the risk is perceived as being higher. How risky a particular project is, and, therefore, how large this *risk premium* should be, are matters which are difficult to handle. In practice, it is necessary to make some judgement on these questions.

Inflation

If you are to be deprived of £100 for a year, when you come to spend that money it will not buy as much in the way of goods and services that it would have done a year earlier. Generally, you will not be able to buy as many tins of baked beans or loaves of bread or bus tickets for a particular journey as you could have done a year earlier. Clearly, the investor needs to feel that this loss of purchasing power will be compensated for if the investment is to be made. This is on top of a return which takes account of the returns which could have been gained from an alternative investment of similar risk.

In practice, interest rates observable in the market tend to take inflation into account. Rates which are offered to potential building society and bank depositors include an allowance for the rate of inflation which is expected in the future.

To summarize on these factors, we can say that the logical investor, who is seeking to increase his or her wealth, will only be prepared to make investments which will compensate for the loss of interest and purchasing power of the money invested and for the fact that the returns which are expected may not materialize (risk). This is usually assessed by seeing whether the proposed investment will yield a return which is greater than the basic rate of interest (which would include an allowance for inflation) plus a risk premium.

Naturally, investors need at least the minimum return before they are prepared to invest. However, it is in terms of the effect on their wealth that they should logically assess an investment project. Usually the investment with the highest percentage return will make the investor most wealthy, but we see later in this chapter that this is not always the case. For the time being, therefore, we shall concentrate on wealth.

Let us now return to the Billingsgate Battery Company example. You will recall that the cash flows expected from this investment, were it to be made, are:

		£000
Immediately	Cost of machine	(100)
1 year's time	Net profit before dep'n	20
2 years' time	Net profit before dep'n	40
3 years' time	Net profit before dep'n	60
4 years' time	Net profit before dep'n	60
5 years' time	Net profit before dep'n	20
5 years' time	Disposal proceeds	20

Let us assume that instead of making this investment the business could make an alternative investment, with similar risk and obtain a return of 20 per cent a year.

You will recall that we have concluded that it is not sensible just to compare the basic figures listed above. It would therefore be useful if we could express each of these cash flows in similar terms so that we could make a direct comparison between the sum of the inflows and the £100,000 investment. In fact we can do this.

A C T I V I T Y ———————————————————————————————————

We know that Billingsgate Battery Company could invest its money at a rate of 20 per cent a year. How much do you judge the present (immediate) value of the expected first-year receipt of £20,000 to be? In other words, if instead of having to wait a year for the £20,000 and being deprived of the opportunity to invest it at 20 per cent, you could have some money now, what sum to be received now would you regard as exactly equivalent to getting £20,000 in a year's time?

———

We should obviously be happy to accept a lower amount if we could get it immediately than if we had to wait a year. This is because we could invest it at 20 per cent (in the alternative project). Logically, we should be prepared to accept the amount which with a year's income will grow to £20,000. If we call this amount PV (for present value) we can say:

$$PV + (PV \times 20\%) = £20,000$$

i.e. the amount plus income from investing the amount for the year equals the £20,000. If we rearrange this equation we find:

$$PV \times (1 + 0.2) = £20,000$$

Note that 0.2 is the same as 20%, but expressed as a decimal. Further rearranging gives:

$$PV = £20,000/(1 + 0.2)$$
$$= £16,667$$

Thus, rational investors who have the opportunity to invest at 20 per cent a year would not mind whether they have £16,667 now or £20,000 in a year's time. In this sense we can say that, given a 20 per cent investment opportunity, the present value of £20,000 to be received in one year's time is £16,667.

If we could derive the present value (PV) of each of the cash flows associated with the machine investment, we could easily make the direct comparison between the cost of making the investment (£100,000) and the various benefits which will derive from it in years 1 to 5. Fortunately we can do precisely this.

We can make a more general statement about the PV of a particular cash flow. It is:

PV of the cash flow of year n = Actual cash flow of year n divided by $(1 + r)^n$

where n is the year of the cash flow (i.e. how many years into the future) and r is the opportunity investing rate expressed as a decimal (instead of as a percentage).

We have already seen how this works for the £20,000 inflow for year 1. For year 2 the calculation would be:

PV of year 2 cash flow (£40,000) $= £40,000/(1 + 0.2)^2$
PV $= £40,000/(1.2)^2 = £40,000/1.44 = £27,778$

Thus the present value of the £40,000 to be received in two years' time is £27,778.

ACTIVITY

Try to show that an investor would be indifferent to £27,778 receivable now, or £40,000 receivable in two years' time, assuming that there is a 20 per cent investment opportunity.

The reasoning is along these lines:

	£
Amount available for immediate investment	*27,778*
Add: Interest for year I (20% × 27,778)	*5,556*
	33,334
Add: Interest for year 2 (20% × 33,334)	*6,668*
	40,002

(The extra £2 is only a rounding error)
Thus because the investor can turn £27,778 into £40,000 in two years, these amounts are equivalent and we can say that £27,778 is the present value of £40,000 receivable after two years.

Now let us deduce the present values of all of the cash flows associated with the machine project and hence the *net present value* of the project as a whole.
The relevant cash flows and calculations are as follows:

Time	Cash flow £000	Calculation of PV	PV £000
Immediately (time 0)	(100)	$(100)/(1 + 0.2)^0$	(100.00)
1 year's time	20	$20/(1 + 0.2)^1$	16.67
2 years' time	40	$40/(1 + 0.2)^2$	27.78
3 years' time	60	$60/(1 + 0.2)^3$	34.72
4 years' time	60	$60/(1 + 0.2)^4$	28.94
5 years' time	20	$20/(1 + 0.2)^5$	8.04
5 years' time	20	$20/(1 + 0.2)^5$	8.04
		Net present value	24.19

We can now say that, given the investment opportunities available to the business elsewhere, investing in the machine will make the business £24,190 better off. What the above is saying is that the benefits from investing in this machine are worth a total of £124,190 today. Since the business can 'buy' these benefits for just £100,000 the investment should be made. Clearly, at any price up to £124,190 the investment would be worth making.

Using discount tables

Deducing the present values of the various cash flows was a little laborious using the approach that we have just taken. Fortunately there is a quicker way. To deduce each PV we took the relevant cash flow and multiplied by $1/(1 + r)^n$. Tables exist which show values of this *discount factor* for a range of values of r and n. Such a table is appended at the end of this chapter. Take a look at it.

Look at the column for 20 per cent and the row for 1 year. We find that the factor is 0.833. Thus the PV of a cash flow of £1 receivable in one year is £0.833. So a cash flow of £20,000 receivable in one year's time is £16,667 (i.e. 0.833 × £20,000), the same result as we found doing it longhand.

ACTIVITY ───

What is the net present value of the Chaotic Industries project from the Activity on page 142, assuming a 15 per cent opportunity cost of finance (discount rate)? (You should use the discount table at the end of this chapter.)

───

Remember that the inflows and outflows are expected to be:

		£000
Immediately	Cost of vans	(150)
1 year's time	Net saving before depreciation	30
2 years' time	Net saving before depreciation	30
3 years' time	Net saving before depreciation	30
4 years' time	Net saving before depreciation	30
5 years' time	Net saving before depreciation	30
6 years' time	Net saving before depreciation	30
6 years' time	Disposal proceeds from the vans	30

The calculation of the NPV of the project is as follows:

Time	Cash flow £000	Discount factor (from the table)	NPV
Immediately	(150)	1.000	(150.00)
1 year's time	30	0.870	26.10
2 years' time	30	0.756	22.68
3 years' time	30	0.658	19.74
4 years' time	30	0.572	17.16
5 years' time	30	0.497	14.91
6 years' time	30	0.432	12.96
6 years' time	30	0.432	12.96
		Net present value	(23.49)

ACTIVITY ───

How would you interpret the result of the previous Activity?

The fact that the project has a negative NPV means that the benefits from the investment are worth less than the cost of entering into it. Any cost up to £126,510 (the present value of the benefits) would be worth paying, but not £150,000.

Figure 7.1 shows how the value of £100 diminishes as its receipt goes further into the future, assuming an opportunity cost of finance of 20 per cent per annum. The £100 to be received immediately has, obviously, a present value of £100. As the time before it is to be received grows larger, the present value diminishes significantly.

From what we have seen, NPV seems to be a better method of appraising investment opportunities than either ARR or PP. NPV fully addresses each of the following:

♦ **The timing of the cash flows.** By *discounting* the various cash flows associated with each project according to when it is expected to arise, the fact that cash flows do not all occur simultaneously is addressed. Associated with this is the fact that

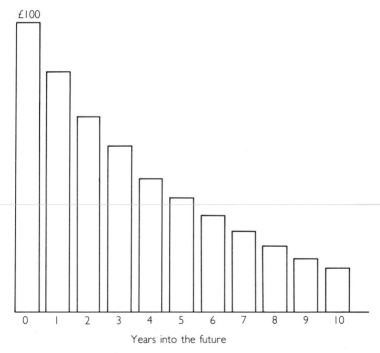

£100

0   1   2   3   4   5   6   7   8   9   10

Years into the future

Figure 7.1   **The present value of £100 receivable at various times in the future, assuming an annual financing cost of 20 per cent.**

by discounting, using the opportunity cost of finance (i.e. the return which the next best alternative opportunity would generate), the net benefit after financing costs have been met is identified (as the NPV).

◆ **The whole of the relevant cash flows.** NPV includes all of the relevant cash flows irrespective of when they are expected to occur. It treats them differently according to their date of occurrence, but they are all taken account of in the NPV and they all have, or can have, an influence on the decision.

◆ **The objectives of the business.** NPV is the only method of appraisal where the output of the analysis has a direct bearing on the wealth of the business. (Positive NPVs enhance wealth, negative ones reduce it). Since most private-sector businesses seek to increase their value and wealth, NPV clearly is the best approach to use, at least out of the methods we have considered so far.

Users of the NPV approach adopt the following rule. Take on all projects with positive NPVs when they are discounted at the opportunity cost of finance. Where a choice has to be made among projects, select the one with the larger or largest NPV.

7.4.4 Internal Rate of Return (IRR)

This is the last of the four major methods of investment appraisal which are found in practice. It is quite closely related to the NPV method in that, like NPV, IRR involves discounting future cash flows.

You will recall that when we discounted the cash flows of the Billingsgate Battery Company machine investment opportunity at 20 per cent, we found that the NPV was a positive figure of £52,260.

ACTIVITY ──

What does the NPV of the machine project tell us about the rate of return which the investment will yield for the business?

───

The fact that the NPV is positive when discounting at 20 per cent implies that the rate of return which the project generates is more than 20 per cent. The fact that the NPV is a pretty large figure implies that the actual rate of return is quite a lot above 20 per cent. We should expect that increasing the size of the discount rate should reduce NPV because a higher discount rate gives a lower discount factor. Thus, future inflows are more heavily discounted, which will reduce their impact on the NPV.

In fact the IRR is the discount rate which will have the effect of producing an NPV of precisely zero.

It is somewhat laborious to deduce the IRR by hand, since it cannot usually be calculated directly. Thus iteration (trial and error) is the only approach. Let us try a higher rate, say 30 per cent, and see what happens:

Time	Cash flow £000	Discount factor	PV £000
Immediately (time 0)	(100)	1.000	(100.00)
1 year's time	20	0.769	15.38
2 years' time	40	0.592	23.68
3 years' time	60	0.455	27.30
4 years' time	60	0.350	21.00
5 years' time	20	0.269	5.38
5 years' time	20	0.269	5.38
			(1.88)

In increasing the discount rate from 20 per cent to 30 per cent, we have reduced the NPV from +£52,600 to −£1,880. Since the IRR is the discount rate which will give us an NPV of exactly zero, we can conclude that the IRR of Billingsgate Battery Company's machine project is very slightly under 30 per cent. Further trials could lead us to the exact rate, but there is probably not much point given the likely inaccuracy of the cash flow estimates.

ACTIVITY ————————————————————

What is the internal rate of return of the Chaotic Industries project from the Activity on page 142? (You should use the discount table at the end of this chapter, and remember that you already know the NPV of this project at 15 per cent.)

Since we know (from a previous activity) that at a 15% discount rate the NPV is a relatively large negative figure, our next trial is using a lower discount rate, say 10%.

Time	Cash flows £000	Discount factor (from the table)	NPV £000
Immediately	(150)	1.000	(150.00)
1 year's time	30	0.909	27.27
2 years' time	30	0.826	24.78
3 years' time	30	0.751	22.53
4 years' time	30	0.683	20.49
5 years' time	30	0.621	18.63
6 years' time	30	0.565	16.95
6 years' time	30	0.565	16.95
		Net present value	(2.40)

We can see that NPV rose about £21,000 for a 5 per cent drop in the discount rate, i.e. about £4,200 for every 1 per cent. We need to know the discount rate for a zero NPV, i.e. a fall of a further £2,400. This logically would be roughly 0.5 per cent. Thus the IRR is close to 9.5 per cent. However, to say that the IRR is about 10 per cent is near enough for most purposes.

The rule for using IRR is that a business using it would require that any project, to be acceptable, must meet a minimum IRR. Logically this minimum should be the opportunity cost of finance. Where there are competing projects, the one with the highest IRR would be selected.

IRR has certain attributes in common with NPV. All cash flows are taken into account and the timing of them is handled logically. The main disadvantage with IRR is the fact that it does not address the question of wealth generation. It could therefore lead to the wrong decision being made. This is because IRR would see a return of 25 per cent being preferable to a 20 per cent IRR, assuming an opportunity cost of finance of 15 per cent. Though this may well lead to the project being taken which could most effectively increase wealth, it could have the opposite effect. This is because IRR completely ignores the *scale of investment*. With a 15 per cent cost of finance £1 million invested at 20 per cent would make you richer than £0.5 million invested at 24 per cent. IRR does not recognize this. It should be recognized that it is not usual for projects to be competing where there is such a large difference in scale. Even though the problem may be rare and that, typically, IRR will give the same signal as NPV, it must be better to use a method (NPV) which is always reliable than to use IRR.

7.5 Some Practical Points

Relevant costs

As with all decision-making, we should only take account of cash flows which are affected by our decision. Cash flows which will be the same irrespective of the decision under review should be ignored. Thus, for example, overheads which will be incurred in equal amount whether the investment is made or not should be ignored, even though the investment could not be made without the infrastructure which the overhead costs create.

Taxation

Tax will usually be affected by an investment decision. The profits will be taxed, the capital investment may attract tax relief, etc. Tax is levied on these at significant rates, and unless tax is formally taken account of, the wrong decision could easily be made.

SELF-ASSESSMENT QUESTION

Beacon Chemicals plc is considering the erection of a new plant to produce a chemical named X14. The new plant's capital cost is estimated at £100,000 and if its construction is approved now, the plant can be erected and commence production by the end of 19X6. £50,000 has already been spent on research and development work. Estimates of revenues and costs arising from the operation of the new plant appear below:

	19X7	19X8	19X9	19X0	19X1
Sales price (£ per unit)	100	120	120	100	80
Sales volume (units)	800	1,000	1,200	1,000	800
Variable costs (£ per unit)	50	50	40	30	40
Fixed costs (£000)	30	30	30	30	30

If the new plant is erected, sales of some existing products will be lost and this will result in a loss of contribution of £15,000 per year over its life.

The accountant has informed you that the fixed costs include depreciation of £20,000 per annum on new plant. They also include an allocation of £10,000 for fixed overheads. A separate study has indicated that if the new plant was built, additional overheads, excluding depreciation, arising from its construction would be £8,000 per year.

The plant would require additional working capital of £30,000.

For the purposes of your initial calculations ignore taxation.

(a) Deduce the relevant annual cash flows associated with building and operating the plant.

(b) Deduce the payback period.

(c) Calculate the net present value using a discount rate of 8%.

Hint: You should deal with the investment in working capital by treating it as a cash outflow at the start of the project and an inflow at the end.

Solution on p. 256.

7.6 Dealing with Risk in Investment Appraisal

We have already considered the fact that risk — the likelihood that what is estimated to occur will not actually occur — is an important aspect of financial decision-making. It is particularly important in the context of investment decisions. This is because of the relatively long time-scales involved: there is more time for things to go wrong between the decision being made and the end of the project.

Various approaches to dealing with risk have been proposed. These fall into the following two categories.

Assessing the level of risk

One popular way of attempting to assess the level of risk is to carry out a *sensitivity analysis* on the proposed project. Here the best available estimates are used for all of the input data. If the result of the analysis, based on these data, is positive, each item of data is examined to see how far its estimated value could be incorrect before the project would become adverse for that reason alone. For example, we found earlier in the chapter that the NPV of the Billingsgate Battery Company investment was a positive value of £52,260. If we were to carry out a sensitivity analysis on this project, we should consider each of the input values — cost of the machine, sales volume and price, individual manufacturing costs, length of the project, discount rate — in turn. We should seek to find the most adverse value which each of them could have before the NPV figure becomes negative. A computer spreadsheet model of the project can be extremely valuable here because it is a simple matter to try various values for the input data and see the effect of each. As a result of carrying out a sensitivity analysis the decision-maker is able to get a 'feel' for the project, which otherwise would probably not be possible.

Thus, sensitivity analysis can be used to identify variables which merit further investigation. The technique can be used to identify variables which need to change by only a small amount for the project to become adverse. Decision-makers can either reject the project because it is not robust enough or undertake further investigations into the crucial factor or factors.

Another means of assessing risk is through the use of statistical probabilities. It may be possible to identify for each of the items of input data a range of feasible values, with the probability of occurrence of each one of the values in the range. Using this information it is possible to derive a weighted average or 'expected' NPV. It is also possible to see how likely it is, in theory, that the NPV will, in the event, turn out to have particular values.

Reacting to the level of risk

The logical reaction to a risky project is to demand a higher rate of return. Both theory and observable evidence show that there is a relationship between risk and the return required by investors. For example, a bank would normally ask for a higher rate of interest on a loan where it perceives the lender to be less likely to be able to repay the amount borrowed. As we saw earlier in this chapter, it is normal to increase the NPV discount rate in the face of a risky investment, i.e. to demand a risk premium. This relationship between risk and return is illustrated in Figure 7.2.

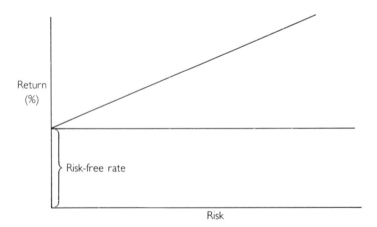

Figure 7.2   Graph of return against risk.

7.7 Management of the Investment Decision-making Process

So far this chapter has been concerned with the process of carrying out the analysis which will enable the decision-maker to select among already identified investment opportunities. This is only part of the process of investment decision-making.

The analytical process is preceded by a search for appropriate opportunities. This means that the business should carry out methodical routines for identifying feasible projects. This may be done through a research and development section or by some other means. One way or another, however, the business must look for opportunities. Failure to do so will inevitably lead to the business losing its competitive position regarding product development, production methods or market penetration.

Similarly, projects which have been analysed as being viable must be managed to actual implementation. Making a decision to invest in the necessary plant to go into production of a new product does not automatically cause the investment to be made and production to go smoothly ahead.

Summary

In this chapter we considered how managers might approach the problem of assessing investment opportunities. We saw that there are basically four methods which are used to any significant extent in practice. These are:

- ◆ Accounting rate of return.
- ◆ Payback period.
- ◆ Net present value.
- ◆ Internal rate of return.

The first two of these are seriously flawed by their failing to take full account of the time dimension of investments. Assuming that the objective of making an investment is to enhance the wealth of the business, the NPV method is, theoretically, far the most superior of the four methods in that it rationally and fully takes account of all relevant information. Since IRR is fairly similar to NPV it tends to give similar signals to those provided by NPV. However, IRR does suffer from a fundamental theoretical flaw which can lead to it giving misleading signals on some occasions. We concluded the chapter by considering some more practical aspects of using the appraisal methods.

EXERCISES ————————————————————————————————————

7.1 The directors of Mylo Ltd are currently considering two mutually exclusive investment projects. Both projects are concerned with the purchase of new plant. The following data is available for each project.

	Project	
	1	**2**
	£	£
Cost (immediate outlay)	100,000	60,000
Expected annual net profit (loss):		
Year 1	29,000	18,000
2	(1,000)	(2,000)
3	2,000	4,000
Estimated residual value	7,000	6,000

The company has an estimated cost of capital of 10 per cent and employs the straight-line method of depreciation for all fixed assets when calculating net profit. Neither project would increase the working capital of the company. The company has sufficient funds to meet all capital expenditure requirements.

(a) Calculate for each project:
    (i) The net present value.
    (ii) The approximate internal rate of return.
    (iii) The payback period.
(b) State which, if any, of the two investment projects the directors of Mylo Ltd should accept, and why.
(c) State, in general terms, which method of investment appraisal you consider to be most appropriate for evaluating investment projects and why.

(Answer on page 265. Answers to exercises 7.2 and 7.3 are given in the Teacher's Manual.)

7.2 C. George (Controls) Ltd manufactures a thermostat that can be used in a range of kitchen appliances. The manufacturing process is, at present, semi-automated. The equipment used cost £540,000 and has a written-down value of £300,000. Demand for the product has been fairly stable and output has been maintained at 50,000 units per annum in recent years.

The following data, based on the current level of output, has been prepared in respect of the product:

	Per unit	
	£	£
Selling price		12.40
Less:		
Labour	3.30	
Materials	3.65	
Overheads: Variable	1.58	
Fixed	1.60	
		10.13
Profit		2.27

Although the existing equipment is expected to last for a further four years before it is sold for an estimated £40,000, the company has recently been considering purchasing new equipment which would completely automate much of the production process. The new equipment would cost £670,000 and would have an expected life of four years at the end of which it would be sold for an estimated £70,000. If the new equipment is purchased the old equipment could be sold for £150,000 immediately.

The assistant to the company accountant has prepared a report to help assess the viability of the proposed change which includes the following data:

	Per unit	
	£	£
Selling price		12.40
Less:		
Labour	1.20	
Materials	3.20	
Overheads: Variable	1.40	
Fixed	3.30	
		9.10
Profit		3.30

Depreciation charges will increase by £85,000 per annum as a result of purchasing the new machinery; however, other fixed costs are not expected to change.

In the report the assistant wrote:

'The figures shown above which relate to the proposed change are based on the current level of output and take account of a depreciation charge of £150,000 per annum in respect of the new equipment. The effect of purchasing the new equipment will be to increase the net profit to sales ratio from 18.3% to 26.6%. In addition, the purchase of the new equipment will enable us to reduce our stock level immediately by £130,000.'

'In view of these facts I recommend purchase of the new equipment.'

The company has a cost of capital of 12 per cent.
Ignore taxation.

(a) Prepare a statement of the incremental cash flows arising from the purchase of the new equipment.
(b) Calculate the net present value of the proposed purchase of new equipment.
(c) State, with reasons, whether the company should purchase the new equipment.
(d) Explain why cash flow forecasts are used rather than profit forecasts to assess the viability of proposed capital expenditure projects.

7.3 The accountant of your company has recently been taken ill through overwork. In his absence his assistant has prepared some calculations of the profitability of a project which are to be discussed soon at the board meeting of your company. His workings, which are set out below, include some errors of principle. You can assume that the statement below includes no arithmetical errors.

	19X7	19X8	19X9	19X0	19X1	19X2
	£000	£000	£000	£000	£000	£000
Sales revenue		450	470	470	470	470
Less: Costs						
Materials		126	132	132	132	132
Labour		90	94	94	94	94
Overheads		45	47	47	47	47
Depreciation		120	120	120	120	120
Working capital	180					
Interest on working capital		27	27	27	27	27
Write off of development costs		30	30	30		
Total costs	180	438	450	450	420	420
Profit/(loss)	(180)	12	20	20	50	50

Total profit/(loss)	(£28,000)	= Return on investment (4.7%)
Cost of equipment	£600,000	

You ascertain the following additional information:

♦ The cost of equipment contains £100,000 being the book value of an old machine. If it was not used for this project it would be scrapped with a zero net realizable value. New equipment costing £500,000 will be purchased on 31 December 19X7. You should assume that all other cash flows occur at the end of the year to which they relate.
♦ The development costs of £90,000 have already been spent.
♦ Overheads have been costed at 50 per cent of direct labour which is the company's normal practice. An independent assessment has suggested that incremental overheads are likely to amount to £30,000 per year.
♦ The company's weighted average cost of capital is 12 per cent.

Ignore taxation in your answer.

(a) Prepare a corrected statement of the incremental cash flows arising from the project. Where you have altered the assistant's figures you should attach a brief note explaining your alterations.
(b) Calculate:
    (i) The project's payback period.
    (ii) The project's net present value.
(c) Write a memo to the board advising on the acceptance or rejection of the project.

Appendix: Present Value Table

Present value of 1, i.e. $(1 + r)^{-n}$

where r = discount rate

n = number of periods until payment

Discount rates (r)

Periods (n)	1%	2%	3%	4%	5%	6%	7%	8%	9%	10%	
1	0.990	0.980	0.971	0.962	0.952	0.943	0.935	0.926	0.917	0.909	1
2	0.980	0.961	0.943	0.925	0.907	0.890	0.873	0.857	0.842	0.826	2
3	0.971	0.942	0.915	0.889	0.864	0.840	0.816	0.794	0.772	0.751	3
4	0.961	0.924	0.888	0.855	0.823	0.792	0.763	0.735	0.708	0.683	4
5	0.951	0.906	0.863	0.822	0.784	0.747	0.713	0.681	0.650	0.621	5
6	0.942	0.888	0.837	0.790	0.746	0.705	0.666	0.630	0.596	0.564	6
7	0.933	0.871	0.813	0.760	0.711	0.665	0.623	0.583	0.547	0.513	7
8	0.923	0.853	0.789	0.731	0.677	0.627	0.582	0.540	0.502	0.467	8
9	0.914	0.837	0.766	0.703	0.645	0.592	0.544	0.500	0.460	0.424	9
10	0.905	0.820	0.744	0.676	0.614	0.558	0.508	0.463	0.422	0.386	10
11	0.896	0.804	0.722	0.650	0.585	0.527	0.475	0.429	0.388	0.350	11
12	0.887	0.788	0.701	0.625	0.557	0.497	0.444	0.397	0.356	0.319	12
13	0.879	0.773	0.681	0.601	0.530	0.469	0.415	0.368	0.326	0.290	13
14	0.870	0.758	0.661	0.577	0.505	0.442	0.388	0.340	0.299	0.263	14
15	0.861	0.743	0.642	0.555	0.481	0.417	0.362	0.315	0.275	0.239	15

	11%	12%	13%	14%	15%	16%	17%	18%	19%	20%	
1	0.901	0.893	0.885	0.877	0.870	0.862	0.855	0.847	0.840	0.833	1
2	0.812	0.797	0.783	0.769	0.756	0.743	0.731	0.718	0.706	0.694	2
3	0.731	0.712	0.693	0.675	0.658	0.641	0.624	0.609	0.593	0.579	3
4	0.659	0.636	0.613	0.592	0.572	0.552	0.534	0.516	0.499	0.482	4
5	0.593	0.567	0.543	0.519	0.497	0.476	0.456	0.437	0.419	0.402	5
6	0.535	0.507	0.480	0.456	0.432	0.410	0.390	0.370	0.352	0.335	6
7	0.482	0.452	0.425	0.400	0.376	0.354	0.333	0.314	0.296	0.279	7
8	0.434	0.404	0.376	0.351	0.327	0.305	0.285	0.266	0.249	0.233	8
9	0.391	0.361	0.333	0.308	0.284	0.263	0.243	0.225	0.209	0.194	9
10	0.352	0.322	0.295	0.270	0.247	0.227	0.208	0.191	0.176	0.162	10
11	0.317	0.287	0.261	0.237	0.215	0.195	0.178	0.162	0.148	0.135	11
12	0.286	0.257	0.231	0.208	0.187	0.168	0.152	0.137	0.124	0.112	12
13	0.258	0.229	0.204	0.182	0.163	0.145	0.130	0.116	0.104	0.093	13
14	0.232	0.205	0.181	0.160	0.141	0.125	0.111	0.099	0.088	0.078	14
15	0.209	0.183	0.160	0.140	0.123	0.108	0.095	0.084	0.074	0.065	15

Further Reading

Arnold, J. and Hope, A., *Accounting for Management Decisions* (2nd edn). Prentice Hall, 1990.
Brealey, R. and Myers, S., *Principles of Corporate Finance* (4th edn). McGraw-Hill, 1991.
McLaney, E., *Business Finance for Decision Makers*. Pitman, 1994.

CHAPTER EIGHT

Budgeting

8.1 Introduction

This chapter is concerned with budgets, their purpose and their construction. It also deals with the role of budgeting in management control.

8.2 Purpose

On completion of this chapter you should be able to:

- Define a budget and show how budgets, corporate objectives and long-term plans are related.
- Explain the interlinking of the various budgets within the business.
- Indicate the uses of budgeting and construct various budgets, including the cash budget, from relevant data.
- Discuss the various aspects of a successful system of budgetary control.
- Reconcile the budget and actual profit figure through variances.

8.3 Budgets, Long-term Plans and Corporate Objectives

In Chapter 1 we saw that it is important that businesses define what it is that they are ultimately seeking to achieve. (You should remember that we identified maximization of the wealth of the business as the single most valid financial objective in the private sector.)

Clearly, just to define a broad objective, such as maximization of the wealth of the business, is not sufficient to achieve the goal. It is necessary to go into more detail as to how the objective is to be gained. Businesses typically do this by producing a long-term plan, perhaps going five years into the future, and a short-term plan perhaps (usually) looking at the following twelve months. The relationship between these three planning devices can be shown graphically, as in Figure 8.1.

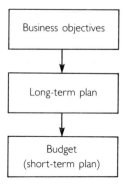

Figure 8.1 Objectives, plans and budgets.

The long-term plan would define the general direction of the business over the next five or so years and would deal, in broad terms, with such matters as:

♦ The market which the business will seek to serve.
♦ Production/service-rendering methods.
♦ What the business will offer to its customers.
♦ Levels of profit sought.
♦ Investments to be made.
♦ Financial requirements and financing methods.
♦ Personnel requirement.
♦ Bought-in goods and services requirements and sources.

The budget would go into far more detail in respect of the forthcoming year and deal with such things as:

♦ Sales and expenses.
♦ Cash flows.
♦ Short-term credit to be given or taken.
♦ Stock-in-trade requirements.

Clearly, the relationship between objectives, long-term plans and budgets is that the objective, once set, is likely to last for quite a long time, perhaps throughout the life of the business (though changes can and do occur). A series of long-term plans identify how the objective is to be pursued, and budgets identify how the long-term plan is to be fulfilled.

An analogy might be found in terms of someone enrolling on a course of study. His or her objective might be to have a working career which is rewarding in various ways. The person might have identified the course as the most effective way to work towards this objective. In working towards achievement of this, passing a particular year of the course might be identified as the immediate target.

Here completion of the entire course is analogous to a long-term plan, and passing each year is analogous to the budget. Having achieved the 'budget' for the first year, the 'budget' for the second year becomes passing that year.

8.4 The Source of Plans and Budgets

It is the function of the management of a business to set long-term plans and budgets. This may be done as a major exercise each five years/year when the plans are made for the next period. Alternatively, during the period of the long-term plan/budget it can constantly be extended. For example, each month the budget for the same month next year is set, thus there will always be fairly detailed plans for a full twelve months into the future; such a budget would be called a *rolling budget*.

It need not be the case that long-term plans are set for five years and that budgets are set for twelve months, and it is up to the management of the business concerned, though these are fairly typical of the time periods found in practice. A business involved in certain industries such as information technology may feel that five years is too long a planning period since new developments can, and do, occur virtually overnight.

The annual budget sets targets for the year for all levels of the business. It is usually broken down into monthly budgets which define monthly targets. In many cases the annual budget will, in any case, be built up from monthly figures.

8.5 Definition of a Budget

A budget may be defined as a financial plan for a future period of time. Financial because the budget is, to a great extent, expressed in financial terms. Note particularly that a budget is a plan, not a forecast. To talk of a plan suggests an intention or determination to achieve the planned targets. Forecasts tend to be predictions of the future state of the environment.

Clearly, forecasts are helpful to the planner/budget-setter. If a reputable forecaster has forecast the particular number of new cars to be purchased in the UK during next year, it will be valuable for a manager in a car manufacturing business to obtain this forecast figure when setting sales budgets. However, the forecast and the budget are distinctly different.

8.6 The Interrelationship of Various Budgets

For a particular business for a particular period there is not one budget but a number of them, each one relating to a specific aspect of the business. It is generally considered that the ideal situation is that there should be a separate budget for each person who is in a managerial position no matter how junior. The contents of all of the individual budgets is, in effect, summarized in master budgets which would typically be a budgeted income statement and balance sheet.

Figure 8.2 illustrates the interrelationship and interlinking of the individual budgets, in this particular case using a manufacturing business as an example.

Starting at the top right of Figure 8.2, the finished stock requirement would be

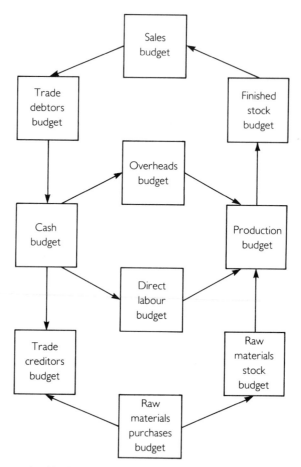

Figure 8.2 **The network of budgets of a manufacturing business.**

dictated partly by the level of sales; it would also be dictated by the policy of the business on finished stockholding. The requirement for finished stock would define the required production levels which would in turn dictate the requirements of the individual production departments or sections. The demands of manufacturing will dictate the materials budget and that will, in conjunction with the business' policy on raw material stockholding, define the stores (raw materials) stock budget. The purchases budget will be dictated by the stores stock budget which will, in conjunction with the policy of the business on creditor payment, dictate the creditors budget. One of the inputs into the cash budget will be from the creditors budget; another will be the debtors budget which itself derives via the debtor policy of the business from the sales budget. Cash will also be affected by selling and distribution costs (themselves indirectly related to sales), by labour and administration costs (themselves linked to production) and by capital expenditure.

Assuming that the budgeting process takes the order in which we have just reviewed it, it might be found in practice that there is some constraint to achieving the sales target. For example, the production function of the business may be incapable of meeting the necessary levels of output to match the sales budget for one or more months. In this case it might be reasonable to look at the possibility of higher production in previous months and stockpiling to meet the higher-demand period(s). Perhaps increasing the production facility might be possible. As a last resort it might be necessary to revise the sales budget to a lower level to enable production to meet the target.

There will not only be the horizontal relationships between budgets which we have just looked at but also vertical ones as well. For example, the sales budget may be broken down into a number of subsidiary budgets, perhaps one for each regional sales manager. Thus the overall sales budget will be a summary of the subsidiary ones. The same may be true of virtually all of the other budgets, most particularly the production budget. Figure 8.1 gives only a very simplified outline of the budgetary framework of the typical business.

All of the operating budgets, which we have just reviewed, are set within the framework of the master budgets, i.e. the budgeted profit and loss account and balance sheet.

8.7 The Uses of Budgets

Budgets are generally regarded as having four areas of usefulness, which we discuss below.

1. They tend to promote forward-thinking and the possible identification of short-term problems

In the previous section of this chapter we saw that a shortage of production capacity may be identified during the budgeting process and that its discovery in plenty of time leaves a number of means of overcoming the problem open to exploration.

2. They can be used to help co-ordinate various sections of the business

It is crucial that the activities of the various departments and sections of the business are linked so that the activities of one department are complementary to those of another. For example, the activities of the purchasing/procurement department of a manufacturing business should dovetail with the raw materials needs of the production departments. If this is not the case then production could run out of stock, leading to expensive production stoppages. Alternatively, excessive stocks could be bought, leading to large and unnecessary stockholding costs.

3.   They can motivate managers to better performance

Having a stated task can motivate performance. It is thought by many people that to tell a manager to do his or her best is not very motivating, but to define a required level of achievement is likely to motivate. It is felt by some that managers are particularly well motivated by being able to relate their particular role to the overall objectives of the business. Since budgets are directly derived from corporate objectives, budgeting makes this possible.

It might seem that requiring managers to work towards predetermined targets will stifle managers' skill, flair and enthusiasm. This danger might exist if targets are badly set. If, however, the budgets are set in such a way as to offer a challenging yet achievable target, the manager is still required to show skill, flair and enthusiasm. It is obviously not possible to allow managers to operate in an unconstrained environment. Having to operate in a way which matches the goals of the business is a price of working in an effective business.

4.   They can provide a basis for a system of control

If senior management wishes to control and monitor the performance of subordinates it needs some standard with which the performance can be compared and against which it can be assessed. There is a temptation, where it is possible to do so, to compare current performance with the previous month's or year's, or perhaps with what happens in another business. However, the most logical yardstick is planned performance. Experience of the past and of what happens elsewhere will be taken into account when budgets are being set.

A definition of control is 'to compel events to conform to a plan'. Even when we talk of controlling a motor car, we mean making the car behave in the manner which the driver planned, even though that plan may have been made less than a second earlier. If there are data available concerning the actual performance for a period (say a month) and this can be compared with the planned performance a basis for control will have been established. Such a basis will enable the use of *management by exception*, a technique where senior managers can spend most of their time dealing with those of their subordinates who have failed to achieve the budget and not having to spend too much time on those who are performing well. It also allows junior managers to exercise *self-control*: by knowing what is expected of them and what they have actually achieved, they can assess how well they are performing and take steps to correct matters where they are failing to achieve.

8.7.1   Example of a Budget — The Cash Budget

We now look in some detail at one particular budget: the cash budget. There are three reasons for using this as an example:

1. It is at least as good an example as is any other budget.

2. Most economic aspects of a business are reflected in cash sooner or later so that the cash budget reflects the whole business more than any other single budget, for the typical business.
3. Very small, unsophisticated businesses (e.g. a corner shop) may feel that full-scale budgeting is not appropriate to their needs, but almost certainly they should prepare a cash budget as a minimum.

Since budgets are documents which are to be used only internally by the business, their style and format is a question of management choice and will therefore vary from one business to the next. However, since managers, irrespective of the business, are likely to be using budgets for similar purposes there is a tendency for some consistency of approach to exist across most businesses. We can probably say that in most businesses the cash budget would possess the following features:

1. The budget period broken down into subperiods, typically months.
2. The budget in columnar form, a column for each month.
3. Receipts of cash identified under various headings and a total for each month's receipts.
4. Payments of cash identified under various headings and a total for each month's payments.
5. The surplus of total cash receipts over payments or of payments over receipts for each month.
6. The running cash balance, which would be obtained by taking the balance at the end of the previous month and adjusting it for surplus or deficit of receipts over payments for the current month.

Typically all of the pieces of information (3)–(6) inclusive would be useful to management for one reason or another.

EXAMPLE ————————————————————————————————————

Suppliers Ltd is a wholesale business. The budgeted profit and loss account for the next six months is as follows:

	Jan.	Feb.	Mar.	Apr.	May	June
	£000	£000	£000	£000	£000	£000
Sales	52	55	55	60	55	53
Cost of goods sold	30	31	31	35	31	32
Salaries and wages	10	10	10	10	10	10
Electricity	5	5	4	3	3	3
Depreciation	3	3	3	3	3	3
Other overheads	2	2	2	2	2	2
Total expenses	50	51	50	53	49	50
Net profit	2	4	5	7	6	3

The business allows all of its customers one month's credit (i.e. goods bought in January will be paid for in February). Sales during December had been £60,000.

The business plans to maintain stocks at their existing level until March, when they are to be reduced by £5,000. Stocks will remain at this lower level indefinitely. Stock purchases are made on one month's credit (the December purchases were £30,000). Salaries and wages and 'other overheads' are paid in the month concerned. Electricity is paid quarterly in arrears in March and June. The business plans to buy and pay for a new delivery van in March. This will cost a total of £15,000, but an existing van will be traded-in for £4,000 as part of the deal. The business expects to start January with £12,000 in cash.

The cash budget for the six months ending 30 June is given below.

Cash Budget for the six months ended 30 June

	Jan. £000	Feb. £000	Mar. £000	Apr. £000	May £000	June £000
Receipts:						
Debtors (note 1)	60	52	55	55	60	55
Payments:						
Creditors (note 2)	30	30	31	26	35	31
Salaries and wages	10	10	10	10	10	10
Electricity			14			9
Other overheads	2	2	2	2	2	2
Van purchase			11			
Total payments	42	42	68	38	47	52
Cash surplus	18	10	(13)	17	13	3
Cash balance	30	40	27	44	57	60

Notes

1. The cash receipts lag a month behind sales because customers are given a month in which to pay for their purchases.
2. In most months the purchases of stock will equal the cost of goods sold. This is because the business maintains a constant level of stock. For stock to remain constant at the end of each month the business must replace exactly the amount of stock which has been used. In March the business plans to reduce its stock by £5,000. This means that stock purchases will be lower than stock usage in that month. The payments for stock purchases lag a month behind purchases because the business expects to be allowed a month to pay for what it buys.

8.8 Preparing Other Budgets

Though each one will have its own idiosyncracies, other budgets will tend to follow the same pattern as the cash budget. Take the debtors budget for example. This would normally show the planned amount owing from credit sales to the business at the beginning and at the end of each month, the planned total sales for each month, and the planned total cash receipts from debtors.

ACTIVITY

Prepare the debtors budget for Suppliers Ltd (see the above Activity) for the six months, January to June.

Debtors Budget for the six months ended 30 June

	Jan. £000	Feb. £000	Mar. £000	Apr. £000	May £000	June £000
Opening balance	60	52	55	55	60	55
Sales	52	55	55	60	55	53
	112	107	110	115	115	108
Less: Cash receipts	60	52	55	55	60	55
Closing balance	52	55	55	60	55	53

This could, of course, be set out in any manner which would have given the sort of information which management would require in respect of planned levels of debtors and associated transactions.

Note how the debtors budget links to the cash budget: the cash receipts row of figures is the same. The debtors budget would similarly link to the sales budget. This is how the linking which was discussed earlier in this chapter is achieved.

ACTIVITY

Antonio Ltd has planned production and sales for the next eight months as follows:

	Production units	Sales units
May	350	350
June	400	400
July	500	400
August	600	500
September	600	600
October	700	650
November	750	700
December	750	800
January	750	750

During the period the business plans to advertise heavily to generate these increases in sales. Payments for advertising of £1,000 and £1,500 will be made in July and October respectively.

The selling price per unit will be £20 throughout the period.

Forty per cent of sales are normally made on two months' credit. The other 60 per cent are settled within the month of the sale.

Raw material will be held in stock for one month before it is taken into production. Purchases of raw materials will be on one month's credit (buy one month, pay the next). The cost of raw material is £8 per unit of production.

Other direct production expenses, including labour, are planned to be £6 per unit of production. These will be paid in the month concerned.

Various production overheads, which during the period to 30 June had run at £1,800 per month, are expected to rise to £2,000 each month from 1 July to 31 October. These are expected to rise again from 1 November to £2,400 per month and to remain at that level for the foreseeable future. These overheads include a steady £400 each month for depreciation.

Overheads are planned to be paid 80 per cent in the month of production and 20 per cent in the following month.

To help to meet the planned increased production, a new item of plant will be bought and will be delivered in August. The cost of this item is £6,600, the contract with the supplier will specify that this will be paid in three equal amounts in September, October and November.

Raw material stock is planned to be 500 units on 1 July. The balance at the bank the same day is planned to be £7,500.

You are required to draw up for the six months ending 31 December:

(a) A raw materials budget, showing both physical quantities and financial values.
(b) A creditors budget.
(c) A cash budget.

Antonio Ltd   Raw Materials Stock Budget for the six months ending 31 December (in units)

	July units	Aug. units	Sept. units	Oct. units	Nov. units	Dec. units
Opening stock	500	600	600	700	750	750
Purchases	600	600	700	750	750	750
	1,100	1,200	1,300	1,450	1,500	1,500
Less: Issues to production	500	600	600	700	750	750
Closing stock	600	600	700	750	750	750

Antonio Ltd   Raw Materials Stock Budget for the six months ending 31 December (in financial terms)

	July £000	Aug. £000	Sept. £000	Oct. £000	Nov. £000	Dec. £000
Opening stock	4,000	4,800	4,800	5,600	6,000	6,000
Purchases	4,800	4,800	5,600	6,000	6,000	6,000
	8,800	9,600	10,400	11,600	12,000	12,000
Less: Issues to production	4,000	4,800	4,800	5,600	6,000	6,000
Closing stock	4,800	4,800	5,600	6,000	6,000	6,000

Antonio Ltd   Creditors Budget for the six months ending 31 December

	July £000	Aug. £000	Sept. £000	Oct. £000	Nov. £000	Dec. £000
Opening balance	4,000	4,800	4,800	5,600	6,000	6,000
Purchases	4,800	4,800	5,600	6,000	6,000	6,000
	8,800	9,600	10,400	11,600	12,000	12,000
Less: Payments	4,000	4,800	4,800	5,600	6,000	6,000
Closing balance	4,800	4,800	5,600	6,000	6,000	6,000

Antonio Ltd   Cash Budget for the six months ending 31 December

	July £	Aug. £	Sept. £	Oct. £	Nov. £	Dec. £
Inflows						
Receipts: Debtors	2,800	3,200	3,200	4,000	4,800	5,200
Cash sales	4,800	6,000	7,200	7,800	8,400	9,600
Total inflows	7,600	9,200	10,400	11,800	13,200	14,800
Outflows						
Payments to creditors	4,000	4,800	4,800	5,600	6,000	6,000
Direct costs	3,000	3,600	3,600	4,200	4,500	4,500
Advertising	1,000	—	—	1,500	—	—
Overheads:						
80%	1,280	1,280	1,280	1,280	1,600	1,600
20%	280	320	320	320	320	400
New plant			2,200	2,200	2,200	
Total outflows	9,560	10,000	12,200	15,100	14,620	12,500
Net inflows/(outflows)	(1,960)	(800)	(1,800)	(3,300)	(1,420)	2,300
Balance c/fwd	5,540	4,740	2,940	(360)	(1,780)	520

Once again we can see how budgets are linked; in this case the stock budget to the creditors budget and the creditors budget to the cash budget.

A C T I V I T Y ───

The cash budget of Antonio Ltd reveals a potential cash deficiency during October and November. Can you suggest any ways in which a modification of plans could overcome this problem?

The following reasons occurred to us:

◆ *Make a higher proportion of sales on a cash basis.*
◆ *Collect the money from debtors more promptly, e.g. during the month following the sale.*
◆ *Hold lower stocks, both of raw materials and of finished stock.*
◆ *Increase the creditor payment period.*
◆ *Delay the payments for advertising.*
◆ *Obtain more credit for the overhead costs, at present only 20 per cent is on credit.*
◆ *Delay the payments for the new plant.*

8.9 Using Budgets for Control — Flexible Budgets

Earlier in this chapter the point was made that budgets can provide a useful basis for exercising control over the business. This is because control is usually seen as making events conform to a plan. Since the budget represents the plan, making events conform to it is the obvious way to try to control the business. In practice, using budgets in this way is very popular. As we saw in Chapter 1, for most businesses the routine is as shown in Figure 8.3.

The steps in the control process shown in the figure are probably easy to understand. The point is that if plans are sensibly drawn up, we have a basis for exercising control over the business. This also requires that we have the means of measuring actual performance in the same terms as those in which the budget is stated. If they are not in the same terms, comparison will not usually be possible. Taking steps to exercise control means finding out where and why things did not go according to plan and seeking ways to put things right for the future. One of the reasons that things may not have gone according to plan is that the plans may prove to be unachievable. In this case, if budgets are to be a useful basis for exercising control in the future, it may be necessary to revise the budgets for future periods to bring targets into the realms of achievability.

This last point should not be taken to mean that budget targets can simply be ignored if the going gets tough. However, for a variety of reasons including unexpected changes in the commercial environment (e.g. unexpected collapse in demand for services of the type in which the business deals), budgets may prove to be totally unrealistic targets. In this case nothing whatsoever will be achieved by pretending that the targets can be met.

By having a system of budgetary control a position can be established where decision-making and responsibility can be delegated to junior management, yet control

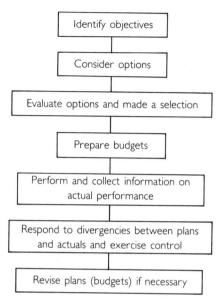

Figure 8.3 The decision-making, planning and control process.

can still be retained by senior management. This is because senior management can use the budgetary control system to enable it to know which junior managers are meeting targets and, therefore, working towards the objectives of the business, and which managers are failing to do so. This enables a *management by exception* environment to be created. Here senior management concentrates its energy on areas where things are not going according to plan (the exceptions — it is to be hoped). Junior managers who are performing to budget can be left to get on with the job.

We shall return to some more practical aspects of this process after we have considered in a little detail one of the above steps, namely comparison of the actual performance with the budget.

8.10 Comparison of Actual Performance with the Budget

Since the principal objective of most private-sector businesses is to enhance their wealth, and remembering that profit is the net increase in wealth as a result of trading, the most important budget target to meet is the profit target. In view of this we concentrate on that aspect of our consideration of making the comparison between actuals and budgets.

The following are the budgeted and actual profit and loss account for Baxter Ltd for the month of May:

	Budget	Actual
Output (production and sales)	1,000 units	900 units
Sales	£ 100,000	£ 92,000
Raw materials	(40,000) (40,000 m)	(36,900) (37,000 m)
Labour	(20,000) (5,000 hours)	(17,500) (4,375 hours)
Fixed overheads	(20,000)	(20,700)
Operating profit	£20,000	£16,900

Clearly the budgeted profit was not achieved. As far as May is concerned this is a matter of history. However, the business (at least some aspects of it) are out of control. Senior management must discover where things went wrong during May and try to ensure that they are not repeated in later months. Thus it is not enough to know that, overall, things went wrong, we need to know where and why.

ACTIVITY

Can you see any problems in comparing the various items (sales, raw materials, etc.) for the budget and the actual performance in order to draw conclusions as to which aspects were out of control?

The problem is that the actual level of output was not as budgeted. This means that we cannot, for example, say that there was a labour cost saving of £2,500 (i.e. £20,000 − 17,500) and conclude that all is well in that area. This is because the level of output was 10 per cent less than budgeted.

One practical way to overcome our difficulty is to 'flex' (i.e. revise) the budget to what it would have been, had the planned level of output been 900 units rather than 1,000 units. In order to do this we need to know which items are fixed and which are variable relative to the level of output. However, with this knowledge, flexing is a simple operation. We assume that sales revenue, material cost and labour cost vary strictly with volume. Fixed overheads, by definition, will not. Whether in real life labour cost does vary in this way is not so certain, but it will serve well enough as an assumption for our purposes.

ACTIVITY

Prepare the flexed budget for Baxter Ltd for a volume of output of 900 units.

On the basis of the assumptions regarding the behaviour of costs, the flexed budget would be as follows:

	Flexed budget
Output (production and sales)	*900 units*
	£
Sales	*90,000*
Raw materials	*(36,000) (36,000 metres)*
Labour	*(18,000) (4,500 hours)*
Fixed overheads	*(20,000)*
Operating profit	*£16,000*

Putting the original budget, the flexed budget and the actual together we obtain the following:

	Original budget	Flexed budget	Actual
Output (production and sales)	1,000 units	900 units	900 units
	£	£	£
Sales	100,000	90,000	92,000
Raw materials	(40,000)	(36,000)	(36,900)
Labour	(20,000)	(18,000)	(17,500)
Fixed overheads	(20,000)	(20,000)	(20,700)
Operating profit	£20,000	£16,000	£16,900

We can now make a more valid comparison between budget (using the flexed figures) and actual. We can now see that there was genuine labour cost saving, even after allowing for the output shortfall.

It may occur to you that we are simply saying that it does not matter if there are volume shortfalls because we just revise the budget and carry on as if nothing had happened. This must be an invalid approach because losing sales means losing profit. The first point we must pick up, therefore, is the loss of profit arising from the loss of sales of 100 units of the product.

ACTIVITY ——————————————————————————————

What will be the loss of profit as a result of the profit arising from the sales shortfall, assuming that everything except sales volume was as planned?

The answer is simply the difference between the original and flexed budget profit figures. The only difference between these two profit figures is the assumed volume of sales, everything else was the same. Thus the figure is £4,000.

We call this difference the *sales volume variance*. It is an *adverse variance* because taken alone, it has the effect of making the actual profit lower than that which was budgeted.

We can therefore say that a variance is the effect of that factor on the budgeted profit. When looking at some particular aspect like sales volume we assume that all other factors went according to plan. It is true to say that:

Budgeted profit

plus

All favourable variances

minus

All adverse variances

equals

Actual profit

ACTIVITY ──

What should the senior management of Baxter Ltd do about the sales volume variance?

───

Enquiries must be made to find out why the volume of sales fell below the budget figure. Only by discovering this information will management be in any position to try to ensure that it does not occur again.

Who should be asked about this variance? The answer would probably be the sales manager. This person should know precisely why this departure from budget has occurred. This is not to say that it was the sales manager's fault. The reason for the problem could easily have been that production was at fault in not having produced the budgeted production, meaning that there were not sufficient items to sell. What is not in doubt is that in the first instance it is the sales manager who should know the reason for the problem.

It is now a matter of comparing the actual figures with the flexed budgeted ones to find out the other causes of the £3,100 (i.e. £20,000 − 16,900) profit shortfall.

Starting with the sales revenue figure, we can see that there is a difference of £2,000 (favourable) between the flexed budget and the actual figures. This can only arise from higher prices being charged than were envisaged in the original budget, because any variance arising from the volume difference has already been 'stripped out' in the flexing process. This is known as the *sales price variance*.

There is an overall or *total direct material variance* of £900 (adverse). Who should be held accountable for this variance? The answer to this question depends on whether the difference arises from excess usage of the raw material, in which case it is the production manager, or whether it is a higher-than-budgeted price per metre being paid, in which case it is the responsibility of the buying manager.

Fortunately we have the means available to go beyond this total variance. We can see from the figures that there was a 1,000 metre excess usage of the raw material. All other things being equal, this alone would have led to a profit shortfall of £1,000 since the budgeted price per metre is £1. The £1,000 (adverse) variance is known as the *direct material usage variance*. Normally this would be the responsibility of the production manager since it is that person's responsibility to supervise the use of the raw material.

The other aspect of direct materials is the *direct materials price variance*. Here we simply take the actual quantity bought and compare what should have been paid for it with what actually was paid for it. For a quantity of 37,000 metres the cost should have been £37,000; it was actually £36,900. Thus we have a favourable variance of £100.

Direct labour variances are very similar in style to those for raw materials. The *total direct labour variance* is £500 (i.e. £18,000 − 17,500). Again, this is not particularly helpful since the responsibility for the rate of pay lies primarily with the personnel manager, whereas the number of hours taken to complete a particular quantity of output is the responsibility of the production manager.

The *direct labour efficiency variance* compares the number of hours which would be allowed for the level of production achieved with the actual number of hours, and costs the difference at the allowed hourly rate. Thus it is $(4,500 - 4,375) \times £4 = £500$ (favourable). The variance is favourable because fewer hours were used than would have been allowed for the actual level of output.

The *direct labour rate variance* compares the actual cost of the hours worked with the planned cost. For 4,375 hours the allowed cost would be £17,500 (i.e. $4,375 \times £4$). Since this is exactly the amount which was paid, there is no rate variance.

The remaining area is that of fixed overheads. Here the *fixed overhead spending variance* is simply the difference between the fixed budget and the actual figures. This is £700 (adverse). In theory this is the responsibility of whoever is responsible for controlling overheads expenditure. In practice this tends to be a very slippery area and one which is notoriously difficult to control.

We are now in a position to reconcile the original budget profit with the actual one, as follows:

	£	£
Budgeted profit		20,000
Favourable variances:		
Sales price variance	2,000	
Direct materials price	100	
Direct labour efficiency	500	2,600
		22,600
Adverse variances:		
Sales volume	4,000	
Direct material usage	1,000	
Fixed overhead spending	700	5,700
Actual profit		£16,900

8.11 Conditions for Effective Budgetary Control

It is probably fairly obvious from what we have seen of control through budgets that if control is to be successful, a system must be established.

ACTIVITY ───────────────────────────────

Jot down a list of points which you feel need to included in any system or routines which will enable control through budgets to be effective. We have not specifically covered these points, but your common sense and, perhaps, your background knowledge should enable you to think of a few.

───

There is no clear-cut correct answer, however most businesses which operate successful budgetary control systems (there are many of such systems) tend to show some common factors. These include the following:

♦ *A serious attitude taken to the system by all levels of management, right from the very top.*
♦ *Clear demarcation between areas of responsibility of various managers so that accountability can more easily be ascribed for any area which seems to be going out of control.*
♦ *Budget targets being reasonable so that they represent a rigorous, yet achievable target. This may be promoted by managers being involved in setting their own targets. It is argued by some people that this can promote the managers' commitment and motivation.*
♦ *Established data collection, analysis and dissemination routines which take the actual results, the budget figures and calculate and report the variances.*
♦ *Fairly short reporting periods, typically a month, so that things cannot go too far wrong before they are picked up.*
♦ *Variance reports being produced and disseminated shortly after the end of the relevant reporting period.*

SELF-ASSESSMENT QUESTION ──────────────────

The following are the budgeted and actual profit and loss account for Baxter Ltd for the month of June:

	Budget	Actual
Output (production and sales)	1,000 units	1,050 units
	£	£
Sales	100,000	104,300
Raw materials	(40,000) (40,000 metres)	(41,200) (40,500 metres)
Labour	(20,000) (5,000 hours)	(21,300) (5,200 hours)
Fixed overheads	(20,000)	(19,400)
Operating profit	£20,000	(£22,400)

Produce a reconciliation of the budgeted and actual operating profit, going into as much detail as possible with the variance analysis.

Solution on p. 257.

8.12 Behavioural Aspects of Budgetary Control

Budgets, perhaps more than any other accounting statement, are prepared with the objective of affecting the attitudes and behaviour of managers. The point was made earlier in this chapter that budgets are intended to motivate managers, and research evidence shows this generally to be true. More specifically:

- The existence of budgets tends to improve performance.
- Demanding but achievable budget targets tend to motivate more than less-demanding targets.
- Unrealistic targets tend to have an adverse effect on managers' performance.
- The participation of managers in setting their targets tends to improve motivation and performance.

It has been suggested that allowing managers to set their own targets will lead to slack being introduced, so making achievement of the target that much easier. On the other hand, in an effort to impress, a manager may select a target which is not really achievable. These points imply that care must be taken in the extent to which managers have unfettered choice of their own targets.

Where a manager fails to meet a budget, care must be taken by that manager's senior in dealing with the failure. A harsh, critical approach may demotivate the manager. Adverse variances may imply that the manager needs help from the senior.

The existence of budgets gives senior managers a ready means to assess the performance of their subordinates. Where promotion or bonuses depend on the absence of variances, senior management must be very cautious.

Summary

We began this chapter by considering the relationship between business objectives and short-term plans. We also considered how those short-term plans or budgets are derived. Next we considered the role of budgeting and how budgets can be used to try to achieve their objectives. After this we considered how budgets are prepared and how budgets for different facets of the business can be made to co-ordinate. Finally we saw how the control aspect of budgeting can be used to help managers to manage both their own performance and that of their subordinates.

EXERCISES ───

8.1 Finetime Ltd, a new business, started production on 1 April. Planned sales for the next eight months are as follows:

	Sales units
May	500
June	600
July	700
August	800
September	900
October	900
November	900
December	800
January	700

◆ The selling price per unit will be a consistent £100.
◆ All sales will be made on one month's credit.
◆ It is planned that sufficient finished goods stock for each month's sales should be available at the end of the previous month.
◆ Raw material purchases will be such that there will be sufficient raw materials stock available at the end of each month precisely to meet the following month's planned production. This planned policy will operate from the end of April. Purchases of raw materials will be on one month's credit. The cost of raw material is £40 per unit of finished product.
◆ The direct labour cost, which is variable with the level of production, is planned to be £20 per unit of finished production.
◆ Production overheads are planned to be £20,000 each month, including £3,000 for depreciation.
◆ Non-production overheads are planned to be £11,000 per month of which £1,000 will be depreciation.
◆ Various fixed assets costing £250,000 will be bought and paid for during April.
◆ Except where specified, assume that all payments take place in the same month as the cost is incurred.
◆ The business will raise £300,000 in cash from a share issue in April.

You are required to draw up for the six months ending 30 September:

(a) A finished stock budget, showing just physical quantities.
(b) A raw materials stock budget, showing both physical quantities, and financial values.
(c) A trade creditors budget.
(d) A trade debtors budget.
(e) A cash budget.

(Answer on page 267. Answers to exercises 8.2 and 8.3 are given in the Teacher's Manual.)

8.2 The manager of an established transport fleet has consulted you regarding the preparation of a flexible budget for the department under his control. One purpose of the budget is to compile an average cost per mile for charging to user departments.

The fleet consists of eight similar vehicles of which two are replaced at the start of each year in a cycle which assumes they have a four-year life. Each vehicle's current cost is £45,000 with an estimated residual value of £9,000.

Typical maintenance costs for each vehicle consist of a service every six months or 10,000 miles (whichever occurs first) costing £250 and spare parts costing £50 in the first year. The cost of spares becomes greater with the age of each vehicle. It has been observed to double with each year of vehicle life.

On consulting other records the manager is able to establish that annual licence and insurance costs are £300 per vehicle. Tyres costing £80 each are changed every 20,000 miles on these four-wheeled vehicles. Fuel is estimated at £1.80 per gallon and each vehicle can achieve 20 miles per gallon.

The annual administration cost of the transport department is part fixed and part variable in relation to the annual mileage covered by all vehicles. The following table shows the prediction of this cost taken from a recent study:

Mileage travelled per annum	Total administration cost
175,000	£55,000
200,000	£60,000
250,000	£70,000

The manager is undecided about the annual workload of his department and for the purpose of budget discussion has put forward three possible levels, namely 20,000, 25,000 and 30,000 miles per vehicle.

(a) Prepare flexible budgets for the transport department covering one year, taking account of the possible range of vehicle mileage. Provide explanations or workings where you consider it appropriate and comment where you consider further information would improve the accuracy of budget preparation.
(b) The manager has read in a recent transport journal 'the more miles travelled the cheaper it becomes'. Comment on this statement.

8.3 A private-sector college has recently been established in London. Amongst its plans is a course in computer literacy. It is a short but intensive course and the price originally proposed is £100 per member. The price is to include a copy of the course manual, currently in production, which is also to be marketed separately. A cost of £15 per copy has been estimated to be relevant for this manual.

The costs of lecturers' fees and travelling expenses have been estimated as £1,020 for the course. For the purpose of planning and costing the course 40 student members per course are predicted.

(a) Determine the budgeted operating profit and break-even number of students for the course as shown above.
(b) Assume that the course was ultimately offered at £95 per member and it attracted

only 30 members for the current season. The course manual, when completed, had a cost of £18 but was still provided within the price charged for the course. Lecturers' costs totalled £950.

Calculate the actual profit achieved for the course and reconcile this with the budgeted profit computed in (a) by computing appropriate variances. Explain your approach to calculating the variances and consider their implications for someone with responsibility for managing this course within the college.

Further Reading

Arnold, J. and Hope, A., *Accounting for Management Decisions* (2nd edn). Prentice Hall, 1990.
Glautier, M. and Underdown, B., *Accounting Theory and Practice*. Pitman, 1991.
Pizzey, A., *Cost and Management Accounting* (3rd edn). Paul Chapman Publishing, 1989.

CHAPTER NINE

The Management of Working Capital

9.1 Introduction

In this chapter we consider the factors which must be taken into account when managing the working capital of a business. Each element of working capital will be identified and the major issues surrounding them will be discussed.

9.2 Purpose

When you have completed this chapter you should be able to:

- Identify the main elements of working capital.
- Discuss the purpose of working capital and the nature of the working capital cycle.
- Explain the importance of establishing policies for the control of working capital.
- Explain the factors which have to be taken into account when managing each element of working capital.

9.3 The Nature and Purpose of Working Capital

Working capital is usually defined as:

Current assets − Current liabilities (i.e. creditors due within one year)

From earlier chapters you will know that the major elements of current assets are:

- Stocks
- Trade debtors
- Cash (in hand or at bank)

The major element of current liabilities is:

- Trade creditors

The size and composition of working capital can vary between industries. For some types of business the investment in working capital can be substantial. For example, a manufacturing company will invest heavily in raw material, work-in-progress and finished goods, and will often sell its goods on credit thereby incurring trade debtors. A retailer, on the other hand, will hold only one form of stock and will usually sell goods for cash.

Working capital represents a net investment in short-term assets. These assets are continually flowing into and out of the business and are essential for day-to-day operations. The various elements of working capital are interrelated and can be seen as part of a short-term cycle. The working capital cycle for a manufacturing business is shown in Figure 9.1.

The management of working capital is an essential part of the short-term planning process. It is necessary for management to decide how much of each element should be held. As we see later, there are costs associated with holding both too much and too little of each element. Management must be aware of these in order to manage effectively. Management must also be aware that there may be other, more profitable, uses for the funds of the business. Hence, the potential benefits must be weighed against the likely costs in order to achieve the optimum investment.

The management of working capital is a significant issue because this item often represents a substantial investment for a business. The following average balance sheet percentages, based on a survey of balance sheets of large UK companies, indicates the relative size of the investment in working capital:

	1990	
	%	%
Fixed assets		85
Current assets		
Stock	20	
Debtors	28	
Cash	13	
	61	
Current liabilities		
Creditors	39	
Dividends, interest and tax owing	7	
	46	15
		100
Equity		74
Long-term liabilities		26
		100

Source: Business Statistics Office, Department of Trade and Industry.

Figure 9.1 The working capital cycle.

In the sections which follow we consider each element of working capital separately and examine the factors which must be considered to ensure their proper management.

9.4 The Management of Stocks

A business may hold stocks for various reasons, the most common being to meet the day-to-day requirements of customers and production. However, a business may hold more than is necessary for this purpose if it is believed that future supplies may be interrupted or scarce. Similarly, if the business believes that the cost of stocks will rise in the future, it may decide to stockpile.

For some types of business the stock held may represent a substantial proportion of the total assets held. For example, a car dealership which rents its premises, may have nearly all of its total assets in the form of stock. In the case of manufacturing businesses, stock levels tend to be higher than in many other forms of business as it is necessary to hold three kinds of stock: raw materials, work-in-progress and finished goods. Each form of stock represents a particular stage in the production cycle. For some types of business, the level of stock held may vary substantially over the year due to the seasonal nature of the industry, e.g. greetings card manufacturers, whereas for other businesses stock levels may remain fairly stable throughout the year.

Where a business holds stock simply to meet the day-to-day requirements of its customers and production, it will often seek to minimize the amount of stock held because there are significant costs associated with holding stocks. These costs include storage and handling, the risk of pilferage, obsolescence and the opportunities forgone in tying up funds in this form of asset. However, a business must also recognize that if the level of stocks held are too low there will also be associated costs.

ACTIVITY ──

What costs might a business incur as a result of holding too low a level of stocks? Try and jot down at least three types of cost.

You may have thought of the following costs:

♦ Loss of sales, from being unable to provide the goods required immediately.
♦ Loss of goodwill from customers, for being unable to satisfy customer demand.
♦ High transportation costs incurred to ensure stocks are replenished quickly.
♦ Lost production due to shortage of raw materials.
♦ Inefficient production scheduling due to shortages.
♦ Purchasing stocks at a higher price than may otherwise have been possible in order to replenish stocks quickly.

In order to ensure that the stocks are properly managed a number of procedures and techniques may be employed. These include the following.

1. **Forecasts for future demand**. In order for there to be stock available to meet further sales a business must produce appropriate forecasts. These forecasts should deal with each product line. It is important that every attempt is made to ensure the accuracy of these forecasts as they will determine future ordering and production levels. The forecasts may be derived in various ways: they may be developed using statistical techniques such as time series analysis, or they may be based on the judgement of the sales and marketing staff.

2. **Financial ratios**. One ratio which can be used to help monitor stock levels is the stock turnover period. This ratio was dealt with in Chapter 3 and, you may recall, is calculated as follows:

$$\text{Stock turnover period} = \frac{\text{Average stock held}}{\text{Cost of sales}} \times 365$$

This will provide a picture of the average period for which stocks are held and can be useful as a basis for comparison. It is possible to calculate the stock turnover period for individual product lines as well as for stocks as a whole.

3. **Recording and reordering systems**. The management of stocks in a business of any size requires a sound system of recording stock movements. There must be proper procedures for recording stock purchases and sales. Periodic stock checks may be required to ensure the amount of physical stocks held is consistent with the stock records.

There should also be clear procedures for the reordering of stocks. Authorization for both the purchase and issue of stocks should be confined to a few senior staff if problems of duplication and lack of co-ordination are to be avoided. To determine the point at which stock should be reordered, information concerning the lead time (i.e. the time between the placing of an order and the receipt of the goods) and the likely level of demand will be required. In most businesses there will be some uncertainty surrounding these factors and so a buffer or safety stock level may be maintained. The amount of safety stock to be held is a matter of judgement and will depend on the degree of uncertainty concerning the above factors. However, the likely costs of running out of stock must also be taken into account.

4. **Levels of control**. Managers must make a commitment to the management of stocks. However, the cost of controlling stocks must be weighed against the potential

benefits. It may be possible to have different levels of control according to the nature of the stocks held. The ABC system of stock control is based on the idea of selective levels of control.

A business may find that it is possible to divide its stock into three broad categories: A, B and C. Each category is based on the value of stock held. Category A stocks represent the high-value items. It may be the case, however, that although the items are high in *value* and represent a high proportion of the total value of stocks held, they are a relatively small proportion of the total *volume* of stocks held. For example, 10 per cent of the physical stocks held may account for 65 per cent of the total value. For these stocks, management may decide to implement sophisticated recording procedures, exert tight control over stock movements and have a high level of security at the stock location.

Category B stocks represent less valuable items held. Perhaps 30 per cent of the total volume of stocks may account for 25 per cent of the total value. For these stocks, a lower level of recording and management control would be appropriate. Category C stocks represent the least valuable items. Say 60 per cent of the volume of stocks may account for 10 per cent of the total value. For these stocks the level of recording and management control would be lower still. Categorizing stocks in this way can help to ensure that management effort is directed to the most important areas and that the costs of controlling stocks are commensurate with their value.

5. **Stock management models**. It is possible to use decision models to help manage stocks. The economic order quantity (EOQ) model calculates the optimum size of a purchase order after taking account of the cost of placing an order and the cost of carrying stocks. The model assumes that stocks will be depleted evenly over time and will be replenished just at the point the stock runs out. This assumption would lead to the 'sawtooth' pattern to represent stock movements within a business (Figure 9.2).

The model reflects the behaviour of costs at varying levels of stock, as shown in Figure 9.3. This figure shows that as the level of stocks and the size of stock orders increase, the annual costs of placing orders will decrease. However, the cost of holding

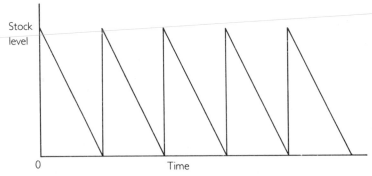

Figure 9.2 Pattern of stock movements over time.

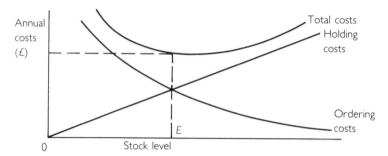

Figure 9.3 Stockholding and stock order costs.

stock will increase. The total costs will fall until the point E which represents the minimum total cost. Thereafter, total costs begin to rise. The EOQ model seeks to identify the point E at which total costs are minimized. The economic order quantity can be calculated by using the following equation:

$$EOQ = \sqrt{\frac{2DC}{H}}$$

where: *D* is the annual demand for the item of stock, *C* is the cost of placing an order, and *H* is the cost of holding one unit of stock for one year.

ACTIVITY

HLA Ltd sells 2,000 units of product X each year. It has been estimated that the cost of holding one unit of the product for a year is £4. The cost of placing an order for stock is estimated at £25. Calculate the economic order quantity for the product.

$$EOQ = \sqrt{\frac{2 \times 2,000 \times 25}{4}}$$

= 158 units (to the nearest whole number)

This will mean that the business will have to order product X about 13 times each year in order to meet sales demand.

The EOQ model has a number of limitations. In particular, it assumes that demand for the product can be predicted with accuracy and that this demand is even over the period. However, this does not mean we should dismiss the model as being of little value. The model can be developed to accommodate the problems of uncertainty and uneven demand, and it is indeed used by businesses to help in the management of stocks.

6. **Just-in-time stock management**. In recent years some manufacturing businesses have tried to eliminate the need to hold stocks by adopting a just-in-time approach.

This method was first used in the US defence industry during World War II but, in more recent times, has been widely used by Japanese businesses. The essence of this approach is, as the name suggests, to have supplies delivered to a business just in time for them to be used in the production process. By adopting this approach the stockholding problem rests with the suppliers rather than the business.

In order for this approach to be successful, it is important for the business to inform suppliers of their production plans and requirements in advance and for suppliers to deliver materials of the right quality at the agreed times. Failure to do so could lead to a dislocation of production and could be very costly. Thus, a close relationship between the business and its suppliers is required.

Although a business will not have to hold stocks there may be certain costs associated with this approach. As the suppliers will be required to hold stocks for the business they may try to recoup this additional cost through increased prices. The close relationship necessary between the business and its suppliers may also prevent the business from taking advantage of cheaper sources of supply when they become available.

9.5 The Management of Debtors

Selling goods or services on credit results in costs being incurred by a business. These costs include credit administration costs, bad debts and opportunities forgone in using the funds for more profitable purposes. However, these costs must be weighed against the benefits of increased sales resulting from the opportunity for customers to delay payment.

Selling on credit is very widespread and appears to be the norm outside the retail trade. When a business offers to sell its goods or services on credit it must have clear policies concerning:

- ◆ Which customers it is prepared to offer credit to.
- ◆ What length of credit it is prepared to offer.
- ◆ Whether discounts will be offered for prompt payment.
- ◆ What collection policies should be adopted.

Each of these issues is considered below.

9.5.1 Which Customers Should Receive Credit?

A business offering credit runs the risk of not receiving payment for goods or services supplied. Thus, care must be taken over the type of customer to whom credit facilities are offered. When considering a proposal from a customer for the supply of goods or services on credit the business must take a number of factors into account. The following 'five Cs of credit' provide a business with a useful checklist:

1. **Capital**.   The customer must appear to be financially sound before any credit is extended. Where the customer is a business, an examination of its accounts should be carried out. Particular regard should be given to the profitability and liquidity of the customer. In addition, any onerous financial commitments must be taken into account.

2. **Capacity**.   The customer must appear to have the capacity to pay amounts owing. Where possible, the payment record of the customer to date should be examined. If the customer is a business, the type of business operated and the physical resources of the business will be relevant. The value of goods which the customer wishes to buy on credit must be related to the total financial resources of the customer.

3. **Collateral**.   On occasions, it may be necessary to ask for some kind of security for goods supplied on credit. When this occurs, the business must be convinced that the customer is able to offer a satisfactory form of security.

4. **Conditions**.   The state of the industry in which the customer operates and the general economic conditions of the particular region or country may have an important influence on the ability of a customer to pay the amounts outstanding on the due date.

5. **Character**.   It is important for a business to make some assessment of the character of the customer. The willingness to pay will depend on the honesty and integrity of the individual with whom the business is dealing. Where the customer is a limited company this will mean assessing the characters of its directors. The business must feel satisfied that the customer will make every effort to pay any amounts owing.

Once a customer has been considered creditworthy, credit limits for the customer should be established and procedures should be laid down to ensure that these credit limits are adhered to.

ACTIVITY ──

Assume you are the credit manager of a business and that a limited company approached you with a view to buying goods on credit. What sources of information might you decide to use to help assess the financial health of the potential customer?

──

There are various sources of information available to a business to help assess the financial health of a customer. You may have thought of some of the following:

- *Trade references.   Some businesses ask a potential customer to furnish them with references from other suppliers who have had dealings with the customer. This may be extremely useful providing the references supplied are truly representative of the opinions of the customer's suppliers. There is a danger that a potential customer will attempt to be highly selective when furnishing details of other suppliers in order to gain a more favourable impression than is deserved.*
- *Bank references.   It is possible to ask the potential customer for a bank reference. Although banks*

are usually prepared to oblige, the contents of a reference is not always very informative. If customers are in financial difficulties the bank will usually be unwilling to add to their problems by supplying poor references.

◆ *Published accounts.* A limited company is obliged by law to file a copy of its annual accounts with the Registrar of Companies. The accounts are available for public inspection and provide a useful source of information.

◆ *The customer.* You may wish to interview the directors of the company and visit its premises in order to gain some impression about the way the company conducts its business. Where a significant amount of credit is required, the business may ask the company for access to internal budgets and other unpublished financial information to help assess the level of risk to be taken.

◆ *Credit agencies.* Specialist agencies exist to provide information which can be used to assess the creditworthiness of a potential customer. The information which a credit agency supplies may be gleaned from various sources including the accounts of the customer, court judgements and news items relating to the customer from both published and unpublished sources.

9.5.2 Length of Credit Period

A business must determine what credit terms it is prepared to offer its customers. The length of credit offered to customers can vary significantly between businesses and may be influenced by various factors. These factors may include:

◆ The typical credit terms operating within the industry.
◆ The degree of competition within the industry.
◆ The bargaining power of particular customers.
◆ The risk of non-payment.
◆ The capacity of the business to offer credit.
◆ The marketing strategy of the business.

The last point may require some explanation. Consider, for example, a business wishing to increase its market share. It may decide to liberalize its credit policy in order to stimulate sales: potential customers may be attracted by the offer of a longer period in which to pay. However, any such change in policy must take account of the likely costs and benefits arising. To illustrate this point consider the following example.

EXAMPLE ──

Torrance Ltd was formed in 19X8 in order to produce a new type of golf putter. The company sells the putter to wholesalers and retailers and has an annual turnover of £600,000. The following data relates to each putter produced.

	£	£
Selling price		36
Variable costs	18	
Fixed cost apportionment	6	24
Net profit		12

The cost of capital (before tax) of Torrance Ltd is estimated at 15 per cent.

Torrance Ltd wishes to expand sales of this new putter and believes this can be done by offering a longer period in which to pay. The average collection period of the company is currently 30 days. The company is considering three options in order to increase sales; these are as follows:

	Option 1	Option 2	Option 3
Increase in average collection period (days)	10	20	30
Increase in sales (£)	30,000	45,000	50,000

You are required to prepare calculations to show which credit policy the company should offer its customers.

In order to decide on the best option the company must weigh the benefits of each against their respective costs. The benefits arising will be represented by the increase in profit from the sale of additional putters. From the cost data supplied we can see that the contribution (i.e. sales less variable costs) is £18 per putter. This represents 50 per cent of the selling price. The fixed costs can be ignored in our calculations as they will remain the same whichever option is chosen.

The increase in contribution under each option will therefore be:

	Option 1	Option 2	Option 3
50% of increase in sales	15,000	22,500	25,000

The increase in debtors under each option will be as follows:

	Option 1	Option 2	Option 3
Planned level of debtors			
630,000 × 40/365	69,041		
645,000 × 50/365		88,356	
650,000 × 60/365			106,849
Less: Current level of debtors			
600,000 × 30/365	49,315	49,315	49,315
	19,726	39,041	57,534

The increase in debtors which results from each option will mean an additional cost to the company. Since the company has an estimated cost of capital of 15 per cent, the increase in the additional investment in debtors will be:

	Option		
	1	2	3
Cost of additional investment (15% of increase in debtors)	(2,959)	(5,856)	(8,630)

The net increase in profit will be:

	Option		
	1	2	3
Cost of additional investment (15% of increase in debtors)	(2,959)	(5,856)	(8,630)
Increase in contribution (see above)	15,000	22,500	25,000
Net increase in profits	12,041	16,644	16,370

The calculations show that option 2 will be the most profitable. However, there is little to chose between options 2 and 3.

The above example illustrates the way in which a business should assess changes in credit terms. However, if there is a risk that, by extending the length of credit, there will be an increase in bad debts or additional collection costs will be incurred, then these should also be taken into account in the calculations.

9.5.3 Cash Discounts

A business may decide to offer a cash discount in order to encourage prompt payment from its credit customers. The size of any discount will be an important influence on whether a customer decides to pay promptly.

From the point of view of the business, the cost of offering discounts must be weighed against the likely benefits in the form of a reduction in the cost of financing debtors and any reduction in the amount of bad debts.

In practice, there is always the danger that a customer may be slow to pay and yet may still take the discount offered. Where the customer is important to the business it may be difficult for the business to insist on full payment. Some businesses may charge interest on overdue accounts in order to encourage prompt payment. However, this is only possible if the business is in a strong bargaining position with its customers. For example, the business may be the only supplier of a particular product in the area.

Williams Wholesalers Ltd at present requires payment from its customers month end after month of delivery. On average it takes them 70 days to pay. Sales amount to £4 million per year and bad debts to £20,000 per year.

It is planned to offer customers a cash discount of 2 per cent for payment within 30 days. Williams estimates that 50 per cent of customers will accept this facility but that the remaining customers, who tend to be slow payers, will not pay until 80 days after the sale. At present the company has a partly used overdraft facility costing 13 per cent per annum. If the plan goes ahead bad debts will be reduced to £10,000 per annum and there will be savings in credit administration expenses of £6,000 per annum.

Should Williams Wholesalers Ltd offer the new credit terms to customers? You should support your answer with any calculations and explanations which you consider necessary.

Solution on p. 258.

9.5.4 Collection Policies

A business offering credit must ensure that amounts owing are collected as quickly as possible. An efficient collection policy requires an efficient accounting system. Invoices must be sent out promptly along with regular monthly statements. Reminders must also be despatched promptly where necessary.

When a business is faced with customers who do not pay, there should be agreed procedures for dealing with them. However, the cost of any action to be taken against delinquent debtors must be weighed against the likely returns. For example, there is little point in pursuing a customer through the courts and incurring large legal expenses if there is evidence that the customer does not have the necessary resources to pay. Where possible, the cost of bad debts should be taken into account when pricing products or services.

Management can monitor the effectiveness of collection policies in a number of ways. One method is to calculate the average settlement period for debtors. You may recall from Chapter 3 that this ratio is calculated as follows:

$$\text{Average settlement period for debtors} = \frac{\text{Trade debtors}}{\text{Credit sales}} \times 365$$

Although this ratio can be useful it is important to remember that it produces an *average* figure for the number of days that debts are outstanding. This average may be badly distorted by a few large customers who are also very slow payers.

A more detailed and informative approach to monitoring debtors is to produce an ageing schedule of debtors. Debts are divided into categories according to the length of time the debt has been outstanding. An ageing schedule can be produced for managers on a regular basis in order to help them see the pattern of outstanding debts. An example of an ageing schedule is set out below:

Customer	Days outstanding			
	1–30 days	31–60 days	61–90 days	>91 days
	£	£	£	£
A Ltd	20,000	10,000	—	—
B Ltd	—	24,000	—	—
C Ltd	12,000	13,000	14,000	18,000
Total	32,000	47,000	14,000	18,000

Thus, we can see from the schedule that A Ltd has £20,000 outstanding for 30 days or less and £10,000 outstanding for between 31 and 60 days. This information can be useful for credit control purposes. The use of computers can make the task of producing such a schedule simple and straightforward. Many accounting software packages now include this ageing schedule as one of the routine reports available to managers.

9.6 The Management of Cash

9.6.1 Why Hold Cash?

Most businesses will hold a certain amount of cash as part of the total assets held. The amount of cash held, however, may vary considerably between businesses.

ACTIVITY

Why do you think a business may decide to hold at least some of its assets in the form of cash?

According to economic theory there are three motives for holding cash:

- *Transactionary motive.* In order to meet day-to-day commitments a business requires a certain amount of cash. Payments in respect of wages, overheads, goods purchased, etc. must be made at the due dates. Cash has been described as the 'life blood' of a business. Unless it 'circulates' through the business and is available for the payment of maturing obligations, the survival of the business will be put at risk. We saw in an earlier chapter that profitability alone is not enough. A business must have sufficient cash to pay its debts when they fall due.
- *Precautionary motive.* If future cash flows are uncertain for any reason it would be prudent to hold a balance of cash. For example, a major customer which owes a large sum to the business may be in financial difficulties. Given this situation, the business can retain its capacity to meet its obligations by holding a cash balance. Similarly, if there is some uncertainty concerning future outlays a cash balance will be required.

♦ Speculative motive.   *A business may decide to hold cash in order to be in a position to exploit profitable opportunities as and when they arise. For example, by holding cash, a business may be able to acquire a competitor business which suddenly becomes available at an attractive price. Holding cash has an opportunity cost for the business which must be taken into account. Thus, when evaluating the potential returns from holding cash for speculative purposes, the cost of forgone investment opportunities must also be considered.*

9.6.2   How Much Cash Should Be Held?

Although cash can be held for each of the reasons identified, it may not always be necessary to hold cash for these purposes. If a business is able to borrow quickly then the amount of cash it needs to hold can be reduced. Similarly, if the business holds assets which can easily be converted to cash (e.g. marketable securities such as shares in stock exchange listed companies, government bonds, etc.) the amount of cash held can be reduced.

The decision as to how much cash a particular business should hold is a difficult one. Different businesses will have different views on the amount of cash which it is appropriate to hold.

ACTIVITY ——

What do you think are the major factors which influence how much cash a business will hold? See if you can think of five possible factors.

———

Factors which influence the decision as to how much cash will be held may include:

♦ The nature of the business.   *Some businesses, such as utilities (water, electricity, gas companies, etc.) may have cash flows which are both predictable and reasonably certain. This will enable them to hold lower cash balances. For some businesses cash balances may vary greatly according to the time of year. A seasonal business may accumulate cash during the high season to enable it to meet commitments during the low season.*

♦ The opportunity cost of holding cash.   *Where there are profitable opportunities it may not be wise to hold a large cash balance.*

♦ The level of inflation.   *The holding of cash during a period of rising prices will lead to a loss of purchasing power. The higher the level of inflation the greater will be this loss.*

♦ The availability of near-liquid assets.   *If a business has marketable securities or stocks which may easily be liquidated the amount of cash held may be reduced.*

♦ The availability of borrowing.   *If a business can borrow easily (and quickly) there is less need to hold cash.*

♦ The cost of borrowing.   *When interest rates are high the option of borrowing becomes less attractive.*

♦ Economic conditions.   *When the economy is in recession businesses may prefer to hold on to cash in order to be well placed to invest when the economy improves. In addition, during a recession, businesses may experience difficulties in collecting debts. They may, therefore, hold higher cash balances than usual in order to meet commitments.*

♦ Relationships with suppliers.   *Too little cash may hinder the ability of the business to pay suppliers promptly. This can lead to a loss of goodwill. It may also lead to discounts forgone.*

9.6.3   Cash Budgets and the Management of Cash

In order to manage cash effectively it is important for a business to prepare a cash budget. This is a useful tool for both planning and control purposes. Cash budgets were considered in Chapter 8 and it is, therefore, not necessary to consider this tool again in detail. However, it is worth repeating the point that the cash budget enables the managers of a business to see the expected outcome of planned events on the cash balance. The cash budget will identify periods when there are expected to be cash surpluses or cash deficits.

When a cash surplus is expected to arise managers must decide on the best use of the surplus funds. When a cash deficit is expected, managers must make adequate provision by borrowing, liquidating assets or rescheduling cash payments/receipts to deal with this. Cash budgets are also useful in helping to control the cash held. The budget represents a target and actual cash movements can be compared with the budget which has been set. If there is a significant divergence between the planned and actual cash movements for a given period, explanations must be sought and corrective action taken where necessary.

To refresh your memory, an example of a cash budget is given below. Remember there is no set format for a cash budget. Managers can determine how the information is presented to them. However, the format set out below appears to be in widespread use. Cash budgets are usually broken down into monthly periods in order to allow a close monitoring of cash movements. In addition, cash inflows are usually shown above cash outflows and the difference between these (i.e. the net cash flow) for a month is separately identified along with the closing cash balance.

EXAMPLE ——————————————————————————————————————

Cash Budget for the six months to 30 November 19X9

	June £	July £	Aug. £	Sept. £	Oct. £	Nov. £
Cash inflows						
Credit sales	—	—	4,000	5,500	7,000	8,500
Cash sales	4,000	5,500	7,000	8,500	11,000	11,000
	4,000	5,500	11,000	14,000	18,000	19,500

	£	£	£	£	£	£
Cash outflows						
Motor vehicles	6,000					
Equipment	10,000					7,000
Freehold premises	40,000					
Purchases	—	29,000	9,250	11,500	13,750	17,700
Wages/salaries	900	900	900	900	900	900
Commission	—	320	440	560	680	680
Overheads	500	500	500	500	650	650
	57,400	30,720	11,090	13,460	15,980	26,930
Net cash flow	(53,400)	(25,220)	(90)	540	2,020	(7,430)
Opening balance	60,000	6,600	(18,620)	(18,710)	(18,170)	(16,150)
Closing balance	6,600	(18,620)	(18,710)	(18,170)	(16,150)	(23,580)

Although cash budgets are prepared primarily for internal management purposes they are sometimes required by prospective lenders when a loan to a business is being considered.

9.6.4 Operating Cash Cycle

When managing cash, it is important to be aware of the operating cash cycle of the business. This may be defined as the time period between the outlay of cash necessary for the purchase of stocks and the ultimate receipt of cash from the sale of the goods. Figure 9.4 shows the operating cash cycle of a business which purchases goods on credit for subsequent resale on credit.

The figure shows that payment for goods acquired on credit occurs some time after the goods have been purchased and, therefore, no immediate cash outflow arises from the purchase. Similarly, cash receipts from debtors will occur some time after the sale is made and so there will be no immediate cash inflow as a result of the sale. The operating cash cycle is the time period between the payment made to the creditor for goods supplied, and the cash received from the debtor.

The operating cash cycle is important because it has a significant influence on the

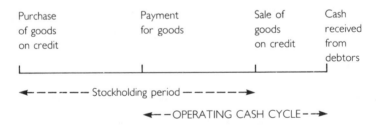

Figure 9.4 The operating cash cycle.

financing requirements of the business. The longer the cash cycle the greater the financing requirements of the business and the greater the financial risks. For this reason, a business is likely to want to minimize the operating cash cycle.

For the type of business mentioned above, the operating cash cycle can be calculated from the financial statements by the use of certain ratios, as follows:

Average stockholding period + Average settlement period for debtors
− Average payment period for creditors

ACTIVITY

The accounts of Freezeqwik Ltd, a distributor of frozen foods, is set out below for the year ended 31 December 19X3.

Profit and Loss Account for the year ended 31 December 19X3

	£000	£000
Sales		820
Less: Cost of sales		
Opening stock	142	
Purchases	568	
	710	
Less: Closing stock	166	544
Gross profit		276
Administration expenses	120	
Selling and distribution expenses	95	
Financial expenses	32	247
Net profit		29
Corporation tax		7
Retained profit for the year		22

Balance Sheet as at 31 December 19X3

	£000	£000	£000
Fixed assets			
Freehold premises at valuation			180
Fixture and fittings at written down value			82
Motor vans at written down value			102
			364
Current assets			
Stock		166	
Trade debtors		264	
Cash		24	
		454	

	£	£	£
Less: Creditors: amounts falling due within one year			
Trade creditors	159		
Corporation tax	7	166	288
			652
Capital and reserves			
Ordinary share capital			300
Preference share capital			200
Retained profit			152
			652

All purchases and sales are on credit.

(a) Calculate the operating cash cycle for the company.

(b) Suggest how the company may seek to reduce the cash cycle.

The operating cash cycle may be calculated as follows:

Average stockholding period =

$$\frac{\text{Opening stock} + \text{closing stock}/2}{\text{Cost of sales}} = \frac{142 + 166/2}{544} \times 365 \qquad 103$$

Average settlement period for debtors =

$$\frac{\text{Trade debtors}}{\text{Credit sales}} \times 365 = \frac{264}{820} \times 365 \qquad \frac{118}{221}$$

Less: Average settlement period for creditors =

$$\frac{\text{Trade creditors}}{\text{Credit purchases}} \times 365 = \frac{159}{568} \times 365 \qquad \frac{102}{}$$

Operating cash cycle   119

No. of days

The company can reduce the operating cash cycle in a number of ways. The average stockholding period seems quite long. At present, average stocks held represent more than three months' sales. This may be reduced by reducing the level of stocks held. Similarly, the average settlement period for debtors seems long at nearly four months' sales. This may be reduced by imposing tighter credit control, offering discounts, charging interest on overdue accounts, etc. However, any policy decisions concerning stocks and debtors must take account of current trading conditions.

The operating cash cycle could also be reduced by extending the period of credit taken to pay suppliers. However, for reasons mentioned below, this option must be given careful consideration.

9.6.5 Cash Transmission

A business will normally wish to receive the benefits from providing goods or services at the earliest opportunity. The benefit received is immediate where payment is made in cash. However, when payment is made by cheque there is normally a delay of 3–4 working days before the cheque can be cleared through the banking system. The business must therefore wait for this period before it can benefit from the amount paid in. In the case of a business which receives large amounts in the form of cheques, the opportunity cost of this delay can be significant.

In order to avoid this delay, a business could require payments to be made in cash. However, this is not usually practical for a number of reasons. Another option is to ask for payment to be made by standing order or by direct debit from the customer's bank account. This will ensure that the amount owing is transferred from the bank account of the customer to the bank account of the business on the day which has been agreed.

It is also possible for funds to be transferred directly to a business bank account. A customer can pay for items using a debit card which results in his/her account being instantly debited and the business bank account being instantly credited with the required amount. This method of payment is being increasingly used by large retail businesses and may well extend to other forms of business.

9.7 The Management of Trade Creditors

Trade credit is regarded as an important source of finance by many businesses. It has been described as a 'spontaneous' source of finance as it tends to increase in line with the level of sales achieved by a business. Trade credit is widely regarded as a 'free' source of finance and therefore a good thing for a business to have. However, there may be real costs associated with taking trade credit.

Customers who pay on credit may not be as well favoured as those who pay immediately. For example, when goods are in short supply credit customers may receive lower priority when allocating the stock available. In addition, credit customers may be given lower priority in terms of delivery dates or the provision of technical support services. Sometimes, the goods or services provided may be more costly if credit is required. However, in most industries trade credit is the norm and, as a result, the above costs will not apply unless, perhaps, the credit facilities are abused by the customer. A business purchasing supplies on credit may also have to incur additional administration and accounting costs in order to deal with the scrutiny and payment of invoices, the maintaining and updating of creditors accounts, etc.

Where a supplier offers discount for prompt payment a business should give careful consideration to the possibility of paying within the discount period. An example may be useful to illustrate the cost of forgoing possible discounts.

EXAMPLE ──

Simat Ltd takes 70 days to pay for goods supplied by its supplier. In order to encourage prompt payment the supplier has offered the company a 2 per cent discount if payment for goods is made within 30 days.

Simat Ltd is not sure whether it is worth taking the discount offered. What is the annual percentage cost to Simat Ltd of forgoing the discount?

If the discount is taken, payment could be made on the last day of the discount period (i.e. the 30th day). However, if the discount is not taken payment will be made after 70 days. This means that by not taking the discount Simat Ltd will receive an extra 40 days' (i.e. 70 − 30) credit. The cost of this extra credit to the company will be the 2 per cent discount forgone. If we annualize the cost of this discount forgone we have:

$$365/40 \times 2\% = 18.3\%*$$

We can see that annual cost of forgoing the discount is quite high and it may be profitable for the company to pay the supplier within the discount period even if it means that it will have to borrow in order to do so.

The above points are not meant to imply that taking credit is a burden to a business. There are, of course, real benefits which can accrue. Provided that trade credit is not abused by a business, it can represent a form of interest-free loan. It can be a much more convenient method of paying for goods and services than paying by cash and, during a period of inflation, there will be an economic gain by paying later rather than sooner for goods and services purchased. For many businesses, these benefits will exceed the costs involved.

* This is an approximate annual rate. For the more mathematically minded the precise rate is:

$$[(1 + 2/98)^{9.125} - 1] \times 100\% = 20.2\%$$

──

9.7.1 Controlling Trade Creditors

In order to monitor the level of trade credit taken management can calculate the average settlement period for creditors. You may recall from Chapter 3 that this ratio was as follows:

$$\text{Average settlement period} = \frac{\text{Trade creditors}}{\text{Credit purchases}} \times 365$$

Once again this provides an average figure which can be distorted. A more informative approach would be to produce an ageing schedule for creditors. This would look much the same as the ageing schedule for debtors described earlier.

Summary

In this chapter we have identified and examined the main elements of working capital. We have seen that the management of working capital requires an awareness of both the costs and benefits associated with each element. Some of the costs and benefits may be hard to quantify in practice, nevertheless some assessment must be made in order to try and optimize the use of funds within a business.

EXERCISES

9.1 Hercules Wholesalers Ltd has been particularly concerned with its liquidity position in recent months. The most recent profit and loss account and balance sheet of the company are as follows:

Profit and Loss Account for the year ended 31 May 19X2

	£	£
Sales		452,000
Less: Cost of sales		
Opening stock	125,000	
Add purchases	341,000	
	466,000	
Less: Closing stock	143,000	323,000
Gross profit		129,000
Expenses		132,000
Net loss for the period		(3,000)

Balance Sheet as at 31 May 19X2

	£	£	£
Fixed assets			
Freehold premises at valuation			280,000
Fixtures and fittings at cost less depreciation			25,000
Motor vehicles at cost less depreciation			52,000
			357,000
Current assets			
Stock		143,000	
Debtors		163,000	
		306,000	

	£	£	£
Less: Creditors due within one year			
Trade creditors	145,000		
Bank overdraft	140,000	285,000	21,000
			378,000
Less: Creditors due after more than one year			
Loans			120,000
			258,000
Capital and reserves			
Ordinary share capital			100,000
Retained profit			158,000
			258,000

The debtors and creditors were maintained at a constant level throughout the year.

(a) Explain why Hercules Wholesalers Ltd is concerned about its liquidity position.
(b) Explain the term 'operating cash cycle' and state why this concept is important in the financial management of a business.
(c) Calculate the operating cash cycle for Hercules Wholesalers Ltd based on the information above. (Assume a 360 day year.)
(d) State what steps may be taken to improve the operating cash cycle of the company.

(Answer on page 269. Answers to exercises 9.2 to 9.4 are given in the Teacher's Manual.)

9.2 International Electric plc at present offers its customers 30 days' credit. Half the customers, by value, pay on time. The other half take an average of 70 days to pay. It is considering offering a cash discount of 2 per cent to its customers for payment within 30 days.

It anticipates that half of the customers who now take an average of 70 days to pay, will pay in 30 days. The other half will still take an average of 70 days to pay. The scheme will also reduce bad debts by £300,000 per year.

Annual sales of £365 million are made evenly throughout the year. At present the company can borrow from its banks at 12 per cent per annum.

(a) Calculate the approximate equivalent annual percentage cost of a discount of 2 per cent which reduces the time taken by debtors to pay from 70 days to 30 days. (This part can be answered without reference to the narrative above.)
(b) Calculate debtors outstanding under both the old and new schemes.
(c) How much will the scheme cost the company in discounts?
(d) Should the company go ahead with the scheme? State what other factors, if any, should be taken into account.

(e) Outline the controls and procedures a company should adopt to manage the level of its debtors.

9.3 Your superior, the general manager of Plastics Manufacturers Limited, has recently been talking to the chief buyer of Plastic Toys Limited, which manufactures a wide range of toys for young children. At present it is considering changing its supplier of plastic granules and has offered to buy its entire requirement of 2,000 kilos per month from you at the going market rate, providing that you will grant it 3 months credit on its purchases. The following information is available:

1. Plastic granules sell for £10 per kilo, variable costs are £7 per kilo and fixed costs £2 per kilo.
2. Your own company is financially strong and has sales of £15 million per year. For the foreseeable future it will have surplus capacity and it is actively looking for new outlets.
3. Extracts from Plastic Toys accounts.

	19X3 £000	19X4 £000	19X5 £000
Sales	800	980	640
Profit before interest and tax	100	110	(150)
Capital employed	600	650	575
Current assets			
Stocks	200	220	320
Debtors	140	160	160
	340	380	480
Current liabilities			
Creditors	180	190	220
Overdraft	100	150	310
	280	340	530
Net current assets	60	40	(50)

(a) Write some short notes suggesting sources of information you would use in order to assess the creditworthiness of potential customers who are unknown to you. You should critically evaluate each source of information.
(b) Describe the accounting controls you would use to monitor the level of your company's trade debtors.
(c) Advise your general manager on the acceptability of the proposal. You should give your reasons and do any calculations you consider necessary.

9.4 The managing director of Sparkrite Ltd, a trading company, has just received summary sets of accounts for 19X2 and 19X3.

Sparkrite Ltd
Profit and Loss Statements for years ended 30 September 19X2 and 19X3

	19X2		19X3	
	£000	£000	£000	£000
Sales		1,800		1,920
Less: Cost of sales				
Opening stock	160		200	
Purchases	1,120		1,175	
	1,280		1,375	
Less: Closing stocks	200		250	
		1,080		1,125
Gross profit		720		795
Less: Expenses		680		750
Net profit		£40		£45

Balance Sheets as at 30 September 19X2 and 19X3

	19X2		19X3	
	£000	£000	£000	£000
Fixed assets		950		930
Current assets:				
Stock	200		250	
Debtors	375		480	
Bank	4		2	
	579		732	
Less: Current liabilities	195		225	
		384		507
		£1,334		£1,437
Financed by:				
Fully paid £1 ordinary shares		825		883
Reserves		509		554
		£1,334		£1,437

The financial director has expressed concern at the deterioration in stock and debtors levels.

(a) Show by using the data given how you would calculate ratios which could be used to measure stock and debtor levels in 19X2 and 19X3.
(b) Discuss the ways in which the management of Sparkrite Ltd could exercise control over:
 (i) Stock levels.
 (ii) Debtor levels.

Further Reading

Brayshaw, R.E., *The Concise Guide to Company Finance and its Management*. Chapman and Hall, 1992.
McLaney, E.J., *Business Finance for Decision Makers* (2nd edn). Pitman, 1994.

CHAPTER TEN

Financing the Business

10.1 Introduction

In this chapter we consider the various forms of finance available to a business. We also consider the factors which determine the type and mix of finance a business employs.

10.2 Purpose

Having completed this chapter you should be able to:

- Identify the main forms of long-term finance available to a business and explain the advantages and disadvantages of each form.
- Identify the main forms of short-term finance available to a business and explain the advantages and disadvantages of each form.
- Identify the factors to be taken into account when deciding the appropriate 'mix' of long- and short-term finance for a business.
- Identify the major internal sources of finance available to a business and explain the advantages and disadvantages of each form.

10.3 Long-term Sources of Finance

For the purpose of this chapter, long-term sources of finance are defined as sources of finance which are not due for repayment within one year. For a company, the major forms of long-term finance are:

- Ordinary shares
- Preference shares
- Loans
- Leases and sale and lease back arrangements

Each of these is considered below. We examine the advantages and disadvantages of each type of finance and also deal with some of the ways in which shares may be issued.

10.3.1   Ordinary (Equity) Shares

Ordinary shares form the backbone of the financial structure of a company. We have seen earlier that ordinary share capital represents the risk capital of a company. There is no fixed rate of dividend, and ordinary shareholders will receive a dividend only if profits available for distribution remain after other investors (preference shareholders and lenders) have received their interest or dividend payments. If the company is wound up, the ordinary shareholders will only receive any proceeds from asset disposals after lenders and creditors and, often, preference shareholders have received their entitlements.

Because of the high risks associated with this form of investment, ordinary shareholders normally require a higher rate of return from the company. Ordinary shareholders also have control over the company. They are given voting rights and have the power to elect the directors and also to remove them from office.

From the company perspective, it is sometimes useful to be able to avoid paying a dividend. In the case of a new expanding company, or a company in difficulties, the requirement to make a cash payment to investors can be a burden. Where the company is financed by equity shares, this problem does not occur. However, the costs of financing equity shares may be high over the longer term for the reasons mentioned earlier. Moreover, the company does not obtain any tax relief on dividends paid whereas interest on borrowings is tax deductible.

10.3.2   Preference Shares

Preference shares offer investors a lower level of risk than equity shares. Provided there are sufficient profits available, preference shares will normally be given a fixed rate of dividend each year and preference dividends will be paid before equity dividends are paid. Where the company is wound up, preference shareholders may be given priority over the claims of equity shareholders. (The documents of incorporation will determine the precise rights of preference shareholders in this respect.) Because of the lower level of risk associated with this form of investment, investors are offered a lower level of return than that offered for equity shares.

There are various types of preference shares which may be issued by a company. *Cumulative* preference shares give investors the right to receive arrears of dividends which have arisen as a result of the company having insufficient profits in previous periods. The unpaid dividends will accumulate and will be paid when the company has generated sufficient profits. *Non-cumulative* preference shares do not give investors the right to receive arrears of dividends. Thus, if a company is not in a position to pay the preference dividend due for a particular period the preference shareholder loses the right to receive the dividend. *Participating* preference shares give investors the right to a further share in the profits available for dividend after they have been paid the fixed rate due on the preference shares and after equity shareholders have been awarded a dividend.

10.4 Role of the Stock Exchange

A public limited company may decide to have its shares listed on a recognized stock exchange. The stock exchange exists to provide a market where shares in particular companies may be bought and sold. From the company viewpoint a stock exchange listing for its shares may have real benefits. Perhaps the most important is that the shares are easily transferable. Investors may be more prepared to invest in a company if it is possible to liquidate their investment easily when required. Share prices are usually determined by the market in an efficient manner and this may also give investors greater confidence to purchase shares. The company may benefit from greater investor confidence by finding it easier to raise long-term finance and by obtaining this finance at a lower cost as investors perceive the shares as being less risky.

A stock exchange quotation can, however, have certain disadvantages. The stock exchange imposes strict rules on listed companies and requires additional levels of financial disclosure to that already imposed by law and by the accounting profession (e.g. half yearly financial reports must be published). The activities of listed companies are closely monitored by financial analysts, financial journalists and other companies and such scrutiny may not be welcome if the company is dealing with sensitive issues or experiencing operational problems. It is often suggested that listed companies are under pressure to perform well over the short term. This pressure may detract from undertaking projects which will only yield benefits in the longer term. If the market becomes disenchanted with the company and the price of its shares falls, this may make it vulnerable to a takeover bid from another company.

10.5 Share issues

A company may issue shares in a number of different ways. The most common methods of issue are as follows:

♦ **Rights issues.** The company may offer existing shareholders the right to acquire new shares in the company in exchange for cash. The new shares will be allocated to shareholders in proportion to their existing shareholdings. In order to make the issue appear attractive to shareholders the new shares are often offered at a price significantly below the current market value of the shares. This is now the most common form of share issue. For companies it is a relatively cheap and straightforward method of issuing shares. In addition, the law now requires shares which are to be issued for cash to be offered first to existing shareholders.

♦ **Offer for sale**. This can involve a public limited company selling a new issue
  of shares to a financial institution known as an issuing house. However, shares
  which are already in issue may also be sold to an issuing house. In this case, existing
  shareholders agree to sell their shares to the issuing house. The issuing house
  will, in turn, sell the shares purchased from either the company or its shareholders
  to the public. The issuing house will publish a prospectus which sets out details
  of the company and the type of shares to be sold, and investors will be invited
  to apply for shares. The advantage of this type of issue from the company
  viewpoint is that the sale proceeds of the shares is certain. The issuing house will
  take on the risk of selling the shares to investors.
♦ **Public issue**. This form of issue involves the company making a direct invitation
  to the public to purchase shares in the company. Typically, this is done through
  a newspaper advertisement. The shares may once again be a new issue or already
  in issue. An issuing house may be asked by the company to help administer the
  issue of the shares to the public and to offer advice concerning an appropriate
  selling price. However, the company rather than the issuing house will take on
  the risk of selling the shares. An offer for sale and a public issue will result in
  a widening of share ownership in the company.

When making an issue of shares, the company or the issuing house will usually
set a price for the shares. However, establishing a share price may not be an easy
task, particularly where the market is volatile or where the company has unique
characteristics. If the share price is set too high, the issue will be undersubscribed
and the company (or issuing house) will not receive the amount expected. If the share
price is set too low, the issue will be oversubscribed and the company (or issuing
house) will receive less than could have been achieved.

One way of dealing with the problem is to make a *tender* issue of shares. This
involves the investors determining the price at which the shares are issued. Although
the company or issuing house may publish a reserve price to help guide investors,
it will be up to the individual investor to determine the number of shares to be
purchased and the price the investor wishes to pay. Once the offers from investors
have been received, a price at which all the shares can be sold will be established
(known as the striking price). Investors which have made offers at or above the striking
price will be issued shares at the striking price and offers received below the striking
price will be rejected. Although this form of issue is adopted occasionally, it is not
popular with investors and is, therefore, not in widespread use.

10.6 Loans and Debentures

Many companies rely on loan capital to finance operations. Lenders will enter into
a contract with the company in which the rate of interest, dates of interest payments
and capital repayments and security for the loan are clearly stated. Security for a loan
may be on particular assets of the company (freehold land and premises is often

favoured by lenders). In some cases, the lender may be prepared to accept personal guarantees from the directors of the company as a form of security. In the event that the interest payments or capital repayments in respect of the loan are not made on the due dates, the lender may have the right, under the terms of the contract, to seize the assets on which the loan is secured and sell them in order to repay the amount outstanding.

One form of long-term loan associated with limited companies is the *debenture*. This is simply a loan which is evidenced by a trust deed. The debenture loan is frequently divided into units (rather like share capital) and investors are invited to purchase the number of units they require. The debenture loan may be redeemable or irredeemable. Debentures of public limited companies are often traded on the stock exchange and the value of the debentures will fluctuate according to the fortunes of the company, movements in interest rates, etc.

ACTIVITY ───────────────────────────────

Why might a company decide to issue loan capital or debentures as part of its capital structure? Try and jot down three advantages of this type of financing.

You might have thought of the following advantages of raising finance in this way:

♦ *Taxation. Loan interest is allowable against taxation. This can make loans a relatively cheap way of financing the company.*

♦ *Service costs. Investors view loans as being less risky than preference shares or equity shares as they have priority over any claims from shareholders and may also have security for their loans. As a result, investors are usually prepared to accept a lower rate of return.*

♦ *Inflation. During a period of rising prices the real value of the capital sum outstanding is reduced and so ultimate repayment will become less burdensome. However, lenders may seek higher rates of interest in order to compensate for the fall in the real value of their investment.*

We saw in Chapter 4 that equity shareholders may benefit from some financial gearing. This is possible where the returns on the funds raised from lending exceeds the costs of servicing the debt.

10.6.1 Convertible Loans and Debentures

This form of loan or debenture gives the investor the right to convert the loan into equity shares at an agreed future date and at an agreed price. The investor remains a lender to the company and will receive interest on the amount of the loan until such time as the conversion takes place. The investor is not obliged to convert the loan or debenture to equity shares. This will only be done if the market price of the shares at the conversion date exceeds the agreed conversion price.

An investor may find this form of investment a useful hedge against risk. This may be particularly useful when investment in a new company is being considered. Initially the investment is in the form of a loan and regular interest payments will be made. If the company is successful the investor can then decide to convert the investment into equity shares.

The company may also find this form of financing useful. If the company is successful the loan becomes self-liquidating as investors will exercise their option to convert. The company may also be able to offer a lower rate of interest to investors because of the conversion option. However, it is difficult to value convertible loans or debentures and a company may find that investors prefer more conventional forms of securities for this reason. There will, of course, be some dilution of control for existing shareholders if holders of convertible loans exercise their option to convert.

10.6.2 Mortgages

A mortgage is a form of loan which is secured on freehold property. Financial institutions such as banks, insurance companies and pension funds are often prepared to lend to businesses on this basis. The mortgage may be over a long period and provides a business with an opportunity to acquire an asset which, until the early 1990s, tended to increase in value faster than the rate of inflation. In addition to the capital gain from holding the freehold property, businesses have also benefited from a decline in the real value of the capital sum because of inflation. However, lenders usually compensate for this fall in value, as mentioned earlier, by increasing the rate of interest payable.

10.6.3 Loan Covenants

When drawing up a loan agreement the lender may impose certain obligations and restrictions in order to protect the investment in the business. Loan covenants (as they are known) often form part of a loan agreement and may deal with such matters as:

- **Accounts**. The lender may require access to the financial accounts of the business on a regular basis.
- **Other loans**. The lender may require the business to ask permission before taking on further loans.
- **Dividend payments**. The lender may require dividends to be limited during the period of the loan.
- **Liquidity**. The lender may require the business to maintain a certain level of liquidity during the period of the loan.

Any breach of these restrictive covenants may have serious consequences for the business. The lender may require immediate repayment of the loan in the event of a serious breach.

ACTIVITY ──────────────────────────────────────

HLA Ltd is a fast-growing company which produces computer software for engineering businesses. In order to finance its proposed expansion programme the company has approached its bank for a long-term loan. If you were the manager of the company's bank what factors would you take into account in deciding whether or not to grant the loan?

──

In answering this activity you may have thought of a number of possible factors. Some of the more important ones are:

◆ **Purpose of the loan.** *The bank manager may wish to know the precise purpose of the loan. Is it to purchase new assets? If so, what type of assets will be purchased? Is it to repay other forms of borrowing? The manager may well ask for some form of business plan from the company to help assess whether the expansion programme has been properly considered. If the loan is for a high-risk venture the bank manager may feel that this is not the type of borrowing which the bank would be interested in and may refer the company to some other source of funds such as a venture capitalist.*

◆ **Ability to repay.** *The ability to repay may be assessed in a number of ways. These include the nature of the business, the financial performance and position of the business, the past record of loan repayments, the likely future demand for the company's products.*

◆ **Security.** *The bank manager will be interested in the nature and value of any security which is being offered in respect of the loan.*

◆ **Existing loans.** *The bank manager will wish to examine any existing loan agreements and the existing level of gearing of the company.*

◆ **Character of key personnel.** *The ability and integrity of key personnel within the company will be an important factor in deciding whether a loan should be granted. The bank manager must have confidence that the company is efficiently managed and that every effort will be made to repay the loan when it is due.*

◆ **Availability of funds.** *The bank may be restricted in its ability to lend to this type of business. Only a certain amount of funds may be earmarked for this type of venture.*

10.7 Preference Shares Versus Loan Capital

Both preference shares and loan capital are non-equity forms of finance and require the company to provide a fixed rate of return to investors. It is worth considering the factors which may be taken into account when deciding between these sources of finance. The main factors are as follows:

◆ **Rate of return.** Preference shares have a higher rate of return than loan capital. From the investor's point of view, preference shares are more risky. The amount invested cannot be secured and the return is paid after the returns paid to lenders.

◆ **Requirement to pay returns.** A company has a legal obligation to pay interest and make capital repayments on loans at the agreed dates. A company will usually make every effort to meet its obligations as failure to do so can have serious consequences. (These consequences were mentioned earlier.) Failure to pay a preference dividend, on the other hand, is less important. There is no legal obligation to pay a preference dividend if profits are not available for distribution. Although failure to pay a preference dividend may prove an embarrassment for the company, the preference shareholders will have no redress against the company if there are insufficient profits to pay the dividend due.

◆ **Taxation**. The taxation system in the UK permits interest on loans to be set against profits for taxation whereas preference dividends may not. Preference shareholders are members of the company and participate in the profits generated through the dividends received whereas lenders are 'outside' the company and interest payable is regarded as an expense. Because of the tax relief which loan interest attracts, the cost of servicing loan capital is usually much less for a company than the cost of servicing preference shares.

◆ **Restrictions**. The issue of loan capital may result in the managers of a company having to accept some restrictions on their freedom of action. We saw earlier that loan agreements often contain covenants which can be onerous. However, no such restrictions can be imposed by preference shareholders.

◆ **Capital base**. Preference shares issued form part of the permanent capital base of the company. If they are redeemed at some future date the law requires that they are replaced, either by a new issue of shares or by a transfer from reserves, in order to ensure that the capital base of the company stays intact. However, loan capital is not viewed in law as part of the permanent capital base of the company and, therefore, there is no requirement to replace any loan capital which has been redeemed by the company.

10.8 Finance Leases and Sale and Lease Back Arrangements

Instead of buying an asset direct from a supplier, a business may decide to arrange for a financial institution, such as a bank, to buy the asset and then agree to lease the asset from the institution. A finance lease is, in essence, a form of lending. Although legal ownership of the asset rests with the financial institution (the lessor), a finance lease agreement transfers virtually all the rewards and risks which are associated with the item being leased to the business (the lessee). The lease agreement covers a significant part of the life of the item being leased and cannot usually be cancelled.

In recent years many of the benefits of finance leasing have disappeared. Changes in the tax laws no longer make it such a tax-efficient form of financing and changes in accounting disclosure requirements make it no longer possible to conceal this form of 'borrowing' from investors. Nevertheless, the popularity of leasing has continued to increase. The reasons for this phenomenon are difficult to understand.

A *sale and lease back* arrangement involves a business in selling freehold property to a financial institution in order to raise finance. However, the sale is accompanied by an agreement to lease the freehold property back to the business to allow it to continue to operate from the premises. The rent payable under the lease arrangement is allowable against profits for taxation purposes. There are usually rent reviews at regular intervals throughout the period of the lease and the amounts payable in future years may be difficult to predict. At the end of the lease agreement the business must either try to renew the lease or find alternative premises. Although the sale of the premises will result in an immediate injection of cash for the business, it will lose benefits from any future capital appreciation on the property. Where a capital gain arises on the sale of the premises to the financial institution a liability for taxation may also arise.

10.9 The Long-term Financing Decision

When making a decision among the various sources of finance available, it must be remembered that the welfare of the equity shareholders is a primary objective of most companies. Hence, the effect of any new source of finance on the equity shareholders' interests must be borne in mind. In the activity which follows you are required to consider the impact of different financing options on the risks and returns to equity shareholders.

ACTIVITY ───────────────────────────────────────

The following is a shortened version of the accounts of Woodhall Engineers plc, a company which is not listed on a stock exchange.

Profit and Loss Account year ended 31 December 19X4

| | 19X4 | 19X3 |
	£m	£m
Turnover	50	47
Operating costs	47	41
Operating profit	3	6
Interest payable	2	2
Profit on ordinary activities before tax	1	4
Taxation on profit on ordinary activities	—	—
Profit on ordinary activities after tax	1	4
Dividends (net)	1	1
Profit retained for the financial year	—	3

Balance Sheet at 31 December 19X4

	19X4 £m	19X3 £m
Fixed assets (less depreciation)	20	21
Current assets		
Stocks	18	10
Debtors	17	16
Cash at bank	1	3
	36	29
Creditors: Amounts falling due within one year		
Short-term debt	11	5
Trade creditors	10	10
	21	15
Total assets less current liabilities	35	35
Less: Long-term loans (secured)	15	15
	20	20
Capital and reserves		
Called up share capital 25p ordinary shares	16	16
Profit and loss account	4	4
	20	20

The company is making plans to expand its factory. New plant will cost £8 million and an expansion in output will increase working capital by £4 million. Over the 15 years' life of the project, incremental profits arising from the expansion will be £2 million per year before interest and tax. In addition, 19X5 profits before tax from its existing activities are expected to return to 19X3 levels.

Two alternative methods of financing the expansion have been discussed by Woodhall's directors. The first is the issue of £12 million 15% debt repayable in year 2000. The second is a rights issue of 40 million, 25p ordinary shares which will give the company 30p per share after expenses.

The company has substantial tax losses carried forward so you can ignore taxation in your calculations. The 19X5 dividend per share is expected to be the same as that for 19X4.

(a) Prepare a forecast of Woodhall's profit and loss account (excluding turnover and operating costs) for year ended 31 December 19X5, and of its capital and reserves, long-term loans and number of shares outstanding at that date assuming:
   (i) The company issues debt.
   (ii) The company issues ordinary shares.

(b) Compute Woodhall's interest cover and earnings per share for the year ended 31 December 19X5 and its gearing on that date, assuming:
(i) The company issues debt.
(ii) The company issues ordinary shares.
(c) What would your views of the proposed scheme be in each of the following circumstances?
(i) If you were a banker and you were approached for a loan.
(ii) If you were an equity investor in Woodhall and you were asked to subscribe to a rights issue.

Your answer to this activity should be as follows:

Forecast Profit and Loss Account for the year ended 31 December 19X5

	Debt issue	Equity issue
	£m	£m
Operating profit	8.0	8.0
Loan interest	3.8	2.0
Profit before tax	4.2	6.0
Taxation	—	—
Profit after tax	4.2	6.0
Dividends (net)	1.0	1.6
Retained profit for the year	3.2	4.4
Capital and reserves		
Share capital 25p ordinary shares	16.0	26.0
Share premium account*	—	2.0
Retained profit	7.2	8.4
	23.2	36.4

* This represents the amount received from the issue of shares which is above the nominal value of the shares. The amount is calculated as follows:

40m shares × (30p − 25p)	= £2m	
No. of shares in issue (25p shares)	64m	104m
Interest cover ratio =		

$$\frac{\text{Profit before interest and tax}}{\text{Interest payable}} \qquad \frac{(4.2 + 3.8)}{3.8} \qquad \frac{(6.0 + 2.0)}{2.0}$$

$$= 2.1 \text{ times} \qquad 4.0 \text{ times}$$

Earnings per share =

$\dfrac{\text{Earnings available to equity}}{\text{No. of ordinary shares}}$	$\dfrac{£4.2m}{64m}$	$\dfrac{£6.0m}{104m}$
	6.6p	5.8p

Gearing ratio =

$\dfrac{\text{Long-term liabilities (LTL)}}{\text{Share capital + Reserves + LTL}}$	$\dfrac{£27m}{£23.2m + £27m}$	$\dfrac{£15m}{£36.4m + £15m}$
	53.8%	29.2%

A banker may be unenthusiastic about lending the company funds. The gearing ratio of 53.8 per cent is rather high and would leave the bank exposed. The existing loan is already secured on assets held by the company and it is not clear whether the company is in a position to offer an attractive form of security for the new loan. The interest cover ratio of 2.1 is also rather low. If the company is unable to achieve the expected returns from the new project, or if it is unable to restore profits from the remainder of its operations to 19X3 levels, this ratio would be even lower.

Equity investors may need some convincing that it would be in their interests to make further investments in the company. The return to equity for shareholders in 19X3 was 20 per cent. The incremental profit from the new project is £2m and the investment required is £12m which represents a return of 16.7 per cent. Thus the returns from the project are expected to be lower than for other activities of the company.

Investors may further discount the expected returns from the new project in view of the uncertainty concerning the future. They may also be unsure whether the company can restore profits from other operations to 19X3 levels. Investors will need to have confidence in the management of the company to undertake this further investment.

10.10 Short-term Sources of Finance

A short-term source of borrowing is one which is available for a short time period. Although there is no agreed definition of what short-term means, we will define it as being up to one year. The major sources of short-term borrowing are as follows.

10.10.1 Bank Overdraft

A bank overdraft represents a very flexible form of borrowing. The size of the overdraft can (subject to bank approval) be increased or decreased according to the financing requirements of the business. It is relatively inexpensive to arrange and interest rates are often very competitive. The rate of interest charged on an overdraft will vary, however, according to how creditworthy the customer is perceived to be by the bank. It is also fairly easy to arrange — sometimes an overdraft can be agreed by a telephone call to the bank. In view of these advantages, it is not surprising that this is an extremely popular form of short-term finance.

Banks prefer to grant overdrafts which are self-liquidating, i.e. the funds supplied will result in cash inflows which will extinguish the overdraft balance. The banks may ask for forecast cash flow statements from the business to see when the overdraft will be repaid and how much finance is required. The bank may also require some form of security on amounts advanced.

One potential drawback with this form of finance is that it is repayable on demand. This may pose problems for a business which is illiquid. However, many businesses operate using an overdraft and this form of borrowing, although in theory regarded as short-term, can often become a long-term source of finance.

10.10.2 Debt Factoring

Debt factoring is a form of service which is offered by a financial institution (a factor). Many of the large factors are subsidiaries of commercial banks. Debt factoring involves the factor taking over the sales ledger of a company. In addition to operating normal credit control procedures, a factor may offer to undertake credit investigations and to provide protection for approved credit sales. The factor is usually prepared to make an advance to the company of up to 80 per cent of approved trade debtors. The charge made for the factoring service is based on total turnover and is often around 2 per cent of turnover. Any advances made to the company by the factor will attract a rate of interest similar to the rate charged on bank overdrafts.

A company may find a factoring arrangement very convenient. It can result in savings in credit management and can release the time of key personnel for more profitable ends. This may be extremely important for smaller companies which rely on the talent and skills of a few key individuals. However, there is a possibility that some will see a factoring arrangement as an indication the company is experiencing financial difficulties. This may have an adverse effect on confidence in the company. For this reason, some businesses try to conceal the factoring arrangement by collecting debts on behalf of the factor.

10.10.3 Invoice Discounting

Invoice discounting involves a business approaching a factor or other financial institution for a loan based on a proportion of the face value of credit sales outstanding. If the institution agrees, the amount advanced is usually about 75 per cent of the value of the approved sales invoices outstanding. The business must agree to repay the advance made within a relatively short period — perhaps 60 or 90 days. The responsibility for collection of the trade debts outstanding remains with the business

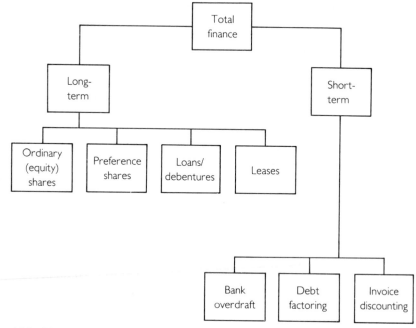

Figure 10.1   Major external sources of finance.

and repayment of the advance is not dependent on the trade debt being collected. The interest rates on the advance made to the business can be quite high and there is a service charge levied on the deal. It can therefore be quite an expensive form of finance. Invoice discounting may be a one-off arrangement whereas debt factoring usually involves a longer-term arrangement with a financial institution.

Figure 10.1 summarizes the main sources of external finance.

10.11 Long-term Versus Short-term Borrowing

Having decided that some form of borrowing is required, the managers must then decide whether long-term or short-term borrowing is more appropriate. There are a number of issues which should be taken into account when making this decision:

- **Matching.**   The business may attempt to match the type of borrowing with the nature of the assets held. Thus, assets which form part of the permanent operating base of the business, including fixed assets and a certain level of current assets, will be financed by long-term borrowing. Assets held for a short period, such as current assets held to meet seasonal increases in demand, will be financed by short-term borrowing (see Figure 10.2).

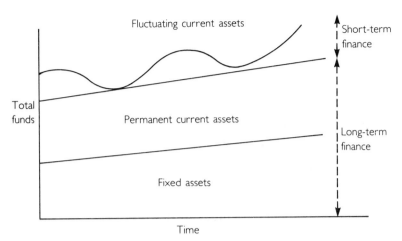

Figure 10.2 **Short- and long-term finance.**

A business may wish to match the asset life exactly with the period of the related loan. However, this may not be possible because of the difficulty of predicting the life of many assets. Some businesses may take up a less conservative position than shown in the diagram by relying on short-term finance to help fund part of the permanent capital base.

- **Flexibility**. Short-term borrowing may be useful in order to postpone a commitment to taking on a long-term loan. This may be seen as desirable if interest rates are high and it is forecast that they will fail in the future. Short-term borrowing does not usually incur penalties if there is early repayment of the amount outstanding whereas some form of financial penalty may have to be paid if long-term debt is repaid early.
- **Refunding risk**. Short-term borrowing has to be renewed more frequently than long-term borrowing. This may create problems for the business if it is already in financial difficulties or if there is a shortage of funds available for lending.
- **Interest rates**. Interest payable on long-term debt is often higher than for short-term debt. (This is because lenders require a higher return where their funds are locked up for a long period.) This fact may make short-term borrowing a more attractive source of finance for a business. However, there may be other costs associated with borrowing (e.g. arrangement fees) to be taken into account. The more frequently that borrowings must be renewed the higher these costs will be.

10.12 Internal Sources of Finance

In addition to external sources of finance there are certain internal sources which a business may use to generate funds for particular activities. These sources usually have the advantage that they are flexible. They may also be obtained quickly — particularly working capital sources — and may not require the permission of other

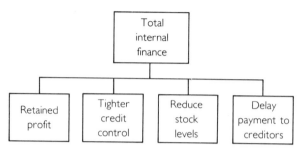

Figure 10.3 **Major internal sources of finance.**

parties. The main sources of internal funds are described below and summarized in Figure 10.3.

10.12.1   Retained Profit

Retained profit is the major source of finance for most companies. By retaining profits within the company rather than distributing them to shareholders in the form of dividends, the funds of the company are increased. It is tempting to think that retained profits are a 'cost-free' source of funds for a company. However, this is not the case. If profits are reinvested rather than distributed to shareholders this means that the shareholders cannot reinvest the profits made in other forms of investment. They will therefore expect a rate of return from the profits reinvested which is equivalent to what they would receive if the funds had been invested in another opportunity with the same level of risk.

The reinvestment of profit rather than the issue of new ordinary shares can be a useful way of raising equity capital. There are no issue costs associated with retaining profits and the amount raised is certain. When issuing new shares, the issue costs may be substantial and there may be uncertainty over the success of the issue. Retaining profits will have no effect on the control of the company by existing shareholders. However, where new shares are issued to outside investors there will be some dilution of control by existing shareholders.

Some shareholders may prefer profits to be retained by the company rather than distributed in the form of dividends. By ploughing back profits, it may be expected that the company will expand and share values will increase as a result. This means that investors will receive their returns in the form of a capital gain rather than a dividend. In the UK, not all capital gains are subject to taxation and the investor has the option over the timing of the sale of shares and the subsequent liability to capital gains tax. However, some shareholders may prefer profits to be distributed in the form of dividends: they may rely on regular dividends to meet their living expenses or may feel that they can invest the profits in better investment opportunities than the company is capable of doing.

10.12.2 Tighter Credit Control

By exerting tighter control over trade debtors it may be possible for a business to reduce the proportion of assets held in this form and to release funds for other purposes. It is important, however, to weigh the benefits of tighter credit control against the likely costs in the form of lost customer goodwill and lost sales. To remain competitive, a business must take account of the needs of its customers and the credit policies adopted by rival companies within the industry.

10.12.3 Reducing Stock Levels

If a business has a proportion of its assets in the form of stock there is an opportunity cost as the funds tied up cannot be used for more profitable opportunities. (This is also true, of course, for investment in trade debtors.) By liquidating stocks, funds become available for other purposes. However, a business must ensure there are sufficient stocks available to meet likely future sales demand. Failure to do so will result in lost customer goodwill and lost sales.

The nature and condition of the stock held will determine whether it is possible to exploit this form of finance. A business may be overstocked as a result of poor buying decisions in the past. This may mean that a significant proportion of stocks held are slow-moving or obsolete and cannot, therefore, be liquidated easily.

10.12.4 Delaying Payment to Creditors

By delaying payment to creditors funds are retained within the business for other purposes. This may be a cheap form of finance for a business, but we saw in the previous chapter that there may be significant costs associated with this form of financing the business.

10.13 Venture Capital

Venture capital is provided by certain institutions to help businesses exploit profitable opportunities. The businesses of interest to the venture capitalist will have higher levels of risk than would normally be acceptable to traditional providers of finance such as the major clearing banks. The risks associated with the business can vary but are often due to the nature of the products or the fact that it is a new business which either lacks a trading record or has new management. Although the risks are higher, the businesses also have potentially higher levels of return — hence their attraction to the venture capitalist. The types of business helped by venture capitalists are normally small or medium-sized rather than large companies listed on the stock exchange.

The venture capitalist will often make a substantial investment in the business and this will normally take the form of ordinary shares. In order to keep an eye on the sum invested, the venture capitalist will usually require a representative on the board of directors as a condition of the investment. The venture capitalist may not be looking for a quick return and may well be prepared to invest in a business for five years or more. This return may take the form of a capital gain on the realization of the investment. When examining prospective investment opportunities, the venture capitalist will be concerned with such matters as the quality of management, the personal stake in the business made by the owners, the quality and nature of the product and the plans made to exploit the business opportunities, as well as financial matters.

SELF-ASSESSMENT QUESTION ──────────────────────────────

Helsim Ltd is a wholesaler and distributor of electrical components. The most recent financial statements of the company revealed the following:

Profit and Loss Account for the year ended 31 May 19X9

	£m	£m
Sales		14.2
Opening stock	3.2	
Purchases	8.4	
	11.6	
Closing stock	3.8	7.8
Gross profit		6.4
Administration expenses	3.0	
Selling and distribution expenses	2.1	
Finance charges	0.8	5.9
Net profit before taxation		0.5
Corporation tax		0.2
Net profit after taxation		0.3

Balance Sheet as at 31 May 19X9

	£m	£m	£m
Fixed assets			
Land and buildings			3.8
Equipment			0.9
Motor vehicles			0.5
			5.2

	£m	£m	£m
Current assets			
Stock		3.8	
Trade debtors		3.6	
Cash at bank		0.1	
		7.5	
Less creditors: amounts falling due within one year			
Trade creditors	1.8		
Bank overdraft	3.6	5.4	2.1
			7.3
Creditors: amounts falling due after one year			
Debentures (secured on freehold land)			3.5
			3.8
Capital and reserves			
Share capital — ordinary £1 shares			2.0
Reserves — profit and loss account			1.8
			3.8

Notes
1. Land and buildings are shown at their current market value. Equipment and motor vehicles are shown at their written down values.
2. No dividends have been paid to ordinary shareholders for the past three years.

In recent months trade creditors have been pressing for payment. The managing director has, therefore, decided to reduce the level of trade creditors to an average of 40 days outstanding. In order to achieve this he has decided to approach the bank with a view to increasing the overdraft to finance the necessary payments. The company is currently paying 12 per cent interest on the overdraft.

(a) Comment on the liquidity position of the company.
(b) Calculate the amount of finance required in order to reduce trade creditors, as shown on the balance sheet, to an average of 40 days outstanding.
(c) State, with reasons, how you consider the bank would react to the proposal to grant an additional overdraft facility.
(d) Evaluate four sources of finance (internal or external, but excluding a bank overdraft) which may be used to finance the reduction in trade creditors and state, with reasons, which of these you consider the most appropriate.

Solution on p. 258.

10.14 The Problem of Overtrading

Overtrading occurs where a business is operating at a level of activity which cannot be sustained by the level of finance which has been committed. This situation usually reflects a poor level of financial control over the business. The reasons for overtrading are varied. It may occur in young, expanding businesses which fail to prepare adequately for the rapid increase in demand for their goods or services. It may also occur in businesses where the managers may have miscalculated the level of expected sales demand or have failed to control escalating project costs. It may occur where the owners are unable to inject further funds into the business and are unable to persuade others to invest in the business. Whatever the reason for overtrading, the problems which it brings must be dealt with if the business is to survive over the longer term.

Overtrading results in liquidity problems such as exceeding borrowing limits, and slow repayment of lenders and creditors. It can also result in suppliers withholding supplies thereby making it difficult to meet customer needs. The managers of the business may be forced to direct all their efforts to dealing with immediate and pressing problems such as finding cash to meet interest charges due, or paying wages. Longer-term planning becomes difficult and managers may spend their time going from crisis to crisis. At the extreme, a business may collapse because it cannot meet its maturing obligations. In order to deal with the overtrading problem, a business must ensure that the finance available is commensurate with the level of operations. Thus, if a business which is overtrading is unable to raise new finance, it should cut back its level of operations in line with existing finance available. Although this may mean lost sales and lost profits in the short term, it may be necessary to ensure survival over the longer term.

ACTIVITY ——

If a business is overtrading, do you think the following ratios would be higher or lower than normally expected?

(a) Current ratio.
(b) Average stockholding period.
(c) Average settlement period for debtors.
(d) Average settlement period for creditors.

Your answer should be as follows:

(a)   The current ratio would be lower than normally expected. This is a measure of liquidity, and lack of liquidity is an important symptom of overtrading.

(b)   The average stockholding period would be lower than normally expected. Where a business is overtrading, the level of stocks held will be low in relation to demand because of the problems of financing stocks. In the short term, sales may not be badly affected by the low stock levels and therefore stocks will be turned over more quickly.

(c)   The average settlement period for debtors may be lower than normally expected. Where a business is suffering from liquidity problems it may chase debtors more vigorously so as to improve cash flows.

(d)   The average settlement period for creditors may be higher than normally expected. The business may try to delay payments to creditors because of its liquidity problems.

Summary

In this chapter we have examined the major sources of long-term and short-term finance available to businesses. We have seen that there are various factors to be taken into account when deciding which source of finance is appropriate to a particular business or a particular set of circumstances. However, as businesses exist primarily for the benefit of their owners, the effect of any financing method on the welfare of the owners must be taken into account.

EXERCISES

10.1 Brunel Instruments Ltd produces precision measurement devices for the oil industry. The balance sheet of the company as at 30 November 19X2 is as follows:

Balance Sheet as at 30 November 19X2

	£m	£m	£m
Fixed assets			
Plant and machinery at cost		36.4	
Less: Accumulated depreciation		12.2	24.2
Motor vehicles at cost		1.2	
Less: Accumulated depreciation		0.6	0.6
			24.8
Current assets			
Stocks and work in progress		18.5	
Trade debtors		21.4	
Bank		1.9	
		41.8	
Less creditors: amounts due within one year			
Trade creditors	12.7		
Proposed dividend	2.4		
Taxation	4.1	19.2	22.6
			47.4
Less creditors: amounts falling due after one year			
10% debentures			15.0
			32.4
Capital and reserves			
£0.50 ordinary shares			10.0
General reserve			4.6
Profit and loss account			17.8
			32.4

A profit and loss account for the year to 30 November 19X2 is as follows:

Abridged Profit and Loss Account for the year ended 30 November 19X2

	£m
Sales turnover	115.4
Profit before interest and taxation	17.9
Interest payable	1.5
Profit before taxation	16.4
Corporation tax	4.1
Profit after taxation	12.3
Dividend	3.6
Retained profit for the year	8.7

The company wishes to expand its production facilities in order to cope with an increase in demand for its products. Although plant and equipment costing £18 million is required it is expected that annual profit before interest and taxation will increase by £5 million.

The directors of the company are considering the following three methods of financing the expansion programme:

(i) The issue of 9 million 50p ordinary shares at a premium of £1.50 per share.
(ii) The issue of 12 million 12% £1 preference shares at par and £6 million 10% debentures at par.
(iii) The issue of 6 million ordinary shares at a premium of £1.50 per share and £6 million 10% debentures at par.

The directors wish to increase the dividend per share by 12p next year whichever financing scheme is adopted.

Assume a rate of corporation tax of 25 per cent.

(a) For each of the financing schemes under consideration:
    (i) Prepare a projected profit and loss account for the year ended 30 November 19X3.
    (ii) Calculate the projected earnings per shares for the year ended 30 November 19X3.
    (iii) Calculate the projected level of financial gearing as at 30 November 19X3.
(b) Briefly assess each of the financing schemes under consideration from the viewpoint of an existing shareholder.
(c) Discuss the major factors to be considered when deciding between preference shares and debentures as a means of increasing the financial gearing of a company.

(Answer on page 270. Answers for exercises 10.2 to 10.5 are given in the Teacher's Manual.)

10.2 Ashcroft plc, a family-controlled company, is considering raising additional funds to modernize its factory. The scheme is expected to cost £2.34 million and will increase annual profits before interest and tax from 1 January 19X4 by £0.6 million. A summarized balance sheet and profit and loss account are shown below. Currently the share price is 200p.

Two schemes have been suggested. Firstly, 1.3 million shares could be issued at 180p (net of issue costs). Secondly, a consortia of six city institutions have offered to buy debentures from the company totalling £2.34 million. Interest would be at the rate of 13 per cent per annum and capital repayments of equal annual instalments of £234,000 starting on 1 January 19X5 would be required.

Balance Sheet at 31 December 19X3

	£m	£m
Fixed assets (net)		1.4
Current assets:		
Stock	2.4	
Debtors	2.2	
	4.6	
Creditors: amounts falling due within one year		
Creditors	2.7	
Corporation tax	0.6	
Proposed final dividend	0.2	
	3.5	
Net current assets		1.1
Total assets *less* Current liabilities		2.5
Capital and reserves:		
Called up share capital, 25p ordinary shares		1.0
Profit and loss account		1.5
		2.5

Profit and Loss Account year ended 31 December 19X3

	£m
Turnover	11.2
Profit on ordinary activities before tax	1.2
Taxation on profit on ordinary activities	0.6
Profit on ordinary activities after tax	0.6
Dividends (net)	0.3
Retained profit for the financial year	0.3

Assume corporation tax is charged at the rate of 50 per cent.

(a) Compute the earnings per share for 19X4 under the debt and the equity alternatives.
(b) Compute the level of profits before debenture interest and tax at which the earnings per share under the two schemes will be equal.
(c) Discuss the considerations the directors should take into account before deciding upon debt or equity finance.

10.3 H. Brown (Portsmouth) Ltd produces a range of central heating systems for sale to builders' merchants. As a result of increasing demand for its products, the directors have decided to expand production. The cost of acquiring new plant and machinery and the increase in working capital requirements is planned to be financed by a mixture of long-term and short-term debt.

(a) Discuss the major factors which should be taken into account when deciding on the appropriate mix of long-term and short-term debt necessary to finance the expansion programme.
(b) Discuss the major factors which a lender should take into account when deciding whether to grant a long-term loan to the company.
(c) Identify three conditions that might be included in a long-term loan agreement and state the purpose of each.

10.4 Telford Engineers plc, a medium-sized Midlands manufacturer of automobile components, has decided to modernize its factory by introducing a number of robots. These will cost £20 million and will reduce operating costs by £6 million per year for their estimated useful life of 10 years. To finance this scheme the company can either:

1. Raise £20 million by the issue of 20 million ordinary shares at 100p.
2. Raise £20 million debt at 14 per cent interest per year, capital repayments of £3 million per year commencing at the end of 19X9.

Extracts from Telford Engineers' accounts appear below:

Summary of Balance Sheet at 31 December

	19X3	19X4	19X5	19X6 (estimated)
	£m	£m	£m	£m
Share capital and reserves	48	61	61	63
Loans	30	30	30	30
	78	91	91	93
Fixed assets	48	51	65	64
Current assets	55	67	57	55

	£m	£m	£m	£m
Less: Amounts due in under one year				
Creditors	(20)	(27)	(25)	(18)
Overdraft	(5)		(6)	(8)
	78	91	91	93
Number of issued 25p shares	80 million	80 million	80 million	80 million
Share price	150p	200p	100p	145p

Summary of Profit and Loss Accounts for years ended 31 December

	19X3	19X4	19X5	19X6 (estimated)
	£m	£m	£m	£m
Sales	152	170	110	145
Profit before interest and taxation	28	40	7	15
Interest payable	4	3	4	5
Profit before taxation	24	37	3	10
Taxation	12	16	0	4
Profit after taxation	12	21	3	6
Dividends	6	8	3	4
Retained	6	13	0	2

For your answer you should assume that the corporate tax rate for 19X7 is 40 per cent, that sales and operating profit will be unchanged except for the £6 million cost-saving arising from the introduction of the robots and that Telford Engineers will pay the same dividend per share in 19X7 as in 19X6.

(a) Prepare for each scheme, Telford Engineers' profit and loss account for the year ended 31 December 19X7 and a statement of its share capital, reserves and loans on that date.
(b) Calculate Telford's earnings per share for 19X7 for both schemes.
(c) Calculate the level of earnings (profit) before interest and tax at which the earnings per share for each scheme is equal.
(d) Which scheme would you advise the company to adopt? You should give your reasons and state what additional information you would require.

10.5 Hatleigh plc is a medium-sized engineering company based in South Wales. The accounts of the company for the year ended 30 April 19X2 are as follows:

Balance Sheet as at 30 April 19X2

	£000	£000	£000
Fixed assets			
Freehold premises at valuation			3,885
Plant and machinery at cost less depreciation			2,520
Motor vehicles at cost less depreciation			1,470
			7,875
Current assets			
Stock: Raw materials		824	
Work in progress		2,120	
Finished goods		5,436	
Debtors		8,578	
		16,958	
Less creditors due within one year			
Trade creditors	2,521		
Bank overdraft	4,776		
Corporation tax	402		
Dividends	600	8,299	
			8,659
			16,534
Less creditors due after more than one year			
10% debentures 19X7–8 (secured on			
freehold premises)			3,500
			13,034
Capital and reserves			
Share capital (25p shares)			8,000
Retained profit			5,034
			13,034

Profit and Loss Account for the year ended 30 April 19X2

	£000
Sales	34,246
Cost of sales	24,540
Gross profit	9,706
Expenses	7,564

	£000
Operating profit	2,142
Interest	994
Profit before taxation	1,148
Corporation tax (35%)	402
Net profit after taxation	746
Dividends proposed	600
Retained profit for the year	146

The company made a one for four rights issue of ordinary shares during the year.

Sales for the forthcoming year are forecast to be the same as for the year to 30 April 19X2. The gross profit margin is likely to stay the same as in previous years but expenses (excluding interest payments) are likely to fall by 10 per cent as a result of economies.

The bank has been concerned that the company has persistently exceeded the agreed overdraft limits and, as a result, the company has now been asked to reduce its overdraft to £3 million over the next three months. The company has agreed to do this and has calculated that interest on the bank overdraft for the forthcoming year will be £440,000 (after taking account of the required reduction in the overdraft). In order to achieve the reduction in overdraft, the chairman of the company is considering either the issue of more ordinary shares for cash to existing shareholders at a discount of 20 per cent, or the issue of more 10 per cent debentures redeemable 19X7–X8 at the end of July 19X2.

It is believed that the share price will be £1.50 and the 10 per cent debentures will be quoted at 82 at the end of July 19X2. The bank overdraft is expected to remain at the amount shown in the balance sheet until that date.

Any issue costs relating to new shares or debentures should be ignored.

(a) Calculate:
   (i) the total number of shares, and
   (ii) the total par value of debentures
   which will have to be issued in order to raise the funds necessary to reduce the overdraft to the level required by the bank.
(b) Calculate the expected earnings per share for the year to 30 April 19X3 assuming:
   (i) the issue of shares, and
   (ii) the issue of debentures
   are carried out to reduce the overdraft to the level required by the bank.
(c) Critically evaluate the proposal of the chairman to raise the necessary funds by the issue of:
   (i) shares, and
   (ii) debentures.

(d) Identify and discuss two other methods of raising the necessary finance (internal or external but excluding a bank overdraft) which may prove appropriate to this company.

Further Reading

Brayshaw, R.E., *The Concise Guide to Company Finance and its Management*. Chapman and Hall, 1992.
McLaney, E.J., *Business Finance for Decision Makers*. Pitman, 1994.

Case Study: Gadabout Travel Ltd

Gadabout Travel Ltd (GT) organizes holidays abroad for UK clients. The company charters planes and books hotels. The charter arrangements are such that the air operators include all UK transport costs, airport charges, etc. in the charter price. The contracts with the hoteliers require them to deal with all local arrangements, including transfers from airports to hotels and local activities where these are a feature of particular holidays. All holidays are booked by clients and paid through UK travel agents. By having to deal only with airlines, hotels and travel agents, the company is able to be administratively streamlined and, its management believe, efficient and price-competitive.

GT's holidays are of two types: summer 'beach' holidays and winter sports holidays. The company charges a flat rate for all holidays, only distinguishing between the beach holidays and the winter sports ones. An unusual feature of GT's holidays is the fact that full payment must be made with the booking. Although this is unusual, GT is able to sustain this policy by being very price-competitive. The management believes that any possible loss of custom through following this policy is outweighed by the knowledge that bookings, once made, are certain from the company's point of view.

Further information about the company and forecasts for next year are as follows:

- ◆ Travel agents deduct a 10 per cent commission from the full price of each holiday before remitting the other 90 per cent to the company at the time of booking.
- ◆ Winter sports holidays have a cost to the customer of £350 each and beach holidays cost £300 each.
- ◆ Flights and hotel accommodation are booked by GT as soon as the booking is received. Airline charges for both types of holiday are £100 per passenger. Hotel charges are £125 for beach holidays and £150 for winter sports holidays. Both airline and hotel charges must be paid in the month in which the holiday was originally due to be taken. If a holiday is cancelled by the time that payment is due to the airline and the hotels, they accept 60 per cent of these amounts in respect of the cancelled places. Airline and hotel charges for later cancellations have to be made

in full. It is not GT's practice to make any refunds to their clients, irrespective of the date of cancellation. The company tends to know from experience what percentage of holidays booked are likely to be cancelled.

♦ At 31 December this year the company has received 660 bookings for winter sports holidays. It is estimated that bookings and cancellations will be as follows:

	Holidays booked		Holidays taken		Holidays cancelled	
	Winter	Beach	Winter	Beach	Winter	Beach
Pre-Jan.	660	—				
Jan.	700	150	540	—	40	—
Feb.	740	980	520	—	50	—
Mar.	120	860	790	—	70	—
Apr.	40	660	230	—	20	—
May	—	450	—	200	—	20
June	—	100	—	370	—	30
July	—	80	—	890	—	80
Aug.	—	80	—	1,070	—	90
Sept.	70	50	—	600	—	60
Oct.	110	—	—	—	—	—
Nov.	360	—	—	—	—	—
Dec.	400	—	—	—	—	—

The holidays cancelled columns of this table show the month for which the cancelled holiday was intended to be taken at the time of booking. Past experience suggests that, of the holidays which are cancelled, 50 per cent will be cancelled before payment is due to the airlines and hotels, and 50 per cent will be cancelled later than this.

GT's outline balance sheet as at 31 December this year is expected to look as follows:

	£	£
Fixed assets		
Freehold land and building		210,000
Equipment and furniture		57,000
		267,000
Current assets		
Prepaid rates	500	
Cash	21,200	
	21,700	
Current liabilities		
Accrued electricity	1,500	
Trade creditors (660 winter sports × (£350 − 10%))	207,900	
	209,400	

	£
	(187,700)
	£79,300

Share capital and reserves	£79,300

In addition to the above plans for bookings, the company management expects the following during next year:

- Salaries will be £20,600 for each month. These will be paid during the month in which they are incurred.
- Electricity is expected to be the same as this year at about £1,500 each quarter, payable on 1 January, 1 April, etc.
- The business rate is also expected to be the same as this year at £2,000 in total, payable in two equal instalments on 1 April and 1 October.
- Repairs are expected to cost about £100 each month, payable in the month concerned.
- Depreciation is to be charged at the rate of 20 per cent on the book value of the equipment and furniture. No depreciation is to be charged on the building.
- Staff will incur costs for travelling on behalf of the company. These are expected to be at the rate of £3,500 each month during the months when holidays are being taken by clients. During each of the other three months the figure will be £500.

The company has always adopted the policy of realizing the profit on a particular holiday in the month in which it is taken.

You are required to prepare a month-by-month cash budget and a budgeted profit and loss account, both for next year, and a budgeted balance sheet as at the end of next year. You should also make some comments on the company's plans and on the policy of waiting until holidays have been taken or were due to be taken before realizing the profit on them.

Solution Guidelines

Cash Budget for next year

	Jan. £	Feb. £	Mar. £	Apr. £	May £	June £
Cash receipts						
Bookings: WS	220,500	233,100	37,800	12,600	—	—
B	40,500	264,600	232,200	178,200	121,500	27,000
	261,000	497,700	270,000	190,800	121,500	27,000
Payments						
Airlines:						
T+LC*	56,000	54,500	82,500	24,000	21,000	38,500
EC*	1,200	1,500	2,100	600	600	900
Hotels:						
T+LC*	84,000	81,750	123,750	36,000	26,250	48,125
EC*	1,800	2,250	3,150	900	750	1,125
Salaries	20,600	20,600	20,600	20,600	20,600	20,600
Electricity	1,500			1,500		
Rates				1,000		
Repairs	100	100	100	100	100	100
Travel	3,500	3,500	3,500	3,500	3,500	3,500
	168,700	164,200	235,700	88,200	72,800	112,850
Surplus/(deficit) for the month	92,300	333,500	34,300	102,600	48,700	(85,850)
Cumulative balance	113,500	447,000	481,300	583,900	632,600	546,750

continued

Cash Budget — *continued*

	July £	Aug. £	Sept. £	Oct. £	Nov. £	Dec. £
Cash receipts						
Bookings: WS	—	—	22,050	34,650	113,400	126,000
B	21,600	21,600	13,500	—	—	—
	21,600	21,600	35,550	34,650	113,400	126,000
Payments						
Airlines:						
T+LC	93,000	111,500	63,000			
EC	2,400	2,700	1,800			
Hotels:						
T+LC	116,250	139,375	78,750			
EC	3,000	3,375	2,250			
Salaries	20,600	20,600	20,600	20,600	20,600	20,600
Electricity	1,500			1,500		
Rates				1,000		
Repairs	100	100	100	100	100	100
Travel	3,500	3,500	3,500	500	500	500
	240,350	281,150	170,000	23,700	21,200	21,200
Surplus/(deficit) for the month	(218,750)	(259,550)	(134,450)	10,950	92,200	104,800
Cumulative balance	328,000	68,450	(66,000)	(55,050)	37,150	141,950

* T+LC is the holidays taken plus the late cancellations, all of which must be paid in full.

EC is the early cancellations (50 per cent of the total cancellations), 60 per cent of which must be paid.

Budgeted Profit and Loss Account for the year ended 31 December next year

	£000	£000
Sales: Holidays sold (net of agents' commission)		
Winter sports (2,080 + 180) × £315	711,900	
Beach (3,130 + 280) × £270	920,700	1,632,600
Hotel charges:		
Winter sports (2,080 + 90) × £150	325,500	
90 × £90	8,100	
Beach (3,130 + 140) × £125	408,750	
140 × £75	10,500	752,850
Airline charges:		
Winter sports (2,080 + 90) × £100	217,000	
90 × £60	5,400	
Beach (3,130 + 140) × £100	327,000	
140 × £60	8,400	557,800
Salaries	247,200	
Electricity	6,000	
Rates	2,000	
Repairs	1,200	
Travel	33,000	
Depreciation	11,400	
		1,611,450
Budgeted net profit for the year		£21,150

Budgeted Outline Balance Sheet as at 31 December next year

Fixed assets

Freehold land and building		210,000
Equipment and furniture (57,000 − 11,400)		45,600
		255,600

Current assets

Prepaid rates	500	
Cash	141,950	
	142,450	

Current liabilities

Accrued electricity	1,500	
Trade creditors (940 winter sports × (£350 − 10%))	296,100	
	297,600	
		(155,150)
		£100,450
Share capital and reserves (79,300 + 21,150)		£100,450

Comments on the Results

- A 20-to-25 per cent return on equity may or may not be considered adequate for the level of risk involved.
- The profit/contribution margin is relatively small.
- Relatively high sensitivity to changes in demand, selling price and costs.
- During much of the year there are major cash surpluses. These need to be carefully managed to gain the maximum benefit from interest payments, without placing the funds at serious risk.
- During September and October there are overdrafts scheduled. Steps need to be taken to deal with this. An overdraft could be negotiated in advance. Perhaps better, steps could be taken to reschedule some of the payments so as to avoid these cash deficits.

Accounting Policy with Reference to Realization of Profit

The generally accepted accounting treatment of revenues is to recognize them when the period in which the work to earn them has substantially been completed, they are capable of objective measurement and it seems probable that the cash will be received.

It could be argued that this position is established in the period in which the booking is made. During that period the bookings with the airlines and hotels will be placed, leaving only the payment to them outstanding, thus it could be argued that the work to earn the revenue has been substantially completed. Since the price is fixed, the revenue is capable of objective measurement. Also cash is received at the time of the customer making the booking.

On the other hand, it is not until the customer actually takes the holiday that the work is fully completed and the process could go wrong in the meantime, leading to extra work and to extra cost. It could be argued that a prudent view should be adopted so that profit is not recognized until the holiday is actually taken. This is probably the view which would be taken in practice.

Ultimately, a major factor in the decision must be the usefulness of the information provided. If it is felt that one approach gives the more valuable information, then this is the approach which would probably be taken. This is particularly the case here because there are quite good arguments, based on accounting conventions, for adopting either policy.

Solutions to Self-assessment Questions

Chapter I, page 12

JJ Limited   Balance Sheet as at . . . .

Assets	£	Claims	£
Freehold shop premises	60,000	Capital	
		(104,800 − 11,000 + 15,500)	109,300
Delivery van	10,000	Commercial Finance	50,000
Stock-in-trade			
(19,000 − 11,000 + 10,000			
+ 12,500)	30,500	Trade creditors	
		(30,000 + 10,000 − 25,000	
		+ 12,500)	27,500
Trade debtors			
(15,000 + 15,500 − 13,000)	17,500		
Cash at bank			
(40,800 + 50,000 + 13,000			
− 25,000 − 10,000)	68,800		
	£186,800		£186,800

Note that the settlement of the trade debtors and creditors is not a matter that affects the capital. This is because the owners' investment in the business has not been affected. For example, the part of the asset of trade debtors (£13,000) simply became part of the asset of cash (£13,000).

Note also that the alterations to the shop premises have no impact on the business sheet yet. This is because there is no change in the assets or claims of the business as a result of entering into the contract.

Chapter 2, pages 41–2

TT Limited   Balance Sheet as at 31 December 19X6

Assets	£	Claims	£
Delivery van		Capital	
(9,500 + 13,000 − 5,000)	17,500	(76,900 − 20,000 + 37,705)	94,605
Stock-in-trade			
(65,000 + 67,000 + 8,000			
− 89,000 −25,000)	26,000	Trade creditors	
		(22,000 + 67,000 − 71,000)	18,000
Trade debtors		Accrued expenses	
(19,600 + 179,000 − 178,000)	20,600	(860 + 690)	1,550
Cash at bank			
(750 − 20,000 − 15,000 −			
1,300 − 13,000 − 36,700 −			
1,820 − 8,000 + 54,000 +			
178,000 − 71,000 − 16,200)	49,730		
Prepaid expenses			
(325)	325		
	£114,155		£114,155

Profit and Loss Account for the year ended 31 December 19X6

	£
Sales (179,000 + 54,000)	233,000
Less: Cost of stock sold	
(89,000 + 25,000)	114,000
Gross profit	119,000
Less:	
Rent (5,000 + 15,000)	20,000
Rates (300 + 975)	1,275
Wages (−630 + 36,700 + 860)	36,930
Electricity (−620 + 1,820 + 690)	1,890
Van depreciation (2,500 + 2,500)	5,000
Van expenses (16,200)	16,200
	81,295
Net profit for the year	£37,705

The balance sheet could now be rewritten in a more stylish form as follows:

TT Limited   Balance Sheet as at 31 December 19X6

	£	£	£
Fixed assets			
Motor van			17,500
Current assets			
Stock-in-trade	26,000		
Trade debtors	20,600		
Prepaid expenses	325		
Cash	49,730		
		96,655	
Less: Current liabilities			
Trade creditors	18,000		
Accrued expenses	1,550		
		19,550	
			77,105
			£94,605
Capital			
Original			50,000
Retained profit			44,605
			£94,605

TT Limited   Cash Flow Statement for the year ended 31 December 19X6

	£	£
Sources of cash (inflows of cash)		
From: Customers for sales (54,000 + 178,000)		232,000
Uses of cash (cash payments)		
To: Suppliers of stock and services		
(15,000 + 1,300 + 36,700 + 1,820 + 8,000 + 71,000 + 16,200)	150,020	
Suppliers of fixed assets	13,000	
Owners (capital withdrawal)	20,000	
		183,020
Net increase in cash during the year		£48,980
Add: Cash balance at 1 January 19X6		750
Cash balance at 31 December 19X6		£49,730

Chapter 3, pages 62–4

The following ratios may be of value in assessing relative profitability and efficiency:

	A plc	**B plc**
ROCE	$\dfrac{(131.9 + 19.4)}{(687.6 + 190)} \times 100 = 17.2\%$	$\dfrac{(139.4 + 27.5)}{(874.6 + 250)} \times 100 = 14.8\%$
Return on owners' equity	$\dfrac{99.9}{687.6} \times 100 = 14.5\%$	$\dfrac{104.6}{874.6} \times 100 = 12.0\%$
Net profit margin	$\dfrac{(131.9 + 19.4)}{1,478.1} \times 100 = 10.2\%$	$\dfrac{(139.4 + 27.5)}{1,790.5} \times 100 = 9.3\%$
Gross profit margin	$\dfrac{459.8}{1478.1} \times 100 = 31.1\%$	$\dfrac{565.5}{1,790.4} \times 100 = 31.6\%$
Average stockholding period	$\dfrac{(480.8 + 592)/2}{1,018.3} \times 365 = 192 \text{ days}$	$\dfrac{(372.6 + 403)/2}{1,224.9} \times 365 = 116 \text{ days}$
Average settlement period for debtors	$\dfrac{176.4}{1,478.1} \times 365 = 44 \text{ days}$	$\dfrac{321.9}{1,790.4} \times 365 = 66 \text{ days}$
Average settlement period for creditors	$\dfrac{271.4}{1,129.5} \times 365 = 87.7 \text{ days}$	$\dfrac{180.7}{1,255.3} \times 365 = 52.5 \text{ days}$
Asset turnover ratio	$= \dfrac{1,478.1}{(447 + 869)} = 1.1 \text{ times}$	$\dfrac{1,790.4}{(601.2 + 833.9)} = 1.2 \text{ times}$

Note: More than six ratios have been calculated in order to provide you with a more comprehensive answer.

The net profit margin of A plc is slightly better than that of B plc although the gross profit margin is slightly worse. This suggests that the overhead expenses of B plc take up a higher proportion of sales revenue. The ROCE of A plc is significantly better and the return on owners equity is also better than B plc. This suggests a more profitable use of resources by A plc.

The average stockholding period of A plc is substantially higher than that of B plc. This may indicate better control over stocks by B plc. The stockholding period of A plc is more than half a year which seems very high for this type of business. The stockholding period of B plc is nearly a third of a year which also seems high.

The average settlement period for debtors of A plc is substantially lower than that of B plc. This may indicate better credit control; however, there may be other reasons. For example, B plc may have liberalized its credit policy in order to increase its market share. The average settlement period for creditors, on the other hand, reveals a quite different situation. For A plc, the average settlement period is nearly three months and is almost twice as long as the average credit period it allows debtors. For B plc, the average settlement period is significantly lower than that of A plc and is also lower than the average settlement period allowed to debtors. The length of the settlement period to creditors of A plc may suggest that the company is experiencing liquidity problems.

The asset turnover ratios for each business are similar and do not indicate significant differences.

Chapter 4, pages 82–4

In order to answer this question you may have used the following ratios:

	A plc	B plc
Current ratio	$\dfrac{869}{438.4} = 2.0$	$\dfrac{833.9}{310.5} = 2.7$
Acid test ratio	$\dfrac{(869 - 592)}{438.4} = 0.6$	$\dfrac{(833.9 - 403)}{310.5} = 1.4$
Gearing ratio	$\dfrac{190}{(687.6 + 190)} \times 100 = 21.6\%$	$\dfrac{250}{(874.6 + 250)} \times 100 = 22.2\%$
Interest cover ratio	$\dfrac{(131.9 + 19.4)}{19.4} = 7.8$ times	$\dfrac{(139.4 + 27.5)}{27.5} = 6.1$ times
Dividend payout ratio	$\dfrac{135.0}{99.9} \times 100 = 135\%$	$\dfrac{95.0}{104.6} \times 100 = 91\%$
Price/earnings ratio	$= \dfrac{£6.50}{31.2p} = 20.8$ times	$\dfrac{£8.20}{41.8p} = 19.6$ times

A plc has a much lower current ratio and acid test ratio than those of B plc. The reasons for this may be partly due to the fact that A plc has a lower average settlement period for debtors. The acid test ratio of A plc is substantially below 1.0 and this may suggest a liquidity problem.

The gearing ratio of each company is quite similar. Neither company has excessive borrowing. The interest cover ratio for each company is also similar. The respective ratios indicate that both companies have good profit coverage for their interest charges.

The dividend payout ratio for each company seems very high. In the case of A plc the dividends announced for the year are considerably higher than the earnings generated during the year which are available for dividend. As a result, part of the dividend was paid out of retained profits from previous years. This is an unusual occurence. Although it is quite legitimate to do this, such action may nevertheless suggest a lack of prudence on the part of the directors.

The P/E ratio for both companies is high which indicates market confidence in their future prospects.

Chapter 5, pages 110–12

Quardis Ltd

Projected Profit and Loss Account for the year ended 31 May 19X1

	£000	£000
Sales		280
Less: Cost of sales		
Opening stock	24	
Purchases	186	
	210	
Closing stock	30	180
Gross profit		100
Wages	34	
Other overhead expenses	21	
Interest payable	12	
Depreciation: Freehold premises	9	
Fixtures	6	82
Net profit before tax		18
Corporation tax (35%)		6
Net profit after tax		12
Proposed dividend		10
Retained profit for the year		2

Projected Balance Sheet as at 31 May 19X1

	£000	£000	£000
Fixed assets			
Freehold premises at cost		460	
Less: Accumulated depreciation		39	421
Fixtures and fittings at cost		60	
Less: Accumulated depreciation		16	44
			465
Current assets			
Stock-in-trade		30	
Trade debtors		42	
		72	

	£000	£000	£000
Creditors: amounts falling due within one year			
Trade creditors	31		
Accrued expenses	7		
Bank overdraft	42		
Corporation tax	6		
Dividends	10	96	(24)
			441
Creditors: amount falling due within one year			
Loan — Highland Bank			95
			346
Capital and reserves			
£1 ordinary shares			200
Retained profit			146
			346

The projected statements reveal a poor profitability and liquidity position for the company. The return on owners' equity for the year is expected to be only 3.5 per cent. This is low, even when compared with risk-free government securities.

The liquidity position at 31 May 19X1 reveals a serious deterioration when compared with the previous year. The current ratio has declined from 1.3 to 0.8 and the acid test (quick) ratio has declined from 0.8 to 0.4.

As a result of preparing these projected statements the management of Quardis Ltd may wish to make certain changes to their original plans. For example, the repayment of part of the loan may be deferred until a later date or the dividend may be reduced in order to improve liquidity. Similarly, the pricing policy of the company and the level of expenses proposed may be reviewed in order to improve profitability.

Chapter 6, pages 134–5

Job costing basis

			£
Materials:	Steel core	10,000 × £1.50	15,000
	Plastic:	10,000 × 0.10 × 0.60	600
Labour	Skilled	10,000 × 10/60 × £4.50	7,500
	Unskilled	10,000 × 5/60 × £3.50	2,917
Overheads		10,000 × 15/60 × 50,000/12,500	10,000
Total cost			36,017
Add: Profit loading		12.5% thereof	4,502
Total tender price			£40,519

Minimum contract price

			£
Materials:	Steel core	10,000 × £2.10	21,000
	Plastic	10,000 × 0.10 × 0.10	100
Labour	Skilled		
	Unskilled	10,000 × 5/60 × £3.50	2,917
Minimum tender price			£24,017

Chapter 7, pages 156–7

Beacon Chemicals Ltd

(a) Relevant cash flows

	19X6	19X7	19X8	19X9	19X0	19X1
	£000	£000	£000	£000	£000	£000
Sales revenue	—	80	120	144	100	64
Loss of contribution		(15)	(15)	(15)	(15)	(15)
Variable costs		(40)	(50)	(48)	(30)	(32)
Fixed costs		(8)	(8)	(8)	(8)	(8)
Operating cash flows		17	47	73	47	9
Working capital	(30)					30
Capital cost	(100)					
Net relevant cash flows	(130)	17	47	73	47	39

(b) Payback period

	19X6	19X7	19X8	19X9
Cumulative cash flows	(130)	(113)	(66)	7

Thus the plant will have repaid the initial investment by the end of the third year of operations.

(c) Net present value

	19X6	19X7	19X8	19X9	19X0	19X1
Discount factor	1.00	0.926	0.857	0.794	0.735	0.681
Present value	(130)	15.74	40.28	57.96	34.55	26.56
Net present value	45.09					

Chapter 8, pages 182–3

The original budget, the flexed budget and the actual are as follows:

	Original budget	Flexed budget	Actual
Output (production and sales)	1,000 units	1,050 units	1,050 units
	£	£	£
Sales	100,000	105,000	104,300
Raw materials	(40,000)	(42,000)	(41,200)
Labour	(20,000)	(21,000)	(21,300)
Fixed overheads	(20,000)	(20,000)	(19,400)
Operating profit	£20,000	£22,000	£22,400

Reconciliation of the budgeted and actual operating profits for June is as follows:

	£	£
Budgeted profit		20,000
Favourable variances:		
Sales volume (22,000 − 20,000)	2,000	
Direct material usage {[(1,050 × 40) − 40,500] × £1}	1,500	
Direct labour efficiency {[(1,050 × 5) − 5,200] × £4}	200	
Fixed overhead spending (20,000 − 19,400)	600	4,300
		24,300
Adverse variances:		
Sales price variance (105,000 − 104,300)	700	
Direct materials price [(40,500 × £1) − 41,200]	700	
Direct labour rate [(5,200 × £4) − 21,300]	500	1,900
Actual profit		£22,400

Chapter 9, page 198

	£	£
Existing level of debtors (£4m × 70/365)		767,000
New level of debtors		
£2m × 80/365	438,000	
£2m × 30/365	164,000	602,000
Reduction in debtors		165,000
Costs and benefits of policy		
Cost of discount (£2m × 2%)		40,000
Less: Savings		
Interest payable (£165,000 × 13%)	21,450	
Administration costs	6,000	
Bad debts	10,000	37,450
Net cost of policy		2,550

The above calculations reveal that the company will be worse off by offering the discounts.

Chapter 10, page 231

(a) The liquidity position may be assessed by using the liquidity ratios discussed in Chapter 4.

$$\text{Current ratio} = \frac{\text{Current assets}}{\text{Current liabilities}} \text{ (i.e. creditors due within one year)}$$

$$= \frac{£7.5m}{£5.4m}$$

$$= 1.4$$

$$\text{Acid test ratio} = \frac{\text{Current assets (less stock)}}{\text{Current liabilities}} \text{ (i.e. creditors due within one year)}$$

$$= \frac{£3.7m}{£5.4m}$$

$$= 0.7$$

These ratios reveal a fairly weak liquidity position. The current ratio seems quite low and the acid test ratio seems very low. This latter ratio suggests that the company does not have sufficient liquid assets to meet its maturing obligations. It would, however, be useful to have details of the liquidity ratios of similar companies in the same industry in order to make a more informed judgement. The bank overdraft represents 67 per cent of the short-term liabilities and 40 per cent of the total liabilities of the company. The continuing support of the bank is therefore important to the ability of the company to meet its commitments.

(b) The finance required to reduce trade creditors to an average of 40 days outstanding is calculated as follows:

	£m
Trade creditors at balance sheet date	1.80
Trade creditors outstanding based on 40 days credit	
40/365 × £8.4 (i.e. credit purchases)	0.92
Finance required	0.88

(c) The bank may not wish to provide further finance to the company. The increase in overdraft will reduce the level of trade creditors but will increase the exposure of the bank. The additional finance invested by the bank will not generate further funds and will not therefore be self-liquidating. The question does not make it clear whether the company has sufficient security to offer the bank for the increase in overdraft facility. The profits of the company will be reduced and the interest cover ratio, based on the profits generated to the year ended 31 May 19X9, would reduce to 1.5 times if the additional overdraft was granted (based on interest charged at 12 per cent per annum). This is very low — so low that a fairly small decline in profits would mean that interest charges would not be covered.

(d) A number of possible sources of finance might be considered. Four possible sources are as follows:

1. *Issue of equity shares.* This option may be unattractive to investors. The return on equity is fairly low at 7.9 per cent and there is no evidence that the profitability of the business will improve. If profits remain at their current level the effect of issuing more equity will be to further reduce the returns to equity.

2. *Issue of loans.* This option may also prove unattractive to investors. The effect of issuing further loans will have a similar effect to that of increasing the overdraft. The profits of the business will be reduced and the interest cover ratio will decrease to a low level. The gearing ratio of the company is already quite high at 48 per cent and it is not clear what security would be available for the loan.

3. *Chase debtors.* It may be possible to improve cash flows by reducing the level of credit outstanding from debtors. At present the average settlement period is 93 days which seems quite high. A reduction in the average settlement period by approximately one-third would generate the funds required. However, it is not clear what effect this would have on sales.

4. *Reduce stock.* This appears to be the most attractive of the four options discussed. At present the average stockholding period is 178 days which seems to be very high. A reduction in this stockholding period by less than one-third would generate the funds required. However, if the company holds a large amount of slow-moving and obsolete stock it may be difficult to reduce stock levels.

Answers to Selected Exercises

Exercise 1.1

Balance Sheet as at the end of the week

Assets	£	Claims	£
Freehold premises	145,000	Capital	
		(203,000 + 11,000 − 8,000 +	
		23,000 − 17,000 + 100,000 +	
Furniture and fittings	63,000	10,000)	322,000
Motor van (+ 10,000)	10,000	Bank overdraft	
		(43,000 − 11,000 − 18,000 −	
		100,000 + 13,000)	(73,000)
Stock-in-trade		Trade creditors	
(28,000 − 8,000 − 17,000		(23,000 + 14,000 − 13,000)	24,000
+ 14,000)	17,000		
Trade debtors			
(33,000 + 23,000 − 18,000)	38,000		
	£273,000		£273,000

Since the bank balance has now moved into the black, we can rewrite this balance sheet as:

Balance Sheet as at the end of the week

Assets	£	Claims	£
Freehold premises	145,000	Capital	322,000
Furniture and fittings	63,000	Trade creditors	24,000
Motor van	10,000		
Stock-in-trade	17,000		
Trade debtors	38,000		
Cash at bank	73,000		
	£346,000		£346,000

Exercise 2.1

(a) It is the profit and loss account which needs to be consulted to see the revenues, expenses and resultant profit or loss for the period. The balance sheet is a list of assets and claims for a period. These assets and claims will be affected by trading events, but it is not possible to see from the balance sheet exactly what has happened.

(b) Capital does increase as a result of the owners introducing more cash into the business, but it will also increase as a result of introducing other assets (e.g. a plot of land) and by the business generating revenues by trading. Similarly, capital decreases not only as a result of withdrawals of cash by owners, but by withdrawals of any other assets (e.g. stock for the owners' personal use) and through trading expenses being incurred. In practice, for the typical business in a typical accounting period, capital will alter much more as a result of trading activities than for any other reason.

(c) The *going concern* convention does not say that you should always assume that the business will go on indefinitely. It says that *in the absence of evidence to the contrary* you should make that assumption.

(d) An accrued expenses is not one that relates to next year. It is one which needs to be matched against the revenues of the accounting period under review, but which has yet to be met in terms of a cash payment. As such it will appear on the balance sheet as a current liability.

(e) This statement does not correctly describe the role of the auditor of a limited company. The auditors of a limited company must form and state an opinion on the truth and fairness of the accounting statements and their compliance with the statutory requirements. They have no power to correct accounts which fail to meet the requirements placed on the auditors. All that the auditors can do is to mention in their report that the accounts do not show a true and fair view, if this should be the case.

Exercise 3.1

The effect of each of the changes on ROCE is not always easy to predict.

 (i) An increase in the gross profit margin *may* lead to a decrease in ROCE in particular circumstances. If the increase in the margin resulted from an increase in price which, in turn, led to a decrease in sales, a fall in ROCE can occur. A fall in sales can reduce the net profit (the numerator in ROCE) if the overheads of the business do not decrease correspondingly.

 (ii) A reduction in sales can reduce ROCE for reasons mentioned above.

(iii) An increase in overhead expenses will reduce the net profit and this, in turn, will result in a reduction in ROCE.

(iv) An increase in stocks held will increase the amount of capital employed by the business (the denominator in ROCE) where long-term funds are employed to finance the stocks. This will, in turn, reduce ROCE.

 (v) Repayment of the loan at the year end will reduce the capital employed and this will *increase* the ROCE.

(vi) An increase in the time taken for debtors to pay will result in an increase in capital employed if long-term funds are employed to finance the debtors. This increase in long-term funds will, in turn, reduce ROCE.

Exercise 4.1

(i) Earnings per share   £4.2/16m   = 26.3p

(ii) Prices/earnings ratio   315p/26.3p   = 12.0

(iii) Dividend yield

$$\frac{\left(\dfrac{£1.3m}{16m}\right)\Big/(1-0.2)}{315p} \times 100\% = 10.2\%$$

(iv) Dividend payout   £1.3/£4.2 × 100%   = 31%

(v) Net assets per share*   £17.4m/16m   = 108.8p

    * Net assets will be equal to the share capital plus reserves which are given in the question.

The company is growing fast. Turnover has more than doubled over two years and profits have nearly doubled during the same period. The net profit margin has increased over the period slightly and is currently 19.7 per cent. The return on owners' equity has risen from 18.3 per cent to 24.1 per cent. In view of these good results, it is rather surprising to find that the company has a fairly modest P/E ratio of 12.0. This suggests that the market does not have a great deal of confidence in the future prospects of the company. Has the market received some adverse news concerning the company or the industry which suggests that the rate of growth and profitability cannot be sustained?

    The chairman of Diversified industries should take the following factors into account when considering the bid:

♦ *Contractual obligations.* Does the company have any onerous contractual obligations with suppliers, lenders or directors of the company?

♦ *Asset quality.* Are the assets of good quality? Do they need replacing in the near future? What are their current realizable values?

♦ *Market.* Is the market for the company's products expanding? What level of competition exists?

♦ *Management.* What is the quality of the company's management? Will key personnel be happy to stay with the company if the bid is successful?

♦ *Strategic fit.* Does the company fit easily with the existing operations of Diversified Industries?

♦ *Finance.* How will the bid be financed? Do the shareholders of Automobile Care require cash, loan stock, shares or some combination of these in payment for their holdings? How much will they be prepared to accept in consideration for their shares?

Exercise 5.1

(a)

Cash Projection for the six months to 30 June 19X5

	Jan. £000	Feb. £000	Mar. £000	Apr. £000	May £000	June £000
Receipts						
Credit sales	100	100	140	180	220	260
Payments						
Trade creditors	112	144	176	208	240	272
Operating expenses	4	6	8	10	10	10
Shelving				12		
Taxation			25			
	116	150	209	230	250	282
Cash flow	(16)	(50)	(69)	(50)	(30)	(22)
Opening balance	(68)	(84)	(134)	(203)	(253)	(283)
Closing balance	(84)	(134)	(203)	(253)	(283)	(305)

(b) Current ratio $\dfrac{[272+(300+340)]}{(305+272)} = \dfrac{912}{577} = 1.6$

Acid test ratio $\dfrac{(300+340)}{(305+272)} = \dfrac{640}{577} = 1.1$

(c) A banker may require various pieces of information before granting additional overdraft facilities. These may include:

- Security available for the loan.
- Details of past profit performance.
- Profit projections for the next twelve months.
- Cash projections beyond the next six months to help assess the prospects of repayment.
- Details of the assumptions underlying projected figures supplied.
- Details of contractual commitment between Prolog Ltd and its supplier.
- Details of management expertise. Can they manage the expansion programme?
- Details of new machine and its performance in relation to competing models.
- Details of funds available from owners to finance the expansion.

Exercise 6.1

(a) and (b)

Deduce the total contribution per product and deduce the contribution per £ of labour and hence the relative profitability of the three products, given a shortage of labour.

Product	Alpha	Beta	Gamma
	£	£	£
Variable costs:			
Materials	6,000	4,000	5,000
Labour	9,000	6,000	12,000
Expenses	3,000	2,000	2,000
Total variable cost	18,000	12,000	19,000
Sales	39,000	29,000	33,000
Contribution	21,000	17,000	14,000
Contribution per £			
of labour	2.333	2.833	1.167
Order of profitability	2	1	3

Since 50 per cent of each budget (and, therefore, £13,500 of labour) is committed, only £6,500 of labour is left uncommitted (i.e. £20,000 − 13,500).

The £6.500 should be deployed as:

Beta	£3,000
Alpha	3,500
	£6,500

Total labour committed to each product and resultant profit as as follows:

Product	Alpha	Beta	Gamma	Total
	£	£	£	£
Labour:				
50% of budget	4,500	3,000	6,000	
Allocated above	3,500	3,000	—	
Total	8,000	6,000	6,000	20,000
Contribution per £ of labour	2.333	2.833	1.167	
Contribution per product	18,664	16,998	7,002	42,664
Less: Fixed costs				33,000
Maximum profit (subject to minor rounding errors)				£9,664

This answer assumes that all costs are variable, except where it is indicated to the contrary. Also that the budgeted sales figures are the maximum sales which can be achieved.

(c) Other factors which might be considered include:

‣ Could all of the surplus labour be used to produce Betas (the most efficient user of labour),

i.e. could the business sell more than £29,000 of this product? It might be worth reducing the price of this product, though still keeping the contribution per labour £ above £2.33, in order to expand sales.
- ◆ Could the commitment to 50 per cent of budget on each product be dropped in favour of producing the maximum of the higher yielding products?
- ◆ Could another source of labour be found?
- ◆ Could the labour-intensive part of the work be subcontracted?

Exercise 7.1

(a) Annual depreciation:
Project 1 (£100,000 − 7,000)/3 = £31,000
Project 2 (£60,000 − 6,000)/3 = £18,000

Analysis of the projects

Project 1 Year	0	1	2	3
	£000	£000	£000	£000
Net profit (loss)		29	(1)	2
Depreciation		31	31	31
Capital cost	(100)			
Residual value				7
Net cash flows	(100)	60	30	40
10% discount factor	1.00	0.909	0.826	0.751
Present value	(100.00)	54.54	24.78	30.04
Net present value	9.36			

Clearly the IRR lies above 10%; try 15%:

15% discount factor	1.00	0.870	0.756	0.658
Present value	(100.00)	52.20	22.68	26.32
Net present value	1.20			

Thus the IRR lies a little above 15%, around 16%.

Cumulative cash flows	(100)	(40)	(10)	30

Thus the payback will occur after about 2 years 3 months (assuming that the cash flows accrue equally over the year).

Project 2 Year	0	1	2	3
	£000	£000	£000	£000
Net profit (loss)		18	(2)	4
Depreciation		18	18	18
Capital cost	(60)			
Residual value				6
Net cash flows	(60)	36	16	28
10% discount factor	1.000	0.909	0.826	0.751
Present value	(60.00)	32.72	13.22	21.03
Net present value	6.97			

Clearly the IRR lies above 10%; try 15%:

15% discount factor	1.000	0.870	0.756	0.658
Present value	(60.00)	31.32	12.10	18.42
Net present value	1.84			

Thus the IRR lies a little above 15%, around 17%.

Cumulative cash flows	(60)	(24)	(8)	20

Thus the payback will occur after about 2 years 3 months (assuming that the cash flows accrue equally over the year).

(b) Assuming that Mylo Ltd is pursuing a wealth maximization objective, project 1 is preferable since it has the higher NPV. The difference between the two NPVs is not significant, however.

(c) NPV is the preferred method of assessing investment opportunities because it fully addresses each of the following:

♦ *The timing of the cash flows.* By *discounting* the various cash flows associated with each project according to when it is expected to arise, the fact that cash flows do not all occur simultaneously is taken into account. Associated with this is the fact that by discounting, using the opportunity cost of finance (i.e. the return which the next best alternative opportunity would generate), the net benefit after financing costs have been met is identified (as the NPV).

♦ *The whole of the relevant cash flows.* NPV includes all of the relevant cash flows irrespective of when they are expected to occur. It treats them differently according to their date of occurrence, but they are all taken account of in the NPV and they all have, or can have, an influence on the decision.

♦ *The objectives of the business.* NPV is the only method of appraisal where the output of the analysis has a direct bearing on the wealth of the business (positive NPVs enhance wealth, negative ones reduce it). Since most private-sector businesses seek to increase their value and wealth, NPV is clearly the best approach to use.

Exercise 8.1

Finished Goods Stock Budget for the six months ending 30 September in units of production

	April (units)	May (units)	June (units)	July (units)	Aug. (units)	Sept. (units)
Opening stock (note 1)	—	500	600	700	800	900
Production (note 2)	500	600	700	800	900	900
	500	1,100	1,300	1,500	1,700	1,800
Less: Sales (note 3)		500	600	700	800	900
Closing stock	500	600	700	800	900	900

Raw Materials Stock Budget for the six months ending 30 September in units

	April (units)	May (units)	June (units)	July (units)	Aug. (units)	Sept. (units)
Opening stock (note 1)	—	600	700	800	900	900
Purchases (note 2)	1,100	700	800	900	900	800
	1,100	1,300	1,500	1,700	1,800	1,700
Less: Production (note 4)	500	600	700	800	900	900
Closing stock	600	700	800	900	900	800

Raw Materials Stock Budget for the six months ending 30 September in financial terms

	April £	May £	June £	July £	Aug. £	Sept. £
Opening stock (note 1)	—	24,000	28,000	32,000	36,000	36,000
Purchases (note 2)	44,000	28,000	32,000	36,000	36,000	32,000
	44,000	52,000	60,000	68,000	72,000	68,000
Less: Production (note 4)	20,000	24,000	28,000	32,000	36,000	36,000
Closing stock	24,000	28,000	32,000	36,000	36,000	32,000

Trade Creditors Budget for the six months ending 30 September

	April £	May £	June £	July £	Aug. £	Sept. £
Opening balance (note 1)	—	44,000	28,000	32,000	36,000	36,000
Purchases (note 5)	44,000	28,000	32,000	36,000	36,000	32,000
	44,000	72,000	60,000	68,000	72,000	68,000
Less: Cash payment	—	44,000	28,000	32,000	36,000	36,000
Closing balance	44,000	28,000	32,000	36,000	36,000	32,000

Trade Debtors Budget for the six months ending 30 September

	April £	May £	June £	July £	Aug. £	Sept. £
Opening balance (note 1)	—	—	50,000	60,000	70,000	80,000
Sales (note 3)	—	50,000	60,000	70,000	80,000	90,000
	—	50,000	110,000	130,000	150,000	170,000
Less: Cash received	—	—	50,000	60,000	70,000	80,000
Closing balance	—	50,000	60,000	70,000	80,000	90,000

Cash Budget for the six months ending 30 September

	April £	May £	June £	July £	Aug. £	Sept. £
Inflows						
Share issue	300,000					
Receipts: Debtors	—	—	50,000	60,000	70,000	80,000
(note 6)	300,000	—	50,000	60,000	70,000	80,000
Outflows						
Payments to creditors	—	44,000	28,000	32,000	36,000	36,000
(note 7)						
Labour (note 3)	10,000	12,000	14,000	16,000	18,000	18,000
Overheads:						
Production	17,000	17,000	17,000	17,000	17,000	17,000
Non-production	11,000	11,000	11,000	11,000	11,000	11,000
Fixed assets	250,000					
Total outflows	288,000	84,000	70,000	76,000	82,000	82,000
Net inflows/(outflows)	12,000	(84,000)	(20,000)	(16,000)	(12,000)	(2,000)
Balance c/fwd	12,000	(72,000)	(92,000)	(108,000)	(120,000)	(122,000)

Notes:

1. The opening balance is the same as the closing balance from the previous month.
2. This is a balancing figure.
3. This figure is given in the question.
4. This figure derives from the finished stock budget.
5. This figure derives from the raw materials stock budget.
6. This figure derives from the trade debtors budget.
7. This figure derives from the trade creditors budget.

Exercise 9.1

(a) The liquidity ratios of the company seem low. The current ratio is only 1.1 and its acid test ratio is 0.6. This latter ratio suggests the company has insufficient liquid assets to pay its short-term obligations. A cash flow projection for the next period would provide a better insight to the liquidity position of the business. The bank overdraft seems high and it would be useful to know if the bank is pressing for a reduction and what overdraft limit has been established for the company.

(b) This term is described in the chapter.

(c) The operating cash cycle may be calculated as follows:

No. of days

Average stockholding period =

$$\frac{\text{Opening stock} + \text{Closing stock}/2}{\text{Cost of sales}} = \frac{(125 + 143)/2}{323} \times 360 \qquad 149$$

Average settlement period for debtors =

$$\frac{\text{Trade debtors} \times 365}{\text{Credit sales}} = \frac{163}{452} \times 360 \qquad \frac{130}{279}$$

Less: Average settlement period for creditors =

$$\frac{\text{Trade creditors}}{\text{Credit purchases}} \times 365 = \frac{145}{341} \times 360 \qquad \underline{153}$$

Operating cash cycle $\qquad \underline{\underline{126}}$

(d) The company can reduce the operating cash cycle in a number of ways. The average stockholding period seems quite long. At present, average stocks held represent almost five months sales. This may be reduced by reducing the level of stocks held. Similarly, the average settlement period for debtors seems long at more than four months sales. This may be reduced by imposing tighter credit control, offering discounts, charging interest on overdue accounts, etc. However, any policy decisions concerning stocks and debtors must take account of current trading conditions.

The operating cash cycle could also be reduced by extending the period of credit taken to pay suppliers. However, for reasons mentioned in the chapter, this option must be given careful consideration.

Exercise 10.1

(a)   Projected Profit and Loss Account under each financing scheme

	(i) £m	(ii) £m	(iii) £m
Profit before			
interest and tax	22.9	22.9	22.9
Interest Charges	1.5	2.1	2.1
	21.4	20.8	20.8
Tax payable	5.4	5.2	5.2
Profit after tax	16.0	15.6	15.6
Preference			
dividend payable	–	1.4	–
Available to			
ordinary			
shareholders	16.0	14.2	15.6
Ordinary			
dividend	8.7	6.0	7.8
Retained profit	7.3	8.2	7.8

EPS under each financing scheme	$\dfrac{16.0}{(20+9)}$	$\dfrac{14.2}{20}$	$\dfrac{15.6}{(20+6)}$
	£0.55	£0.71	£0.60
Gearing ratio	$\dfrac{15}{(47.4+7.3+18)} \times 100$	$\dfrac{33}{(47.4+8.2+18)} \times 100$	$\dfrac{21}{(47.4+7.8+18)} \times 100$
	20.6%	44.8%	28.7%

(b) Scheme (ii) provides the highest EPS and also produces the highest gearing ratio. Thus, the highest level of return to ordinary shareholders brings the highest level of risk. However, the interest cover ratio under this scheme is high (11.9 times) and, providing the profits achieve expected levels, the additional gearing should not be an undue burden on the company. Scheme (i) brings the lowest return to ordinary shareholders and also produces the lowest level of gearing. The EPS of £0.55 under this scheme is also lower than the current level of EPS of £0.62. Scheme (iii) provides a 'middle way' in terms of EPS and gearing, although the EPS achieved is still lower than the current level.

(c) The following factors should be considered when deciding between preference shares and debentures:

- *Commitment to pay.* Debenture interest must be paid irrespective of the profitability of the business. Failure to do so can have grave consequences for the business. However, preference dividends are only payable where there are profits available.
- *Returns.* Preference shares usually require a higher level of return than debentures. From the investor's viewpoint, debentures are a less risky form of investment because of priority in payment and the fact that some form of security is given by the company.
- *Taxation.* Interest on debentures is allowable against taxation, whereas preference dividends are not. From the company viewpoint, this makes debentures more attractive.
- *Management decisions.* A debenture may have a number of restrictive covenants associated with it (e.g. dividend and directors' remuneration limits, minimum liquidity requirements and maximum gearing levels). As a result, management will have a restricted ability to make certain decisions while the debenture is outstanding. Preference shareholders, on the other hand, cannot impose such restrictions on management.
- *Capital redemption.* Preference shares and debentures may both be redeemable. In the former case, however, the permanent capital base must be maintained by transfers to a capital reserve or by issuing new shares. There is no such legal requirement when debentures are redeemed.

Index